T0227914

# Security for Service Oriented Architectures

# Security for Service Oriented Architectures

## Walter Williams

**CRC Press**
Taylor & Francis Group
Boca Raton London New York

CRC Press is an imprint of the
Taylor & Francis Group, an **informa** business
AN AUERBACH BOOK

CRC Press
Taylor & Francis Group
6000 Broken Sound Parkway NW, Suite 300
Boca Raton, FL 33487-2742

First issued in hardback 2017

© 2014 by Taylor & Francis Group, LLC
CRC Press is an imprint of Taylor & Francis Group, an informa business

No claim to original U.S. Government works

ISBN-13: 978-1-4665-8402-0 (pbk)
ISBN-13: 978-1-1384-6843-6 (hbk)

**Visit the Taylor & Francis Web site at**
**http://www.taylorandfrancis.com**

**and the CRC Press Web site at**
**http://www.crcpress.com**

Library of Congress Cataloging-in-Publication Data

Williams, Walter (Telecommunications engineer)
    Security for service oriented architectures / Walter Williams.
        pages cm
    Summary: "Providing a comprehensive guide to security for web services and SOA, this book covers in detail all recent standards that address web service security, including XML Encryption, XML Signature, WS-Security, and WS-SecureConversation. It also reviews recent research on access control for simple and conversation-based web services, advanced digital identity management techniques, and access control for web-based workflows. With illustrative examples and analyses of critical issues, the book is a solid reference on web service standards, a practical overview for researchers looking for innovative new directions,and a suitable textbook on advanced topics in computer and system security"-- Provided by publisher.
    Includes bibliographical references.
    ISBN 978-1-4665-8402-0 (paperback)
    1. Service-oriented architecture (Computer science) 2. Computer networks--Security measures. 3. Computer security. I. Title.

TK5105.5828.W55 2014
005.8--dc23                                                                        2013047689

# Contents

# In Gratitude

This book came from meeting Hal Tipton in an International Information Systems Security Certification Consortium (ISC)²-sponsored educational material workshop. After working with him for three days on creating materials to be used in the preparation for the Systems Security Certified Practitioner (SSCP) examination, he asked me to consider submitting a chapter for the *Information Security Management Handbook*. This book is a child of that chapter and its successor in the following edition. The reason for the follow-up article was that serious advances had happened in the testing of SOAs for vulnerabilities during the months between the writing and publication of the first article. Regrettably, Hal died shortly after submitting the second article. He was a good man who did much to advance this profession and my own career. One of the things he taught me was to invest in the profession by creating educational material, or in other words, to give to those entering or advancing in information security through sharing both my experience and expertise. Thus, when CRC Press approached me about turning the articles into a book, with the encouragement of my wife, I readily agreed. I dedicate this volume to the memory of Hal Tipton.

Volumes of this length and complexity do not come quickly or without significant help. There are so many I need to thank both personally and professionally. First, my wife Margo and children Kayla and Hannah, who all sacrificed quality time that could have been spent with me and who put up with me as I wrote and edited this text. Professionally, I need to thank Lazz McKenzie, Peter Souza, Vik Solem, John Burke, David Caplin, Peter Zatko, Chris Wysopal, Paul Nash, Pat Cain, Hallett German, Val Milshtein, Scott Tousley, Chris Hoff, Craig Cato, John Ekburg, Gene Curcio, Mayank Prakash, Art Schloth, Ed Levis, Glen Gregory, Karen Stopford, Matt Truenow, Jeff Bardin, Allan Lam, Manish Jain, Julie Fitton, Iris Seri, David Burdelski, Miles Freedman, Tim Carruthers, Peter Lindstrom, Dewey Sasser, David Dumas, Ed Norris, Robin Wheeler, and other members of the New England Chapter of the Information Systems Security Association (ISSA) who have helped with my career.

# 1
# INTRODUCTION

As applications become more complex and distributed, it is increasingly important that security be considered during the design phases. While there are a lot of books and articles on point solutions that would flow from this integration, such as threat profiling and how to block injection attacks, there is more to consider in the design of an application than how to leverage some of the excellent tools that have been developed to enhance the security of our applications.

Applications, especially those that are distributed across corporate boundaries, benefit from being developed within a comprehensive design or an architecture. While there is a lot of literature on how to develop these software architectures and service-oriented architectures (SOAs), their treatment of security is focused on the use of tools within the architecture.

Information security also benefits from an architecture. However, traditional security architectures are most often focused on infrastructure and consider software as no more than applications that require integration into the policies and standards of an organization, leveraged within approved procedures.

This volume seeks to provide both security and software architects with a bridge between these two architectures, with the goal of providing a means to develop software architectures that leverage security architectures.

Each of the chapters within this volume could be and has been covered in book-length manuscripts. This volume does not attempt to duplicate or condense those texts but rather to draw them together to show how building software architectures within security architectures allows the development of more scalable and resilient applications, which become a trusted platform for their execution of business functionality.

Because architectures are only effective when designed with the capabilities and limitations of the technology in mind, as well as the business goals and design philosophy, this volume will look at, in some detail, how protocols and application components work and interact in the context of the decisions that need to be made in a distributed application. I will explore the various web services standards as well as SOAs, which are not web services based, but only to expose sufficient detail about the operation of each of the technology frameworks, standards, protocols, messages, and assertions, so that an architect is made aware of the decisions that need to be made regarding their approach to application design. I will look at not only the construction of an architecture but also the possible ways by which to attack an architecture, by exploiting those same frameworks, standards, protocols, messages, and assertions that businesses depend upon to conduct their business.

None of the standards is explored in sufficient detail to allow this book to be used as source material for application development. Such a book would be beyond any one person to pull together and would be obsolete when it is published. In fact, the chapters on penetration are likely out of date as the publisher and I work on bringing the book to print. All good security architects keep themselves up to date on such matters, and this volume represents a point in time, and it is of the past.

However, architecture and the ideas that go into architectural design are not so fleeting. I hope that this book brings together both software and security architects and facilitates their collaboration during the design phases of the next generation of applications.

# 2

# FOUR KINDS OF ARCHITECTURES

## 2.1 Architecture

An architecture is a deliberate and holistic design. Architectures are used in information technology to provide benefits of synergy between the various components and layers of technology. In the absence of an architecture, an implementation of technology will be of necessity ad hoc. This implementation may meet a specific narrow set of requirements but may fail to interoperate with other deployed technologies, or worse, require duplication of components already implemented but incompatible with this specific technology.

Architectures, when well designed, provide a framework for all current and future technologies, guaranteeing interoperability and ensuring compatibility. As such, well-designed architectures are technology at a high level of abstraction.

There are four architectures that need to be considered as complementary within information technology: infrastructure architecture, software architecture, data architecture, and security architecture. While it is possible to have software, infrastructure, data, and security without an architecture unifying them and possible to have each without an architecture in their deployment, the design and implementation of each and all three into an architectural framework allow for an organization to develop an application, which is designed to be secure, scalable, and support business needs and objectives.

The impact of not having a data architecture is that application performance will always be slow, and eventually, the application will not scale. The impact of not having an infrastructure architecture is that the application will be more vulnerable to attack and the back-end systems will be harder to maintain. Cloud deployment is not an architecture, and deploying to the cloud without an architecture just adds to the chaos. The impact of not having a security infrastructure is that not only is your company more likely to have a data breach, but it is also more likely that you will learn about this from your customers. Finally, if you do not have an application architecture, you will have an application that becomes increasingly hard to maintain, is vulnerable to attack, and has both performance and scalability issues.

So, it may be possible to develop, deploy, and maintain applications and systems without an architecture. It is just a bad idea.

## 2.2 Infrastructure

Infrastructure architectures are foundational of both security and software architectures, providing a platform to guarantee the scalability and serviceability of all software and services run within it. These architectures consist of hardware, networks, protocols, operating systems, and storage. A service-oriented architecture (SOA), for the most part, is infrastructure agnostic. While both web services and Web 2.0 depend on the Internet protocols, SOAs may also leverage other protocols to integrate with platforms and services that are not available over HTTP, SOAP, or even TCP/IP. That capacity to access application capabilities regardless of protocol or infrastructure is a key strength of an SOA. This infrastructure independence does not preclude a need to understand infrastructure architecture.

In contemporary infrastructures, there are four basic infrastructure models:

- Public cloud
- Hybrid
- Private cloud
- Private

Many current infrastructures are best categorized as hybrid architectures, leveraging components of public and private clouds as well as private infrastructures.

There is a lot of industry debate on the validity of the term "private cloud." Much like other undebated jargon found in this volume, I am going to abstain from the debate and attempt to represent what the architecture looks like and why it is an important consideration.

To understand a private cloud, first you must understand cloud as an infrastructure. Fundamental to all cloud technologies is that they are service oriented and depend on SOAs to be well designed to be successful. There are many cloud technologies:

- Infrastructure as a service (IaaS)
- Platform as a service (PaaS)
- Software as a service (SaaS)
- Storage as a service (STaaS)
- Security as a service (SECaaS)
- Data as a service (DaaS)
- Database as a service (DBaaS)
- Test environment as a service (TEaaS)
- Desktop virtualization
- Application-programing interface (API) as a service (APIaaS)
- Back end as a service (BaaS)

IaaS provides to the customer hosting, networks, security, storage, database, API, and back end, all bundled into one comprehensive service. While not all IaaS offerings contain all those capabilities, and there will be a difference between how comprehensive each service group will be within any IaaS offering, IaaS offerings provide customers everything they need (in theory) to host their application.

PaaS provides basic hosting and storage. While there may be security components, they are all on the host. No network components are available, including firewalls, intrusion prevention system/intrusion detection and prevention system (IDS/IPS), load balancing, and so on. Databases, virtual machines, and so on are all on the host provided.

SaaS provides applications to the customer. That application may process credit card payments for other organizations, hotel reservations associated with major events, data analytics for sales, identity theft protection, and so on. These applications provide specific expertise to other organizations that may leverage their capability. They need to be hosted some place, however, and may be hosted in a private cloud, hybrid configuration, or public cloud using either PaaS or IaaS or perhaps just APIaaS.

SaaS most readily benefits from being built as an SOA, but it does not have to provide an interface for other applications to call it a service. The application could provide just a basic web front end to its capabilities and remain an SaaS platform. However, most companies that offer their business expertise within publicly available applications have recognized that exposing an API to their application so that it may be called a service by other applications offers a unique opportunity to expand the business. Where the business lacks the expertise to extend their software through an API, they may leverage an APIaaS provider that will build and maintain the API for them.

STaaS provides exactly a place to put large amounts of data, structured or otherwise, where it is available especially in the event of a disaster. Usually, they bundle into their offerings encryption capabilities, though key management remains a challenge. If the provider manages the keys for you, then they have full access to the data. The most viable solution to this I have seen is that data are encrypted locally before they are sent to the STaaS provider; this way not only are you managing your keys but the STaaS vendor also never has the keys located on their system. The downside to this is that you have to find another mechanism to provide offsite storage for your encryption keys.

SECaaS vendors provide everything from managed virtual private networks (VPNs), firewalls, web application firewalls (WAFs), distributed denial-of-service (DDoS) protection, secure authentication, identity, and access management to incident management. With some of these providers, you retain access to rule management and configuration; with others this is not available. The primary challenge is that the vendor may not be able to provide you with access to their logs, and thus, your ability for security event management may be compromised unless you purchase a suite of security as a service solution, which includes both central logging and event management.

DaaS providers provide specific data such as individual credit history and reports, background checks, and other information that are not generally available but are generally useful. These vendors often provide no native logic for access to their data but provide access to the raw data only.

DBaaS vendors provide not only highly available high-speed databases but also database administration and data architecture as components of their service. This can permit a small organization that cannot afford the high cost of database licensing and DBA support staff to have access to highly available scalable databases. In writing contracts with DBaaS providers, it is imperative that a clause defining data ownership is clearly specified and that the customer put in place an alerting mechanism every time the vendor needs access to the customer data; otherwise, the customer sacrifices any claim to data integrity, confidentiality, authenticity, or control over their data.

I am not going to touch on either test environment as a service or virtual desktop as a service. Neither concerns the deployment of a production service-oriented application other than a test environment, which could, in theory, provide a platform for application test. APIaaS, however, provides a service front end for back-end applications where the company has an expertise that they wish to market but not the expertise to expose this as a service securely.

Hybrid infrastructures combine the use of some of the above services with often a data and database back end, which is internal, exposed through an API (which may or may not be built as a service and may or may not be put in place by an APIasS provider). Private clouds, however, keep the entirety of the infrastructure in house, exposing perhaps only the presentation layer of the application. To run a private cloud is to do more than just to leverage virtual machine technology; it is to leverage all the dynamic deployment and management techniques available in the public cloud.

The architectural team will want to consider which, if any, of these services they wish to leverage, using them underneath the application architecture. However, the decision to put an application into the cloud does not preclude making decisions regarding the layout of the infrastructure, which is the primary job of the infrastructure architect.

This layout will be designed to meet requirements for responsiveness as well as security and platform. Some decisions will be based on security, such as if the data are very sensitive and the risk of data breach is unacceptable, then the use of DBaaS will not likely be open to consideration, but security as a service may be leveraged to have the specialized expertise of the service provider available. If the requirements for performance and uptime are high, use of either platform as a service or even infrastructure as a service may be considered for at least the presentation layer of the application, if not the business layer.

Ideally, the infrastructure architecture is segregated into multiple networks with border firewalls at the edge of each tier. The layout of the networks will closely approximate the application architecture but will reflect considerations of the technology deployed. As an example, while there may be a network dedicated to the presentation layer, it may be segregated into two actual networks, one containing an application proxy and the other containing the actual web servers separated by a web application firewall or a load balancer or both. Sometimes, the load balancer will be placed in front of the application proxy, and in some infrastructure designs, there will be no application proxy.

Where the components of the infrastructure are shifted to the cloud, the presence of a border firewall becomes at once critical to limit the traffic to only authorized devices but is also somewhat irrelevant as a simple IP address spoof might be sufficient to subvert such protections. Traffic between cloud and private systems must be not only over encrypted protocols but the digital signatures of the encryption keys should also be cryptographically validated to prevent such spoofing attacks from succeeding. Ideally, both sides of the encrypted tunnel are signed.

Where cloud services are used to host application components, whether they be APIaaS, PaaS, or IaaS, corporations surrender control of the firewall rules for key components of their application architecture to other organizations, and ironically many SECaaS vendors cannot work within others' clouds, limiting the enterprises' options to those security services provided by service providers whose specialties are not security.

Infrastructure nuances can impact security goals of availability. As an example, adding redundant network interfaces with additional IP addresses may not achieve the goal of providing fault-tolerant network interfaces, depending on the platform. Not all operating systems can fall over from one network interface to another. Just like a deep understanding of an application's components is required to build an application architecture that meets all business's needs, the infrastructure architect must have a deep understanding of the behavior of all components to design an effective architecture.

As this volume is concerned with the relationship between a particular kind of application architecture and security architectures, I am not going to explore further the concepts and challenges of an infrastructure.

## 2.3 Software Architectures

Software architectures are the structures of software, their elements, and the relationship between them. They are developed to reduce the complexity of software design by designating the components at an abstract level, with the goals of increasing the quality of communication regarding software development for people who do not develop software and increasing the value of these software components through reuse. They are designed to bring about the goals of business requirements through the understanding of the uses of the application and how best to leverage technology to meet both.

Application architectures often involve making trade-offs between functionality, performance, and security in the design, all of which are critical to the success of the business. The classic application architect will always choose functionality over performance and security, and for good reason, if the application cannot deliver on function, no one will care how fast or how secure it is.

SOAs represent a particular type of application architecture, but there are others. A classic application architecture is the thin client architecture. This application architecture is behind the development of applications on mainframes and many of the original web applications. In a thin client architecture, all business logic is hosted on a server and all the client does is represent to the user the interface into the application's logic and both collect and provide the application's information. Another application architecture is client/server, wherein a feature-rich client is distributed to computers, which then access the features and data resident on a server. In this application architecture, the business logic is distributed with the client so that some processing of information happens locally in the client and other activities happen on the server. Usually, the server is reserved for sensitive and lengthy transactions. Many Web 2.0 applications use this architecture.

The next few sections of this chapter will dive into the components of an application architecture and explore what makes an SOA so useful and compelling. Regardless of application architecture, there are some common elements to all architectures. The key principles of an application architecture are its design philosophy, the presentation layer, the business layer, the data, service, workflow, and communications layers.

### 2.3.1 Key Principles

There are two design philosophies that will drive software architectures: design to last or design to change. Applications that are designed to last become cornerstones of business processes but are often orphaned on outdated technology with dwindling support staff as the application ages. Eventually, these applications become "legacy" applications, continuing to provide business value but without the ease of use associated with innovations.

Applications that are designed to change must consider which components are best reused and which are best replaced. Designing with change in mind involves careful consideration as to which parts of the application are most susceptible to change and which parts of the application are most vulnerable to change.

To minimize this risk, application architects often use design and modeling tools such as the Unified Modeling Language to both capture requirements and design decisions and measure their impact.

Use of higher-level frameworks often make the best sense as they provide a reusable base on which you can build a product, focusing on what is unique about your application. The problem with using such frameworks is that you are dependent on market forces. If you choose a framework, which is then abandoned by the supporting vendor, as Microsoft abandoned Silverlight in 2011, you may be faced with the necessity of changing frameworks, sunsetting the application, or converting it to legacy status. An SOA can extend the life of a legacy system, providing a scalable interface to systems too valuable to sunset.

One key principle that reduces the risk of obsolescence is the principle of loose coupling. By designing a modular application with minimal relationships between front-end interfaces, back-end business logic, and data processing, you can improve both maintainability and interoperability. SOAs are based on this principle.

Another area where SOAs assist architects in their design is in the need to develop an architecture in an iterative and incremental fashion. The ability to design and build components, test, and validate and then either revise the architecture when assumptions are proven unfound or expand the architecture as assumptions are validated.

One element that is common to most modern application architectures is that an application consists of layers that provide special services and the interfaces between those layers. These layers are the presentation layer or the user interface, the service layer, the business layer, the data layer, and any data sources. Crosscutting these layers are security, operations, and communications, which leads to the intersections with a security architecture, operational infrastructure and architecture, and communications frameworks.

Similar to how a security architecture will look to enforce separation of duties, an application architecture will look to enforce separation of concerns. By componentizing the design, maintenance on the application is simplified, and code reuse can be optimized. One must carefully delineate the boundaries to minimize the couplings between components and prevent component overlap.

An object, procedure, or component should be designed with a single purpose. By adhering to the single responsibility principle, you reinforce the separation of concerns. You also enable the development team to effectively implement agile project management and development techniques. You can only adhere to this principle, however, if a very clear understanding of what each distinct purpose is. It is not uncommon to set the boundaries of a task too wide to result in a multifaceted code.

Related to this is the principle of nonduplication of functionality. If, in another component of the application, you need to have a similar feature to the one already designed with a slightly different result, modify the existing component to have this result as one of its use cases. Simplicity of design can be overdone, resulting in code bloat and confusion as to which of the many similar modules performs the specific function that is needed.

Application design should enforce the principle of least knowledge, wherein an application component should not need to know the inner workings of another application component even where dependencies exist.

Another key design philosophy could easily be described as the avoidance of needless features. Designing the application for only what is needed does not add anything, no matter how much fun it may be to design or use. This design principle is frequently ignored, resulting in application bloat and often security vulnerabilities.

Operational and security concerns should be built into the application design. Key items such as metrics and logs should be part of the design, and quality assurance (QA) testing should validate that the metrics produced provide the desired indicators of application performance and state.

Component design should be consistent with the application layer. There is no need to develop code for the presentation layer in a service layer object. While one would think that this would fall naturally from the development of coding to a single purpose, it is not uncommon to misunderstand the purpose of a component during the requirements gathering or fail to distinguish the boundaries of a component properly.

Communication between the layers should be consistent and managed. Each layer should be able to communicate only with the adjacent layers; otherwise, the application will become too complex and hard to manage. This can also lead to security vulnerabilities, especially when the presentation layer communicates with the data layer directly.

An important consideration for the architecture is the purpose of the application. If the application is a mobile application designed for a phone, then it must be designed to have a very lightweight interface. If the application is designed for use in a browser, then it may have a very feature-rich and potentially heavy interface.

Finally, one must consider those elements that cross the layers:

- Instrumentation
- Authentication
- Authorization
- Exception management
- Communication
- Caching
- Logging

The careful reader will have noticed that three of those concerns are key components of the security architecture. These should be designed with that architecture in mind so that they may provide more than just authentication, authorization, and logging and become part of a comprehensive management of business risk.

*2.3.2 Presentation Layer*

The presentation layer is the layer at which both an individual and an attacker will use an application. It is very important to consider both user stories when designing the application's presentation layer as every point of input is a specific source of authentication and authorization into the business logic of the application and when under attack, may also become an interface without authorization into other layers of the application including the data layer.

Presentation layers are usually composed of two fundamental objects: the user interface components and presentation logic. The presentation logic may include style sheets or other items that are independent of user action such as graphics, colors, and the locations of elements on the interface. A common mistake that is made by application developers and architects is to use the presentation logic for authentication and authorization functions. While it would seem a logical leap that because all interface elements in which users interact with the application have by default the secondary function of points of authentication and authorization to perform the functions for which they are presented to the user, the logic to process these core security functions will not be located in the presentation layer in a well-designed application.

When the actual authentication and authorization logic is included in the presentation logic, it is more readily attacked. Especially in applications developed in the Web 2.0 framework using AJAX (which is not so much a language as a way of using a language—or a framework imposed on a language for which it was not designed), the authentication logic is often fully exposed, allowing an attacker to present to the application the expected responses of an authorized transaction without the actual authentication that should trigger such a response.

Application architects tend to concern themselves with specific design issues in the presentation layer to optimize the user experience. These would be issues of:

- Data caching
- Communication
- Composition
- Error handling
- Navigation

Data caching is one of the most important techniques to improve the speed of data, image, and experience rendering. An important consideration is that certain data such as social security numbers or credit card numbers should never be cached. The extra security is worth the speed penalty, which should be minimal.

Communication issues are important to manage as not all requests will result in short-term responses, and different techniques need to be deployed based on the speed of the running logic. When code runs past a user's expectations, this may cause the user to reinitialize the sequence, causing the code to take even longer to respond. Application architects design application communications with either many small requests to pull together a large response or one large request. This latter technique is usually used when the user does not have to wait on the completion of the request.

Communication issues can also provide a point of attack into the application layer if the communication system is overloaded through either repetition of request or reinitialization of long requests. These are application layer denial of service attacks.

Long-running requests should be asynchronous and provide feedback to the user on the progress. Allowing the user to cancel such a thread is a polite thing to do. When you need to return a large amount of information, a common and valued technique is to display data as they become available. This is only possible when the many small request strategies are utilized. However, this is a rather undesirable strategy where you have a high-frequency change environment with many data dependencies in the transaction, as this could render results inaccurate because the rest of the data are still being queried unless strong data locking mechanisms are deployed.

The design considerations regarding composition have less to do with security than other design considerations of the presentation layer. The dynamically generated content has the benefit of being customizable. One mistake that is rather common is to have the logic for the components to be rendered located in the presentation layer. As this is often linked to the authorization of the individual, it is likely that an attacker could then use this logic to elevate privileges and gain access to unauthorized functionality. It is extremely important to remember that all the presentation layer logic is exposed to the attacker for inspection at run time through an attack proxy.

While some polite notice of an error condition should be rendered, especially when the error is regarding information that was omitted or improperly submitted in the application's use, these messages should be as devoid of content as possible. As always, the business logic for error trapping and message rendering should not be in the presentation layer logic but rather passed to it from other layers of the application. Error messages should send messages to the business layer for handling, checking to see if a service or database failure caused the exception as examples.

When designing for application flow, an architect looks to optimize the use of the application so that it is easy and logical and nothing is missed in the capability of the product and that all dependencies are addressed before the use of the application is advanced. Here, care must be taken to ensure that the business logic cannot be subverted and that things cannot be done out of the intended order or with data not intended. Most important, validation of input needs to be taken so that there is a confidence that data dependencies come from within the application or valid user input, not from code manipulation or injection. If the application is being written using the J2EE framework, HTTP Data Integrity Validator (HDIV) can be used as an invaluable tool to prevent malicious manipulation of the presentation layer. If .net is used as an alternative framework, then the Web Protection Library can be used to prevent injection attacks and other malicious modifications of the presentation layer.

### 2.3.3 Business Layer

Some application architects dispute the need for a business layer and would claim that all business logic should be handled either in the data layer or in the presentation layer. This is a two-tier application architecture. Having worked in companies with applications written for this architecture, I can speak for the ability to secure such an application architecture. I can also speak for the challenges to maintain code developed under such narrow constraints.

When business logic is coupled with presentation logic, it is hard to maintain and grow either. Changes in the visual presentation of the application are necessarily more complex and prone to mistakes. Changes in the data model and communication become mired in a need to preserve logic tied to an outdated data model. Application support and maintenance under these conditions eventually deteriorate to the point where application changes become odious and the business either begins to suffer in its reputation with its customers due to an increasing amount of bugs or the business halts investment in the application, and all development is relegated to the role of patch/fix.

The security of the two-tier application which I was encharged with protecting was ensured mostly through the deployment of a third tier of infrastructure in the form of a web application firewall. This provided a limited ability to mask security vulnerabilities by blocking the behavior that would allow exploitation. However, as the number of bugs within the application grew, masking the vulnerabilities became increasingly problematic as the techniques used to block these vulnerabilities would actually prevent business logic within the presentation layer from functioning.

Creating a three-tier application architecture allows the development and maintenance of business logic without being impinged by the constraints of an application interface or encumbered by the need to interact directly with the data model.

Many application architects divide the business layer into two main components: the business facade and the actual business logic. The business facade provides an abstraction of the other three components to facilitate and simplify communication with the business layer. The business logic consists primarily of workflow and data manipulation and validation. Other architects put forward the design philosophy that this division is simply due to poor understanding of the location of the presentation layer and the communications layer in relation to the business logic.

### 2.3.4 Data Layer

The data layer comprises both the actual data and the code used to manipulate and query that data. This, however, is not meant to imply that the data layer of an application architecture is the data architecture. However, the data architecture must be understood and properly integrated into the application, and this is done through the data layer. This code may be static or dynamic in nature. Where static, such as with a database-stored procedure, there is the opportunity to optimize the language for efficiency and accuracy. The problem is that this depends on you knowing in advance and planning for all possibilities, and that is not always possible. Thus, all data access technologies have the capacity to be dynamic or static.

There are multiple data access technologies, each with different strengths. XML is, as an example, both a data access technology and a data description language and works well for data access where data relationships are not well known. Structured Query Language (SQL) is a structured language for accessing structured data where data relationships are well known. Other languages leverage unstructured syntax for accessing data where the structure is not known in advance. Google uses natural language syntax to access the data it indexes on the Internet to provide fast and mostly accurate results to searches for which there can be no preplanning. The choice of data access language involves a knowledge of the strengths and weakness of the language to access the data in question.

Other issues that must be considered in the design of the data layer include batching of commands to improve performance; the handling of binary objects, especially large ones; and the handling of exceptions, transactions, and validation.

Batching reduces the load on a database by combining multiple commands into a single database connection. As many databases have a threshold on connections rather than on queries, batching can reduce the load on a database more effectively than the best indexing scheme.

Binary large objects (BLOBs) are a special case and are rarely queried directly but are often part of the response to a query. Thus, it is not uncommon to place BLOB data into the presentation layer where it can be summoned quickly, often placing frequently retrieved BLOBs into a data cache.

As entire volumes have been written regarding data architectures, there is no way that I can do the subject justice in one short chapter. However, the issues regarding data queries are a subject that should be addressed simply because of the frequency at which this is leveraged maliciously. One area that should be out of scope of this volume, however, is the nature of the data schema, regardless of whether the schema is a star schema, object-oriented, hierarchical, binary tree or a relational, service-oriented applications interface with the data layer as a logical whole. However, this does not mean that data are never removed from the data layer. On the contrary, XML is a data description language and may actually be used as a database. Thus, any time that properties, variables, or attributes are leveraged through queries or provided through XML parsing and use, the application is accessing the data layer. This leads to the realization that there are different kinds of data and that the data required for business logic need to be kept separate from the data that provide information to the user of the application.

Wherever possible, connections should be batched to prevent an inadvertent denial of service from the happy problem of a lot of people using the application. I have witnessed the impact of each new use of the application opening a fresh connection to the database due to the architect's mistaken assumption that this would best preserve the ability to track and respond to the use of the application by the customer. As the application became a success, its design limited its scalability and performance, setting a ceiling on how many customers could use it simultaneously while system resources purchased to support large user loads went underutilized.

The application should take advantage of connection pooling, leveraging a trusted security layer, which offloads authentication but preserves identity and passes authorization to the underlying database. However, it is imperative that the authorization for the data requested be validated before returning it to ascertain that there has been no compromise at other layers of the application architecture. A simple data validation check for authorization would prevent many attacks, which provide access to the password table of the database, something for which no end user should have authorization.

Error handling is problematic at the data layer. If you introduce retry logic, you risk both self-inflicted and malicious denial of service on your application where a badly formed query continues to not return data, tying up precious data connections.

Application logic and data logic are often contradictory in structure. Object-oriented programming has problems interacting with structured data models that do not exist when interacting with an object-oriented database. Where application and data modeling are divergent, consider putting in place translation logic in the communication and messaging layer of the application logic. Failure to do so can lead to malicious use by allowing manipulation of the encapsulation of object-oriented code where hidden elements can be exposed and manipulated to access data.

Finally, data queries can be either dynamic or static. Security best practice of using static stored procedures is often not flexible enough for an application's business requirements. When queries must be dynamically generated, great care should be taken to ensure that they are parameterized and that variables are strongly typed. String concatenation should be avoided due to its vulnerability to injection attacks.

### 2.3.5 *Workflow*

An application's workflow is the logic through which events happen in a desired sequence. Frequently planned out in a logic tree or a flow chart, it may be as simple as select product, place into shopping cart, check out, pay for purchase, and receive confirmation. The trouble is that if you mandate this workflow, then none of your customers can ever order more than one product per order, a strategy designed to quickly drive a company bankrupt.

There are three basic kinds of workflow, each driven by the nature of the application and need for data manipulation. The workflow example I used above is an example of a simple sequential workflow. Sequential workflows may have conditional branching, but all events must follow a clearly defined sequence. While not appropriate for an e-business application that is consumer facing, it may be very appropriate for an event creation and management solution.

For applications that depend on tracking state, where a stage of the application must be completed before the next phase must begin, you have the so-called machine state workflow. This kind of workflow is appropriate for application wizards, such as the DCPromo application that transforms a Windows server into a domain controller. SOAs benefit from using a machine state workflow as each service can readily communicate the service state.

The third kind of workflow, which is driven by the data state, can also be leveraged by SOAs that are more transitionally oriented. An example of a simple form of this workflow would be certificate issuance and signing.

A clever attacker, who represents to later states of the application in which prior and dependent steps have been completed successfully, can subvert all workflows. This is why, especially for a distributed and service-oriented application, it is essential that the design not only keep workflow elements hidden from the browser state but also not using cookies or other tokens, which may be subject to manipulation. Regardless of the use of data state of the system state, these states must be communicated in a way that cannot be replayed or falsified.

### 2.3.6  Communications and Messaging

While the design elements of a good communications system are essential to any SOA, for that matter, any distributed system, good communications improve application reliability and performance for any multitiered application.

There are many communications mechanisms, each with their distinct traits and advantages. Message-based communications are often used when crossing physical or process boundaries due to their ability to be queued in case of system failure or network interruption. Message queues can support transactional systems and allow for reliable once-only delivery.

Object-based communications are often used only when logical boundaries need to be crossed, such as between tiers of a multitiered application that is not distributed across corporations; however, they can be used to great effect in an SOA due to their ability to encapsulate information. Another technique for applications that are not distributed in nature is to use direct communication such as method calls. However, this restricts the ability to segregate an application into multiple tiers.

There are different communications and messaging techniques, each of which provides the application architect distinct advantages in moving information within the application components.

1. Duplex messages are two-way communications sent independently.
2. Fire and forget are messages sent with no reply required or expected.
3. Reliable sessions are messages sent end to end regardless of the intermediaries.

4. Request/response are like duplex messages in so far as they are messages between two components, but each message requires a distinct and dependent response.

Messaging systems often have different components and can represent a mini-architecture within the application architecture. They may contain channel adapters, which are components that can access the API and application data directly, publishing messages based on the data and invoking functionality through API calls.

A message bus is often used to connect disparate applications through messaging. This approach to distributed systems is an alternative to an SOA, which is also based on messaging. A messaging bridge may also be made available to connect different messaging systems and replicate messages between them.

There are also multiple mechanisms for message delivery to be considered. Messages may be sent with only one recipient in mind, in a point-to-point system. Messages may be widely broadcast to any subscriber of the application, which remains unaware of the recipient.

*2.3.7  Service Layer*

A service layer is a method of providing access to application functionality regardless of the presentation layer, as it has as its users other applications. In general, the service layer is a message-based layer, which is both slower and more flexible than a direct API, which might be exposed. Interaction with the service layer is often asynchronous, with messages routed, modified, and delivered in a potentially different order from which they are sent. An application can expose services without being designed as an SOA, so no assumptions regarding exposing services as requiring the full rigors of an SOA need to be made when designing an application for which there is a business requirement for exposed services.

The service layer should be scoped to perform an application function and not as a narrow component. It should be designed as customer agnostic, in as generic terms as possible, with the broadest representation of the application functionality made available. Like with all application layers, it should not expose other layers of the application and should be separated from the infrastructure as much as possible.

The service should be able to detect and manage invalid requests as well as repeated messages and handle these gracefully. Most important, and to reiterate, a service must be able to handle messages in an asynchronous manner. Much like the data layer, a service layer benefits from processing message requests in bulk, or in batches, rather than in small discrete quantities.

As a unique interface into the application, a service layer must be concerned with many of the same issues as a presentation layer:

- Authentication and authorization
- Communication
- Exception management

However a service must also manage many of the same concerns as the messaging layer of the application:

- Message construction
- Message end point
- Message protection
- Message routing
- Message transformation
- Message validation

Message validation is a key security issue. Messages should be validated for length, range, format, type, as well as expected data. If all messages are not validated, then the application may not be reliable but nevertheless secure. Schemas can be used to validate data, and in an SOA, a validation service can be developed and exposed.

### 2.4 Service-Oriented Architecture

To properly understand what an SOA is, it is helpful to understand where it sits as an architecture and the problem that an SOA tries to solve. An SOA, first, is an application architecture. Unlike other applications, in a pure SOA, all application layers comprise services. This is not to imply that the entire application runs at the service layer.

SOA was developed to solve the problem of how to connect disparate systems in a way that they could function together in a systematic manner. These systems, or applications, each provide to the organization the value for which they are designated, but often this value would be enhanced if either the processing or the results could be integrated with the information processing of other applications.

SOAs are not the first attempt to solve the problem of how best to leverage the capability of disparate systems in a unified and comprehensive way.

### 2.4.1 Distributed Computing and Services

The message-oriented model (MOM) was developed with the idea of distributing the components of a system among existing and emerging applications and platforms. Messages were used to connect these systems, implemented through specialized platforms called message queues. Message queues are very reliable; however, they require not only a system to manage them but also a staff to maintain the messaging system. Most important, support for the message queues had to be built into all the application components, restricting the implementation of a system built on an MOM architecture to the internal needs of a single corporate infrastructure.

As a software architecture, MOM depends on every component being designed with MOM in mind, instead of leveraging the capabilities of the existing applications in a synergistic manner.

To provide this synergy, each application in an SOA is treated as if it can only perform one specialized function or as if it were an element in the larger software. This specialized function is called a service. Thus, each service functions as an element of the SOA, where the structure and the defined relationship between the elements must transcend application and often corporate boundaries. This allows for the creation and deployment of large distributed applications.

SOAs can leverage messages the same way an MOM can, as a means to transport information from one service to another for processing.

To be considered as a service, the functionality of an application must possess distinct characteristics. First, the functionality to be considered as a service must have complete autonomy; more specifically, this must be limited to a narrow function. It must be able to complete this function without the need for any other component. Second, this function must be directly accessible remotely via some protocol. It is not sufficient for the functionality to be embedded deep within the application and be dependent on other components to provide the business value. If the application functionality depends on, as an example, additional user input to provide the desired business functionality, it is ineligible to participate as a service unless this can be abstracted and presented to the application as part of the message.

The service must be able to present an informal specification of the purpose, functionality, constraints, and usage of the service. This specification, often called a contract, is often represented in a formal language such as Interactive Data Language (IDL) or Web Services Description Language (WSDL). This contract may provide (though is not required to do so) a detailed semantic description of how to call the service. This semantic description does not need to be limited by WSDL or IDL constraints, even when wrapped by WSDL or IDL.

A service must expose an interface to service clients. This interface will consist of service stubs or application front ends. Front ends may be a web page or an API.

Behind this front end is the actual implementation, the code that performs the actual business logic consisting of application code, configuration, and perhaps data structures.

SOAs that began to be developed as businesses realized that other companies' applications provided a better solution to meet their requirements than their own internally developed systems. They realized that they could provide better products to their customers if they found a way to leverage the capabilities and expertise of other companies for components that were not part of the core competency of their own company.

As an example, a travel company might recognize that MapQuest's maps (or Google Maps) were vastly superior to their own, and because their homegrown map application was not how they brought in new business but still provided a desired component to their customers, it would benefit everyone if there was a way to leverage the capabilities of the other companies' superior product.

SOAs abstract the diverse applications, protocols, systems, and data into four key concepts:

- Application front end
- Service
- Service repository
- Service bus

An application front end is the owner of the business process the application provides and other services can use. It is the interface, the API, the graphical user interface (GUI).

A service is an implementation that provides business logic and data; a service contract that specifies functionality, usage, and constraints, which must be observed by any client; and an interface that exposes the functionality. A service repository stores the service contract of the individual services.

A service bus connects all the services and application front ends with each other. If two participants need to communicate, they do so via the service bus, which uses the service descriptions found in the service contracts to govern how to format the messages, which call the application front end or interface. While similar to the concept of a software bus as defined in Common Object Request Broker Architecture (CORBA), the components of the service bus do not have to have been designed to interoperate in the fashion in which the service bus defines their relationship within the context of the implementation. Each service may have been designed around distinct and alternative business requirements, but because the implementation is exposed as a service, it may be reused to fulfill emerging and new needs.

Thus, each service may serve different roles across different service buses while providing the same discrete unit of business logic, which allowed it to be defined as a service.

There are various technologies that can be applied in the implementation of an SOA. Some of these are more appropriate for internal enterprise-specific projects; others may be applied to any project with any scope.

Precisely because of the common architecture, there are issues that transcend the individual technologies that must be considered when establishing a security architecture appropriate for the protection of the business and its objectives as supported by the specific implementation of an SOA. Before we can explore the relationship between the SOA and security architectures, we need to explore specific variations of SOAs.

*2.4.2 Process-Oriented SOA*

Data integrity is a key factor in the success of many SOAs, as data are transferred from service to service. However, the integrity of data is not sufficient to guarantee that the service returns the correct results due to the complexity of business processes that span multiple systems and often involve multiple corporations. A process-oriented SOA is an SOA designed with the primary goal of managing the integrity of process. Process integrity involves not only the integrity of the assets but also their utility throughout the architecture.

The principles of entity, domain, and referential integrity are borrowed, where appropriate, from relational databases. Entity integrity requires that each row in a table be uniquely identified. Domain integrity requires that certain data be within a valid range (such as the date of purchase of an item not being in the future or before the date of which the item was first placed on sale). Referential integrity refers to the validity of the relationship between different data sets, preserving as an example the names of the residents in relationship to their appropriate residence.

Where data must be processed across multiple systems through the use of their services, there is the risk of inconsistencies that impact the validity of both the data and the use of the data in all services. There might be technical failures, business exceptions, and special cases that impact the integrity of the process. Because the process is not centrally controlled, the impact of the failure of any particular component may be high.

There have been a number of techniques applied to solve this problem, each with their own merits and issues. The most common approach is to apply logging and tracing. This is similar to the use of transaction logs in a transactional system, allowing for recovery to a valid state in the event of a failure. The problem is that it is difficult for logging and tracing to resolve issues that relate to logical processes, which span the multiple systems involved in an SOA.

Online transaction processing systems were developed to enable large numbers of users to manipulate shared data concurrently. Such systems are based on the concept of transactions on a unit of work that transforms data from one state to another. A unit of work is presumed to be atomic or indivisible, consistent (move from one consistent state to another), in isolation where no process is visible to any other, and durable where committed updates are permanent. Such systems depend on a central control mechanism that resolves conflicts. Such a central control mechanism is often unavailable to an SOA that leverages services from multiple organizations.

The two-phase commit protocol (2PC) was developed to allow online transactional processing to span multiple systems. A transaction coordinator is implemented as part of a transaction monitor. This enforces that in the first phase of the processing all relevant locks have been acquired and that the state of the data has been properly captured. Dependent on the results of this examination, the transaction coordinator informs the participating systems if they should roll the transaction forward or back. These systems "vote" on how to handle the data; a single abort vote will cause the entire transaction to be rolled back.

All of these mechanisms of tracking changes to data are predicated on some assumptions that often do not apply in an SOA. One is that that it is possible to ensure the isolation to the data; another is that the transaction is short term. Neither can be assumed in an SOA, where the various services may be entirely ignorant of access and use of data by other services, and transactions are often long lived. SOAs are also often implemented on discontinuous networks, and none of the above mechanisms are designed to operate under such conditions.

Two techniques scale well to address the issues of process integrity. The first is that of persistent queues with transactional steps. Persistent queues, which follow the data, can guarantee consistency of the individual steps of the process, where errors are handled by a dequeue, and the error is returned with the data. Such systems depend heavily on the presence of a message-queuing system and are more often implemented in internal SOAs where such systems are present.

The second is transactional chains and compensation. Complex workflows are created through individual process steps (transaction chains), where failures are dealt with through compensating transactions that logically undo a prior transaction. Each transaction is made visible to each service so that data may be made available to a compensating control.

Another approach has been the development of a process-centric service, which may or may not use persistent queues or transactional chains. This service operates as both client and server within the service bus and maintains the process state throughout the entire service bus.

### 2.4.3 Web Services or an Externally Focused SOA

Unlike an internal SOA, a web service-based SOA cannot rely on a single monolithic service bus. To this end, web services are

| Service Registry (UDDI) | Business Process (BPEL) | Quality of Service | | | | | | |
|---|---|---|---|---|---|---|---|---|
| | Service Implementation | | | | | | | |
| | Service Description (WSDL) | | | | | | | |
| | Service Protocol (SOAP, REST) | Security / WS-Security | Coordination & Transactions / WS-Atomic Transact & WS-Business Activity | Reliable Messaging / WS-Reliable Messaging | Message Correlation / WS-Addressing | Introspection / WS-Inspection | Event Model / WS-Event Model | Management / ESB Management Features |
| | Service Bus | | | | | | | |

**Exhibit 2.1**  Web 2.0 and SOA (web services). *Abbreviations:* BPEL, Business Process Execution Language; REST, Representational State Transfer; SOA, Service-oriented architectures; SOAP, Simple Object Access Protocol; UDDI, Universal Description, Discovery and Integration.

based on slightly different principles than a traditional SOA. Each service needs to be reusable, stateless, autonomous, abstract, discoverable, and loosely coupled. Instead of a formal service bus, you have a service integration layer, which operates as a logical or virtual service bus.

Services engage with this service integration layer and with each other through a formal contract, which defines the terms of information exchanged and provided supplemental service description. Since services need to be discoverable, they make themselves known through a service provider. Services also need to know which service to call and thus will have a service requester. These roles can be and often will be reversed as the role of the service changes within the larger workflow from client to server. There may be more than one service provider through which a workflow must pass before it arrives at its ultimate destination; these are called intermediary services. Intermediary services may or may not do more than discover the next step in the workflow, depending on the nature of the service and the contract it has as a service provider.

Web services tend to be broken down into one of a set of roles:

- Utility service
- Business service
- Controller service
- Proxy service
- Wrapper service
- Coordination service
- Process service

The nature of the service offered, how to engage it, and the results to be expected are all defined in a specialized XML document present on the service provider. This document will be written in the WSDL. The WSDL functions as the integration layer of the web service, providing the basis for other services to discover how to engage the particular service.

Some implementations of web services will register themselves in a central registry of services using a specification called the Universal Description, Discovery and Integration (UDDI). UDDI repositories provide a marketplace of generic services and are often hosted by major corporations.

Many protocols can be used and are used to communicate between the various web services over TCP/IP. The most common is SOAP. SOAP provides a standard message format that consists of an XML document capable of hosting remote procedure call (RPC) and document-centric data. SOAP can be easily leveraged by both synchronous and asynchronous data exchange models. SOAP, as a raw protocol set, does not define a preset language, allowing the application designer to create a language specific to the architecture.

An alternative to SOAP-based web services is the Representational State Transfer (REST)-based web services. REST leverages the existing vocabulary of the HTTP or other robust application layer protocols with existing vocabularies. SOAs based on REST are easier to implement but less flexible.

With second-generation web services, or Web 2.0, a limited vocabulary was developed to provide a common framework for common constructs that all business services rely on, such as business process or workflow, security, reliability, policies, and attachments. These standards, managed by the Organization for the Advancement of Structured Information Standards (OASIS), are called the WS or web services standards.

The most common kind of web services is the XML web service. Like all web services, the communications of an XML-based web service leverages the Internet protocols for communications but most commonly uses SOAP. Equally important is that all data are expressed and communicated via documents formatted in the XML.

Another commonly found version of web services is called Web API (often called Web 2.0). Web services in the Web API model do not depend on XML for data communications, often leveraging HTML instead, utilizing HTTP as the transport protocol. Applications built on this version of an SOA have one key distinct assumption not always found in other SOA implementations: that the services are stateless. They use REST, instead of messaging or operations like a more traditional SOA and limit operations to the well-known operations of HTTP (GET, POST, PUT, DELETE).

### 2.4.4 Enterprise Service Bus

An enterprise service bus is the technical infrastructure of the distributed environment. It is composed of an XML-based communications protocol with a message-oriented middleware core to perform the actual message delivery. There are a variety of message bus frameworks in common use. Message bus frameworks such as Enterprise JavaBeans within the J2EE specification and Microsoft's .net are based on the capabilities of an application architecture. Others rely on either message queues or object-oriented communication infrastructures such as CORBA. In practice, a successful enterprise service bus is not a single product, no matter how flexible or how many communications protocols it supports, but one that supports accessing services on a meta level, which can leverage the capacities of all application architectures, allowing .net, Enterprise JavaBeans, and other diverse applications to function within a single business process.

### 2.5 Security Architecture

Security architectures are an abstraction of the protections provided to software and infrastructures to provide confidentiality, availability, and integrity of information. These can be layered on top of software and infrastructure as complementary, or they can be integral to the design and implementation of either or both.

Unlike in many application architectures, SOAs are usually designed with security in mind. However, it is an internally focused security rather than the integration into a larger security architecture.

In the absence of an architecture, security is often relegated to be no more than the security components of an infrastructure, namely, the controls on protocol usage and flow, with a nod to the need to authenticate. Sometimes, software applications will also consider the requirement for authorization as well as authentication.

Security architectures are more complex than this and were often developed to solve issues of maintaining confidentiality in military and government systems where the consequences of a failure of the security system might be loss of life. Unlike other architectures in consideration in this volume, security architectures are not founded in technology, though they govern its implementation.

Just like an SOA is only one kind of software architecture, there are many different security architectures. However, before we explore these architectures, we must explore certain governing principles that are foundational to all security architectures.

Fundamentally, information security is concerned with a class of risk management, specifically, management of risk regarding business information. Each information security architecture is designed to address risk in a particular manner, so the selection of the risk tolerance of an organization often drives the choice of security architecture.

Second, there are six properties of information that may be at risk. This model for information security is fondly called the Parkerian hexad after Donn Parker who extended the triad of confidentiality, integrity, and availability, after demonstrating how they are incomplete to properly secure information. The goals of the model are to guarantee:

- Confidentiality
- Integrity
- Availability
- Utility
- Control
- Authenticity

Confidentiality is the property of information that restricts knowledge of that information to only those who have valid and approved access to that information. This is the attribute of information most commonly associated with information security.

Integrity is the property of information that guarantees that information has not been altered without authorization. A failure to maintain information integrity is often the hardest to detect and can have tremendous impacts as a failure of integrity can cause loss of trust in the application.

Availability is the property of information that provides access to the information by authorized individuals at all times for which those individuals have been authorized access. Almost everything within software and the underlying infrastructure is designed with providing availability to information to authorized individuals as a key component of the service.

Utility is the property of information that ensures that the information is usable to those individuals to whom access and use is authorized. Data may be encrypted, thus confidential, unchanged, thus have integrity, be accessible to the authorized persons—though only in the encrypted state, remain in the control of the organization, and remain authentic but not be usable to anyone due to an inability to decrypt the information.

Control or possession is the property of information that guarantees that only authorized individuals have had access to the information containers. If, as an example, a thief has access to encrypted data, control of that data is lost without necessarily compromising confidentiality.

Authenticity is the property of information that guarantees the ownership of the information. As an example, the authenticity of a will is verified through the signature of both the deceased and the witnesses.

Some security architectures only concern themselves with issues of confidentiality, integrity, and availability, approaching utility as a form of availability, control as a form of confidentiality, and authenticity as a form of integrity.

Another property that must be understood before security architectures are considered is the principle of least privilege. This principle is implicit in the property of confidentiality and availability that an individual must only have access to that to which there is a clear and defined need, and that the access granted is no more than that which is required to meet this need.

A seventh element can be added but is traditionally thought of as derived from a combination of others is privacy. I would argue that doing so comes from misunderstanding what privacy is. Privacy controls have more to do with the use of the data than just keeping it confidential. It is not enough to preserve the confidentiality of customers' data; you cannot use, as an example, their e-mail address to send advertisements without providing those customers with a means to have their e-mail address retained by you without receiving advertisements. Nor can you share it under a nondisclosure agreement (NDA) without their consent, even if the party bound by the NDA will also keep it confidential.

Security architectures are built from various models that are chosen for their appropriateness for the risk tolerance of the organization. These models are based on controlling the three common basic principles of data: confidentiality, integrity, and availability, though the better models also allow the control of utility, control, authenticity, and privacy.

### 2.5.1 Construction of a Security Architecture

The models that have been discussed are some of the tools used by security architects. Security architectures, however, do not start with models or other tools; security architectures start with policy. Policy is the fundamental remediation of information security risk within an organization. They are high-level documents, which detail the rules of conduct within the various functions of the business related to the storing, processing, and distribution of information.

As policies specify neither technology nor its implementation within an organization, standards and procedures are created to enforce the implementation of policy within an organization. Standards define what is implemented, and procedures define how it is used.

Policies are not static documents; when well written they are collaborative affairs derived from the input of many individuals within the organization. They stem from the results of a risk assessment, which will contain a business impact analysis. From this, an initial draft will be created, reviewed with the stakeholders, approved by the appropriate level of management, and then distributed.

Other components of a security architecture will be user awareness and training, compliance, security assessments and audits, and the organization of security regarding personnel, applications, and infrastructure.

Thus any discussion of the integration of the service-oriented architecture into a security architecture must begin with an organization's policy and associated tolerance for risk of a compromise of confidentiality, loss of integrity, failure of availability, loss of control, failure of utility, or inauthenticity of information.

## 2.5.2 Risk Management

There are many ways to perform a risk analysis, but they all have the same end game: to permit an organization sufficient understanding of the risks to their organization to manage it appropriately. Risk is a topic that is not easily understood. As an example, "There is a risk that hackers in the anonymous organization may attack our organization" is an inaccurate statement. Not because members of the anonymous organization will not attack, but because that is not an expression of a risk, it is an expression of the chance of a threat acting.

Risks are more than the threat that an organization may be attacked. When security analysts define the risk to the organization, they are discussing the probability that not only will a threat against an organization materialize but also there will be damage to the organization as a result of this.

Regardless of whether risks are expressed in formulaic terms or in more abstract terms such as "high," "medium," or "low," or even in colors, an organization that takes action to manage information security risks is an organization that is putting in place security controls.

There are four controls stemming from the only possible responses to risk: remediation, transference, avoidance, or acceptance. Organizations, however, often perceive risk differently from a security professional will, and will articulate language such as "we need to take risks." This is risk acceptance at its most basic and a key strategy of most businesses. If risks are not taken when opportunity is presented, then the business will not grow and prosper. The other side of that coin is that in taking a risk, the business may fail. Most information security professionals are very risk adverse and will always caution regarding that chance for failure. This may explain why no chief security officer ever became a chief executive officer.

Controls, which enforce risk remediation, are not the same as risk avoidance. They exist to allow the organization to engage in the chosen risky behavior, while reducing (not eliminating) the risk of failure. Risk avoidance, on the other hand, is choosing not to engage in the behavior to begin with.

Risk transference is a process that every adult does when they purchase an insurance policy. They are transferring the risk to an external organization at a fee. That organization is betting that the risk will not happen until they have collected enough fees to make the payout against the consequences less than their profit.

The challenge of risk management is to choose effective controls that remediate the risk less expensively than the cost of the impact. To reduce the risk of the impact of a computer virus on an organization, the organization could choose as its remediation strategy to prevent connectivity to the Internet. They could easily justify this strategy as having no cost to the business while providing tremendous success at remediating the risk while increasing the productivity of the work-place. However, the loss of capability to effectively communicate with customers and vendors via e-mail would seriously cripple the productivity of the organization, and if e-mail was permitted, but nothing else, then the inability to patch systems would keep the company vulnerable to the first e-mail virus that came along.

Impact, therefore, is not just damage done. There is also the potential for the loss of productivity. The time spent recovering from the attack, the time spent in putting in place controls that should prevent a second attack (and likely would have prevented the first) is time that was planned for other tasks whose deliverables now must slip. This kind of unbudgeted expense pulls funding from planned projects, which may not be able to be completed.

While most controls implemented are an effort at risk remediation, there are many different kinds of remediation. Some controls are preventative, some are detective, and some have both functions. As an example, most antimalware software functions to both detect the presence of malware and prevent it from functioning. An example of a control that is purely detective would be an intrusion detection system. A disk encryption system is an example of a control that is purely preventative.

Those controls are technological in nature. Information security is not a technological discipline. Unlike other information services, information security is focused first on people and processes, with a tertiary focus on technology. Unfortunately, too many organizations focus on the technological aspect of information security, the firewalls, antivirus, encryption, and so on. Their testing is limited to penetration testing and perhaps an annual test of the ability to recover from a disaster.

The controls needed by an application, regardless of architecture, are more than just technological in nature. There are process controls such as how an organization determines who has authorization to use the application, procedural controls such as how to return data to an organization after termination of contract, as well as the various technological controls, which will be the focus of this volume.

As the implementation of an application needs to integrate it into the larger security architecture of the entire organization, not just those components of information security concerned with technology, I will spend some time expanding on those aspects of information security.

### 2.5.3 Organization and Management

While at first glance it would appear that the organization and management of information security would have little impact on the architecture of applications, this would be an erroneous assumption. Much of the impact depends on where security sits within the software development life cycle, and much of that depends on where information security fits within an organization.

Information security usually falls in one of the following branches of an organization: as a separate and distinct entity under a chief security officer, as part of the engineering organization underneath a chief technology officer or director of engineering, or underneath information technology under a chief information officer. Where information security is part of the information technology office, it will have the least impact on the organization and the development of business products. This relationship will often be adversarial as the security program will find flaws within the application during the penetration test that could have been caught during the development life cycle. These become high-profile bugs that are embarrassing to the development and QA teams. They are often not addressed until there is a security breach due to the lack of respect held for information security within the organization.

Where information security is more valued within an organization and therefore more trusted, it will be positioned so as to be equivalent to the rest of product development within engineering and given the opportunity to review code and test the application before it is released. This may slow down deployment of new code, as the testing is often considered part of the QA process, but the bugs are caught and addressed with much less expense than organizations where the only security testing preformed is during the annual penetration test.

Where information security does not sit within the technology department of the organization, information security requirements are considered during product design and architecture. While this may happen within some organizations that place information security lower within the organization, when information security sits as a peer to the engineering organization, it has the authority to insist that its concerns are as important to the organization as any other business unit.

It is in these organizations that applications are always designed to be secure as well as functional. Both static analysis of the code and dynamic testing of the application are part of or in parallel to the QA process, and the penetration test remains as a vital part of the process.

While readers of this chapter may make the assumption that if information security does not sit at the executive level, there is no hope of either a truly secure application or the kind of integration of application architecture within security architecture that this book has as its core thesis. However, this is not the case. That kind of integration can happen in organizations where security has less prestige. Many chief technology officers or directors of engineering value information security highly and require that there are security requirements considered for each new business function and incorporate information security testing at all phases of their application development life cycle. It is in these organizations that the development of an SOA, which is secure as well as functional, has the chance of succeeding.

### 2.5.4 Third Parties

The management of third parties is a key component of the success of both an SOA and information security program. There is an implicit requirement to have a service contract in each WSDL, which outlines how the third party can interface with the service. These contracts are an extension of the contract that exists between the organizations.

These contracts will have conditions regarding the quality, responsiveness, and availability of the service to be provided as well as the security of the data transmitted and processed.

The application should be designed to validate that the contracts as presented in the third-party WSDL meet the specifications outlined in the business contract and that any WSDL contracts published by the organization meet the contractual language to which the organization has obligated itself.

While it may be the responsibility of the software architect to ensure that the contract presented in the WSDL accurately reflects the terms of the legal contract, it is the responsibility of the information security team to ascertain that the contract presented in the WSDL cannot be broken.

Even if the contract as represented in the WSDL is sound, there could be other items that invalidate a service contract. As an example, failure to maintain Payment Card Industry Data Security Standard (PCI DSS) compliance would invalidate any contract where maintaining such compliance is required. The security team must monitor third-party adherence to all the terms of their contract, and the application architecture must be flexible to change on the invalidation of a service provider due to the failure to maintain the contract. This is where a well-constructed SOA can provide tremendous resiliency to change as the work involved in changing a service provider is minimal compared to the work involved in calling a different vendor's proprietary API set.

### 2.5.5 Asset Management

The flip side to risk management is asset management. While too many people in information technology confuse assets with servers and switches, when a control is put in place to prevent an adverse impact, it is to protect an asset to the company.

To protect and manage your assets, you must first understand them. While many business applications have assets, the asset is often not the source code. Depending on the application, the asset is more likely to be the data and the business logic used to manipulate that data so that it becomes information.

This logic, often captured in the workflow layer, represents the business expertise of the business put into a tangible form. As this logic is only a component of the sum total of the services provided by most enterprises, the loss of control of the source code may not be a worry to the business owner, especially as deriving the logical workflow from source code is a nontrivial task.

A matter of greater concern is that a malicious user can manipulate assumptions made in the business logic often. Thus, the logic and its assumptions must be understood and tested by the information security architect.

While the data collected by the application may or may not have any value to the hosting entity, the information derived from this data will often have tremendous value. Even the hit statistics provides the marketing staff key information they need to govern the success of a campaign and grow the business. As such, the security architect needs to understand all the data associated with the business application, not just the data that the application is explicitly designed to collect and process. Appropriate controls must be designed and put in place to guarantee as appropriate the confidentiality, control, utility, availability, authenticity, and integrity of all business data. These assets must be identified, classified, and managed.

### 2.5.6 Information Classification

For organizations to manage their information properly, they must understand the nature of the information they are trying to manage. Information classification programs are designed to help a company identify the information it possesses and the risk to the organization should a threat agent be able to access and act on the information.

Classification schemes need to have nothing to do with the need to protect the information in question to be useful to the organization. The Dewey Decimal System is a very effective and flexible classification system in use by many organizations with similar goals.

Legal issues regarding data definition and handling are often key requirements in the classification schemes. Military organizations and those organizations, which do business with the military must classify their data accordingly. Those organizations which do business in the European Union or with individuals who are citizens of the European Union must consider EU privacy laws in their classification schemes, as most organizations which do business with the citizens of Massachusetts must content with MA General Law 201c.

When it comes to classification schemes that are useful in determining the nature of the protections, which must be applied, the most fundamental classification is if the information in question is public or internal. If the information is public, that does not mean that the organization does not need to put into place protections on the information, just that confidentiality of the information will not be a property that must be managed.

The classification of private information, outside of military organizations, has come to have specific legal and regulatory meaning and should be avoided as a classification unless used for information governed under one of the many privacy laws, which may be in scope for the organization in question. Security and application architects must meet with legal experts on the subject of data classification and handling.

"Restricted" is a classification term which may be used to refer to the data for which the principle of need to know, need to use is most strictly applied.

It is often useful to classify information as confidential; however, this begs the question: Who is entitled to access this confidential data? Thus, the classification of "Confidential" is not sufficient to the application of access control for the information.

Many organizations borrow levels of confidentiality as a means to establish the appropriate security controls. This leads to classifications such as "Top Secret" and "Highly confidential" where the organization establishes a matrix of individuals authorized to access such material.

"For Internal Distribution Only" is a very useful classification, which defines an audience and for which access controls may be readily applied.

"Proprietary" is another classification term that can be useful, depending on the organization. However, while the term designates ownership, it does not designate any special handling of the information.

Ideally, the classification system designates who can have access to what and why under what conditions. Most information classification systems are less specific than this but provide a framework for implementing such controls as encryption, limited access, and so on.

As the architects of a distributed SOA design both the data and application architecture, it is imperative that data classification schemes be understood and followed, lest the very architecture become a mechanism for data disclosure and leakage.

### 2.5.7 *Identity Management*

While I will write at great length on the mechanics of identity management and federation in later chapters, it is important to understand the architectural issues involved in identity management both as they arise from information security and business requirements and impact application design and development.

There are four basic phases of identity management: registration, privilege management, revocation, and audit. The registration phase involves the creation of credentials that are to be assigned to an individual who will hold them as a custodian. Privilege management involves the authorization of those credentials for specific rights and capabilities within the application.

Revocation may involve the revocation of rights or privileges within an application or the ability to access the application or even the loss of the credential as an allowed or existent credential, which depends on circumstance. Revocation of rights or privileges may happen on change of role within an organization, termination, failure to use the assigned credentials, or any other change of status. Often a revocation of rights is followed by a revocation of access, and then a loss of credentials.

Audit is that process through which the current status of entitlements and accounts is checked to see if they are still authorized for the entitlement level assigned and if the accounts in existence have current authorized custodians.

In an ideal scenario, identity management is a process independent of but usable by the application in question. Various identity and access management architectures and designs are available to the application and security architect, but not all will be viable options to each company, nor under all circumstances.

Identity management may be outsourced to an external service provider, may be controlled through a single sign-on framework that integrates applications with a centralized authorization and identity store, may be integrated with a centralized directory service such as Active Directory or LDAP, and may be located within the application through databases or directories local and specific to the application.

Outsourcing identity management to an external identity provider such as openID allows individuals to utilize credentials they have already established to access your application and service. This is a common strategy for applications that provide limited services free to prospective customers and have a broader service class for paying customers. LinkedIn, Facebook, LiveJournal, Google, Yahoo, Verisign, and WordPress among many others offer external identity services as an option for their customers.

Single sign-on frameworks such as CA SiteMinder or Oracle Identity provide a single credential that can be used to access multiple applications hosted by the corporation. These can be used internally, providing the same credentialed authentication to a diverse series of internal applications or may be exposed externally through an e-business service layer.

While it is not required, single sign-on frameworks often utilize a centralized directory service such as LDAP, x500, or Active Directory. Directories are superior to databases for credential stores for a number of reasons. They are read-optimized, while databases are write-optimized. They permit a compare operation without a requirement for access to the password, preventing many of the injection attacks that have plagued applications that depend on databases for their credentials. They are extremely scalable both horizontally and vertically and are designed to be distributed. They readily provide attributes regarding the identity without a performance impact, even with repeated queries for additional information, and their hierarchical structure can be used for resource-based authorization models, as can their ability to group identities into deliberate security groupings based on role, department, function, or other logical organization.

The main problem with keeping the credentials record separate from the application database is speed. Each authorization check needs to query either the directory or session information passed from the browser. In a service-oriented application, all the information for the authorization needs to be present within the XML. Unless there is an exposed directory service (very unlikely), the architects of a service-oriented application must design a distributed authentication and authorization framework, likely using security assertion markup language (SAML), leveraging openID or similar which supports SAML, or permitting the passing of credentials within the application's XML, which are then validated against a local account store.

Use of local account stores in the web service layer is the common solution where a legacy application has been extended to have a service layer in addition to an existing presentation layer, and the reuse of the existing credential store is a requirement. Local account stores are also used where account mapping is a requirement for proper access control. Where the accounts are external but the authorization model is resource based or there are no attributes that can be provided to ensure appropriate authorization, local accounts are necessary. These are internal identity shells mapped to external credentials through a common attribute, often e-mail address or some unique identifier.

The fact that the credential store is local does not restrict the application and security architects from leveraging SAML, and the use of SAML will permit a faster and more secure authentication. However, not all service interfaces support SAML, and even where they do, there could be comparability issues preventing its use.

Regardless, in a distributed application, no matter what the authentication technique, the credentials need to either be distributed or made globally available to all components of the application so that both authentication and authorization checks may be performed at the local service.

The most scalable credential to meet all of these requirements is certificates using public key cryptography. The public key may be stored locally without fear of compromise, unlike passwords, and XML readily supports signing of text by a private key. LDAP and x500 directories schema provide support for public key storage and also support authentication using public/private key pairs. Where public key cryptography cannot be supported, such as where the authentication token needs to be forwarded to other service providers, SAML provides a very secure security token that can meet all of the identified requirements, depending on the implementation. If an organization is to enter into a partnership with other organizations exchanging either public key certificates or SAML tokens, they can rest assured that as long as the key and token management is sound, that they have an authentication and authorization model, which can be trusted.

With service-oriented applications, where it is often another application authenticating, the normal issues around key management are more easily solved. This has led to a widespread use of public key authentication within SOAs.

It should be noted that where a password is sent in an XML document, it should be both hashed to prevent alteration and encrypted if the XML is not sent over a secure network. As Secure Sockets Layer/Transport Layer Security (SSL/TLS)-encrypted tunnels are vulnerable to a very real man-in-the-middle threat, you may not choose to trust SSL/TLS as secure, just as private. In that case, the password should also be encrypted, as it is a trivial matter with modern computers to brute force a hash, even when salted. That need to encrypt the password to ensure its security makes the argument for using public key authentication very compelling.

### 2.5.8 Security Awareness and Training

Security awareness is the process through which an organization makes its contractors, employees, officers, and other authorized agents aware of its security policies and practices. While such a program is an essential component of a security architecture, there is little need to integrate an SOA into this part of the larger security architecture.

For the most part, awareness and training concerns regarding the development and implementation of security within an SOA will be to guide the development staff in threat profiling and sound coding practices. Ironically, this book also fits within the scope of a security awareness program, and the author hopes that it remains useful to organizations' awareness campaigns. After all, security awareness is sharing your expertise and experience with others so that they may make decisions that reduce risk rather than increase it as their actions and decisions may have unexpected consequences.

### 2.5.9 Physical Security

SOAs exist to transcend the physical barriers of a single corporate entity and thus are not strongly impacted by this otherwise key component of an information security architecture. However, the ability to transcend physical boundaries is also problematic when you consider that this could also transcend geopolitical boundaries. There are real implications to the architecture of any application from the diverse laws of any nation state as well as the European Union, so any application architecture must comply with these laws as applicable.

One law that has a real impact on data architectures is the law of the European Union, which requires that no private data regarding its citizens be stored outside of its boundaries, save as where that individual has knowingly consented to that information being stored in that location, or the company has demonstrated the ability to comply with the EU privacy laws. The US department of commerce has established the Safe Harbor program to assist US-based companies to demonstrate compliance with these laws. As one of the regulations is that the company must, on request, remove that private data from their system, any application's architecture must have a mechanism to preserve the integrity of the transaction in the absence of these data, should it be removed.

In the light of revelations that nation states are both suspected aggressors against corporate security controls and seek to collect information on the activities of its citizens, corporations need to carefully consider the laws regarding lawful intercept as well as search and seizure in the layout of their distributed applications. Governments also regulate what information regarding their citizenry may be stored outside of national borders without their consent. These laws and practices must be understood by the security architect who must ensure that in the event of a lawful seizure of corporate assets, the company can still provide to its customers the services to which it has contractually obligated itself.

### 2.5.10 Communications and Operations Management

Communications and operations management have no more to do with applications and application architectures than security awareness does; this domain of information security has more to do with how the support organization is run than with anything. By mandating the existence of procedures and standards and the adherence to these in daily operations and communications, a service level is guaranteed, as is availability.

However, in designing an application, it is imperative that the application architects keep operations management in mind as they design and build applications. The application should provide a service interface for measuring performance and responsiveness. It should, at least, provide a mechanism for tracking memory usage and alert on both memory and processor use thresholds, which are defined as being normative ceilings. Ideally, it should provide other operations metrics that can be used as per the business requirements to measure performance, availability, and utility and provide a mechanism for debugging when needed.

### 2.5.11 *Perimeters and Partitioning*

The concept of a perimeter is the most commonly understood component of a security architecture. Derived from the military doctrine of protecting the borders of countries, corporate resources are segregated from external resources through the application of controls that prevent full interaction between internal and external resources.

An SOA was designed to be perimeter agnostic, with much of the application's transport transcending any corporate perimeter. This has led the security think tank, the Jericho Forum, to advocate an abandonment of the concept of the perimeter as an architectural concept within information security. While there are other items, namely, the threat of malware brought into the enterprise by incautious employees, which make the reliance on formal security perimeters a problematic architectural construct, a successful distributed application architecture such as an SOA must leverage the concept of perimeter, only differently.

Abstractly, each WSDL defines the security perimeter of an SOA, along with how to successfully transverse it. However, one does not need to rest on the protections defined within the applications' authorization checks. Those will not protect against attacks designed to overwhelm the perimeter with an attack on availability.

Various vendors design XML firewalls to prevent denial-of-service attacks against such attacks. These devices provide protection at the application layer against all the attacks, which I will outline later in the volume. As with other firewalls, the mere presence of an XML firewall will not give sufficient protection. A good architecture will be designed to be as secure as possible even without the firewall, as there may be attacks that find a way to circumvent the firewall and attack the application directly.

The presence of an XML firewall, however, does potentially slow down application traffic. When you consider that a modern security perimeter might include the following layers, application responsiveness is at risk:

- Load balancer
- Application firewall
- Network firewall
- Intrusion prevention system
- XML firewall
- Database firewall

These can be deployed in various combinations, as there is merit to placing the application firewall behind the network firewall or the intrusion prevention system in front of the network firewall. In what I like to refer to as the belt-and-suspenders philosophy of security perimeters, there should be a second network firewall by a different vendor behind the first segregating the service and web layer of the application from the data layer.

One solution to the issue of application response time is to combine the functionality of multiple defensive techniques onto a single box, so that, as an example, the network firewall functions as an intrusion prevention system, or the application firewall is also a load balancer. Sometimes, this aggregation of features can be accomplished in an exemplary fashion, and at other times the secondary functionality of the device is not utilized but replaced by a fully functional additional device after experience in operating the secondary functionality exposes its weaknesses.

As with everything else, it is a question of risk management and budget. If performance is more important than security, then lowering the application hops by utilizing a multipurpose device makes sense. If security is more important, then it is rather rare that the functionality of a special purpose device is not superior to the secondary functionality of a multipurpose security appliance.

The subtle irony is that the adaptation of a perimeter-agnostic approach to application design in distributed applications such as

SOAs can actually lead to a heavier investment in perimeter security protections.

## 2.5.12 Access Control

Access control is basically the process of taking the answer to the question of who or what is permitted to view, modify, delete, and report on what and making certain that only those and that which should have access does.

There are two basic processes involved in access control: authentication and authorization. Most people confuse the two as they are not aware of the authorization checks but encounter authentication on a periodic and regular basis, and hence, they are not aware of the secondary process.

While the identity management process provides the list of who or what as well as the location to find the credentials (LDAP, SQL, X500, etc.), that identity store may or may not be referenced during either the authentication or the authorization process.

That statement is probably surprising. How can you have authentication without reference to the identity store? Some applications leverage single sign-on frameworks, which preauthenticate a credential and then pass onto the application a token such as a cookie, which allows the application to authenticate the credential and perhaps authorize it for access to both data and functionality.

## 2.5.13 Authentication

Authentication is the process of representing through predetermined credentials that a person or application is entitled to use functionality and data of the application. There are many kinds of credentials that can be used for this process. In gross, they are something you have, something you know, something you are, somewhere you are, or some combination of the above. Multifactor authentication involves two or more of the above kinds.

Multiples within a category do not count as multifactor. As an example, a user account name and a password are both something you know, and therefore, though you may have both, requiring both does not constitute multifactor authentication.

User accounts and passwords are two common examples of something you know. While they may be (but should not be) written down, they are supposed to be committed to memory. Another kind of thing known is what is called a shared secret, shared because you are not alone in your knowledge of this credential. Shared secrets are often used in password reset routines or help desk functions to allow the technician to verify that the person with whom they are talking is the person they are trying to reach.

There are not many things you have or can be given, which can be leveraged for an SOA's authentication needs. One such object is a one-time pad token such as the RSA secure ID. However, the nature of this is such that while it could be used at one authentication point, it would have to be supplemented by other objects. X509 certificates or Pretty Good Privacy (PGP) certificates may be readily used. The best way to leverage such certificates is to have the private key used to sign an object sent in the XML and then send that object within the XML as the authentication token. This practice does weaken the use of public key cryptography, unless other mechanisms are deployed to prevent malicious reuse. Other objects, such as an IP address, media access control (MAC) address, and computer serial number, while spoofable, may be used and readily passed from component to component.

Something you are, while often used as a secondary credential in the physical security layer to gain access to the data center, is the least applicable to use within a distributed application such as an SOA. However, where morphed, which is a special kind of hashing designed for biometric credentials, the credential may be passed through the XML to all components as an authentication token. This practice would be common in military implementations of SOAs.

Unfortunately, somewhere you are is used rather widely. While geolocation is a poor authentication token, it is often used to restrict access from certain nation states thought of as hostile. While theoretically bypassable through a proxy, proxy use is often detectable and often equally restricted. While such practices may exclude customers of organizations such as AOL, they may also readily exclude a share of malicious users. This credential is widely used in mobile apps to attempt to deliver location-specific services. While a bit more reliable over cell phone carrier networks than by IP addressing, this relative success has its own price.

When the credential of somewhere you are located is used, it opens up privacy and legal issues, as does the use of the credential of something you are. In the collection of these credentials, you are best served by hashing them with a strong salt and only storing that hash in your logs. This way your data cannot be summoned by the government as part of a criminal investigation.

### 2.5.14 Authorization

Authorization is both a business and a technical process. Usually, due to time constraints they are loosely coupled and time independent, with the business practice often happening months in advance. The business practice of authorization is the one that matters wherein the credential is granted the access to the permitted application functions and data. This is often done through placing the credential into the appropriate group.

The technical process is ideally executed on each application transaction but is more often performed on first authentication. This is the process through which the application examines what the credential is permitted access to against the request and either grants or denies the request.

While it is ideal from an information security perspective to verify authorization with each query and transaction as, after all, the permissions may have changed in the last two seconds, it is more common to perform a global authorization check on all but access to sensitive components of the application, where a second check is performed. This global check is most often stored in a temporary location such as a variable or a cookie.

Authorization in a service-oriented application is more often checked on each transaction than with other applications, because the application and data components are distributed and the transaction may be asynchronous.

While the technical aspect of the authorization check may be more securely validated, the business aspect of a distributed application is more problematic. Especially when components of the application are distributed across companies, any change in status needs to be communicated quickly and effectively. This is often accomplished through loosely coupling authorization with the validation of the credential.

Where identity management is distributed, the business authorization is most often set on a per-component basis. This can be communicated through properties of the SAML assertion, to allow for dynamic validation on each transaction, or communicated through an out-of-band mechanism, with the business authorization updated periodically rather than instantaneously. Thus, SOAs benefit greatly from the federation of identity. We discuss this at length later in this volume.

### 2.5.15 Separation of Duties

Separation of duties is a security architectural principle meant to convey a process more than anything. It means that the same people who do development should not perform quality assurance testing, security testing, performance testing, product deployment, product support, operating system support, and so on. Access is restricted according to one's responsibility. This works well in large companies, but in small companies, there has to be some blurring of responsibilities. It is common in small firms to find that a single team performs the quality, performance, and sometimes the security testing and that a single team does product deployment and support, sometimes mixed in with operating system support. The key is to keep developers from testing and supporting the product.

While this is a core component of a sound security architecture, it has more to do with the development and support of an application than it does with the architecture of an application. Separation of duties involves making certain that developers are not able to make changes in a production environment but depend on an application support team, which rolls tested changes into production on a planned basis. While a key factor of application stability and availability, this concept is probably irrelevant to most SOAs.

### 2.5.16 Principles of Least Privilege and Least Authority

The principle of least privilege, however, is one that all well-designed applications should be able to support. This is a concept implemented in an authorization framework insofar as no individual is granted more access or rights than are strictly needed to meet the requirements of their position. This may be managed by having each capability independently assignable to each role in the application or through grouping these capabilities into logical aggregates. While the second approach is much more scalable and manageable, it does imply the potential of individuals having more capabilities than they strictly need if the aggregation is poorly mapped out.

Related is the principle of least authority. This provides to the application just the required permissions it needs to run effectively on the platform. This is hard to implement, but when implemented properly, it provides a secure system. Many operating systems use "jails" to implement the principle of least authority, as within the jail, the application may operate with any level of permission but it cannot (in theory) break out of the jail. In practice, this rarely if ever works well. Restricting the access to the right level of authority allows a more effective way to isolate a security breach of an application from becoming a security breach of an operating system, and so on.

### 2.5.17 Systems Acquisition, Development, and Maintenance

The security requirements regarding systems acquisition, development, and maintenance are not related to the architecture of any application except where they are designed to meet and maintain those capacities for an organization.

### 2.5.18 Confidentiality Models

*2.5.18.1 Lattice Models*   Lattice-based models seem to establish a one-way information flow wherein users are assigned security clearances, and data are classified by sensitivity. The system compares the clearance versus the sensitivity and grants access accordingly. The most famous of the lattice-based models is the Bell–LaPadula model, where access is granted only when the clearance is equal to or higher than the classification. Owners of information may choose to grant access to only those with a need to know but access cannot be granted without proper clearance.

A more flexible confidentiality model does not consider the classification of data but rather the operation to be performed on data.

Individuals are granted read, write, edit, and/or delete access. This kind of access control model is an information flow model, not a lattice model but may be amended to a lattice.

An example of an information flow model is the Graham–Denning model. Here, three properties are to be tracked: object, subject, and rights. An individual may be granted create and/or delete for an object or a subject, and may or may not be granted access to read access rights, grant access rights, delete access rights, and/or transfer access rights.

The Brewer–Nash model can be applied as an enhancement to other security models of confidentiality. In this model, access may not be granted to objects when access is already granted to objects owned by competitors. This model aims to prevent conflicts of interest.

This last model is of great interest to service providers and is readily applied within an SOA meant to provide administrative or maintenance access to services utilized by competitors who both leverage the same service application.

### 2.5.19 Nonrepudiation

Nonrepudiation is the capability of being able to prove that an action was taken by an individual or application at a particular time. This is one of the harder things to implement in an SOA due to the distributed and asynchronous nature of the transactions. Strict identity-bound logging of each transaction must be kept and made available centrally for all components, ideally in a way that can show the forking and asynchronous nature of the application flow during each specific transaction.

In practice, this is rarely done, as a single enterprise cannot impose its logging requirements on the others in the distributed application. Exposing a logging service within each object of the SOA is probably the best solution, as the calling entity can then access the materials they need to determine who did what and when under what authorization.

### 2.5.20 Integrity Models

The Biba Integrity model is based on the same principles of the Bell–LaPudula model but is applied to integrity rather than confidentiality. Here there are graduations of integrity, wherein based on the security level of the actor, access may be granted to the simple integrity property: read, or the * property where writes are permitted. Writes are permitted only where the security property of the subject is equal to or higher than that of the object. This prevents data of lower integrity corrupting data of higher integrity.

The Clark–Wilson integrity model is explicitly designed for the change controls suitable to a transaction system and therefore more suitable for an SOA. Like an information flow model, no changes are permitted to unauthorized subjects, and no unauthorized changes are permitted to authorized subjects. The model enforces the maintenance of internal and external consistency.

Within the Clark–Wilson model, internal integrity involves guarantees that the system performs only what is expected with every operation. External consistency involves enforcing that the data within the system are consistent with similar data external to the system through the application of well-formed transitions.

Within the model, each data item is defined and changes are allowed only by a limited set of operations (such as a service or application). These items are defined as follows:

- Constrained data items, where data integrity is protected.
- Unconstrained data items, where data integrity is not protected.
- Integrity verification procedures, procedures to guarantee integrity.
- Transformation procedures, those procedures allowed to change a constrained data item.

Subjects and objects are labeled accordingly and the application is developed so that the procedures act as an intermediate layer between subjects and objects. Through restricting access to constrained data items only through transformative procedures, data integrity is assured even when the data are changed.

### 2.5.21 Service Clark–Wilson Integrity Model

The Clark–Wilson is readily adopted to fit the needs of an SOA, which has led to a recent publication of a Service Clark–Wilson integrity model by Majd Mahmoud Al-kofahi as part of his dissertation entitled "Service Oriented Architecture (SOA) Security Models."

Al-kofahi proposes that within an SOA, there is a service whose function is to govern information flow, seeking out the appropriate service to perform the data transaction that he calls a root service. His argument is that all data should be classified as either constrained data items (CDIs) or unconstrained data items (UDIs) and that each service is assigned the tasks of processing a set of CDIs. There are two kinds of procedures used to maintain the integrity of the service and the CDIs. They are Integrity Verification Procedures (IVPs), and Transformation Procedures (TPs). The IVPs are used to verify that the data and the service are in an expected state before the start of any transaction, and the TPs are used to perform the functions of the SOA, moving the CDIs from one valid state to another.

TPs consist of a set of Service Transformation Procedures (STPs) where each STP is the specific transformational procedure between layers of the service architecture. For a TP to move services from one valid state to another, all applicable STPs must have completed successfully. If after all TPs are performed, all IVPs are still in an expected state even in an error condition, then the root service is considered to be a well-formed service.

In addition to the existing rules of the Clark–Wilson model, Al-kofahi proposes two new rule types:

- Enforcement rules
- Certification rules

Enforcement rules are those rules enforced by the service and transactions. Certification rules are those rules imposed by the security officer or system owner regarding data and process integrity. Certain certification rules are recommended to enforce data and process integrity. The first two are basic rules that would need to be enforced even if there was no risk of data or process integrity being compromised.

Certification rule 1: All CDIs are processed by a service, and each service is responsible for performing updates and modifications to its assigned CDI.

Certification rule 2: Each service must have a well-defined contract that enforces all relevant certification and transaction rules.

The third certification rule exists to solve a problem, which is unique to distributed loosely coupled services of an SOA. In an SOA, multiple transactions can happen at the same time in different services that have no mutual dependency; the Service Clark–Wilson integrity model must contend with the issue of concurrency, especially as it is possible that multiple services could perform transformative procedures on the same CDI at the same time. Thus, Al-kofahi proposes certification rules 3 and 4.

Certification rule 3: If CDIs can be processed by two or more services concurrently, then all services associated with a CDI must be certified to ensure the mutual consistency of the updated CDI.

Certification rule 4: Concurrent TPs must be certified to maintain consistency of all services and CDIs once the transformations are complete.

Al-kofahi understands that to maintain both process and data integrity, the model must consider conditions of the authentication and authorization part of the integrity model. One issue that is unique to an SOA is that you cannot presume that a single identity or credential is used throughout the entire TP. Therefore, he proposes the following certification and enforcement rules.

Certification rule 5: All TPs and secure file transfers (SFTs) must be certified to be valid, that is, they must leave the CDI in a valid state, even in the case of an error. To facilitate this, the security officer must make the CDI that provides input into an SFT explicit and exclusive. The identity and its authorization to perform the transaction would be at least two of these CDIs.

This leads to the first of a number of proposed enforcement rules.

Enforcement rule 1: Each service must authenticate the identity of all subjects attempting to execute a TP. All propagations of this identity across all dependent services for the TP must be authenticated for each STP.

Enforcement rule 2: Each service must maintain a list of relations that relate a subject, a TP, an STP, and all CDIs, which these processes may reference on behalf of each valid identity.

Related to this enforcement rule is Al-kofahi's proposed certification rule 6 that all STPs must be certified to be part of a well-formed TP, and that this certification must capture all the dependencies between each service and subservice called by the TP.

As transactions in an SOA are asynchronous, may be concurrent yet must retain the integrity of both data and process, Al-kofahi proposes a certification rule as sufficient to enforce transactional sequencing.

Certification rule 8: Within each TP, the order in which STPs are performed must be certified to maintain global consistency of all the services and data items.

To maintain the transactional sequence, and allow for both audit and recovery, each service must maintain a dependency table that records all dependencies between different services as regards a specific TP or use a specific service to maintain this.

Enforcement rule 4: Each service must maintain a dependency table recording all dependencies between different services in a service network.

This enforcement rule, as it will be seen, is a problematic requirement in many web service applications, especially those using a Web 2.0 design.

To permit both transaction auditing and recovery, Al-kofahi proposes certification rule 9.

Certification rule 9: All TPs and STPs must be certified to write to an append-only CDI (a log) all information required to both permit the nature of the transaction to be reconstructed and, if necessary, facilitate recovery to a valid state in the case of an error.

Integrity verification procedures are responsible for validating that all CDIs of an SOA are in a valid state before beginning a new transaction or transformation. To ensure this, Al-kofahi proposes two more certification rules.

Certification rule 10: IVPs must properly ensure that all CDIs are valid when an IVP is run.

Certification rule 11: A well-formed service must be certified to ensure that all subservice CDIs remain in a valid state and that the global consistency is valid regardless of failure or error condition within any STP.

Finally, the system must only act on a CDI. If a UDI is presented to a service, it must be upgraded to a CDI or be rejected.

Certification rule 12: Any STP or TP that takes a UDI as a potential input must be certified to perform only valid transformations or else no transformations for any possible value of that UDI. The transformation should take the input from a UDI to a CDI or reject the UDI.

*2.5.22  Security Assessments and Audits*

There are two kinds of security assessments: an assessment of adherence to policy and process and an assessment of the soundness of the technical controls implemented. The first kind of assessment is commonly called an audit, where the presence of the mandated form of the control is tested for, such as verifying that all logs are written to a central log server so that they cannot be modified by anyone without causing a security incident.

The second kind of assessment is commonly called a penetration test, wherein the technological controls are attacked as if by a malicious entity or threat. I have devoted a chapter in this volume as to how to perform a penetration test against an SOA; however, it is likely that before this volume comes to print, there will already be new techniques not covered within these pages as new attack methodologies are always being developed.

As SOAs are being designed, careful consideration should be paid to how to tie together an event history. Especially for those SOAs for which process integrity is a key business requirement, leveraging the integrity model to create a process history which tracks who, what, where, when, how, and under what authorization could allow a comprehensive transaction log to be generated as a by-product of the business logic. A common decision is to develop a service where transaction histories are written. This service can be used both to roll back transactions, if needed, as well as to record what was done.

*2.5.23  Incident Management*

Information security professionals must plan for failure and their response. The need for security incident management comes from the recognition that historically any determined and skilled aggressor will find a way to break through any security model. That reality will drive the information security professional to call for the strongest of protections, knowing that a less stringent security model will be implemented than desired due to a need to worry about small things such as application functionality and response time.

As a service-oriented application is being designed, it needs to support the capacity of performing security incident management.

This starts with good logging. The logs should capture who did what to what, when, under what authorization, where they came from, and link into what was done next.

It also should be designed to alert the security response team when it is being used maliciously. If the password field is suddenly flooded with text such as 'or = 1', then an alert should be sent that someone is trying to break into the specified account. On a similar basis, an alert should sound if someone tries such techniques after they have logged in. The trouble is that the more sophisticated attacks, and the ones more likely to succeed, are hard to detect. If authorizations are stored in application headers in an encoded fashion, a skilled hacker will find these and manipulate these in an attempt at elevation of privilege. The only way to catch these attacks is to, if possible, have alerts triggered on odd authorization strings or if you actively check on authorization for each transaction and alert when an attempt is made to access something for which they should not have access.

Having alerts built into the application on attempts to circumvent security controls can only be accomplished if the application and security architects go through an exercise called threat profiling. Threat profiling is the process of going through an application using an attack proxy looking for those components of the application that a malicious user may try to attack and then determining what the attack would look like and how it may be detected. Sometimes, actual application vulnerabilities may be discovered in a threat-profiling exercise, allowing the development team the opportunity to mark this as a bug and work toward resolution.

### 2.5.24 Business Continuity

If UDDI had caught on, then SOAs would provide ideal solutions to the business continuity problem of what do you do when your provider goes away. As I discuss later, UDDI was a bad idea for other reasons. However, there are other aspects of the service approach for application design that make sense for business continuity planning. When you engage a service, the WSDL, which is a public document, provides the mechanism to communicate effectively and efficiently with the target service, making it cost effective and efficient to swap providers who provide similar services.

Thus, a sound SOA has a secondary service for any critical third-party services already engaged, with its service contract understood. In the event of a catastrophic failure of the preferred partner, the application transparently calls the secondary and continues to function.

SOAs, however, also have to be designed to survive internal disasters and continue providing the services for which they are designed. This is harder in the absence of UDDI's ability to direct a client to a service's alternative location. As the frequency of disasters is significantly less frequent than that of attempts at malicious use, the sacrifice is well worth it. The Domain Name System (DNS) probably provides the most scalable solution, with the use of aliases to a host of globally dispersed and load-balanced service gateways to the same service interface. This would allow your service to continue to provide service in the event of a disaster.

*2.5.25 Compliance*

All organizations must comply with the laws of the countries in which they do business as well as various local and international laws where applicable. Some organizations must also remain in compliance with various regulations and standards that, though not legally mandated, are a prerequisite for conducting business. Two such standards are the PCI DSS and the U.S. Government's Federal Information Processing Standards (FIPS).

Compliance concerns may mandate that certain controls be implemented. As an example, compliance with PCI DSS requires that all payment card data must be sent over public networks and must be over encrypted channels; so any SOA build that must store, process, or transport payment card data must use encrypted transports.

A key element of compliance efforts is in the licensing of the use of third-party code. Most modern applications make heavy use of open-source application code. Service-oriented applications tend to make heavy use of the open-source schemas found at http://www.w3.org. Later in this volume, I review many of the schemas and service objects provided by http://www.w3.org, which are relevant to the security controls implemented by service-oriented applications.

## 2.6 Data Architectures

No small part of me wants to write here "Data architectures do not matter for either application or security architectures," and within limits, I would be correct to do so. No matter what the data architecture, the data layer of the application should abstract that for the entire application, and the application should be designed so that the access to data is strictly controlled so that it is impossible to connect to data except through the application, effectively using the application to impose the security controls on data.

As true as that statement would be, it would only be true from a particular path of egress. The database administrator would still require access directly to data, as might others. Also, the data layer cannot be properly designed without knowledge and understanding of the data architecture.

The trouble is that of all the architectures I have discussed, this is the most volatile and subject to change. While it may be a buzzword, which is as of this writing making executives cringe, the challenges associated with big data have irrevocably changed the assumptions that data architectures are based on, the languages that are used to access and represent data, as well as the platforms and databases in which data are stored.

I am not among those who would define all databases as either relational or other, and even the "NoSQL" camp has altered their definition of the term to be "not only relational" instead of "no SQL to be found here."

Let us back up and cover some fundamentals of data architecture. Data can be organized, but it does not have to be. Data may be organized so that relationships between categories of data are represented in the structuring. This is a relational database. Most relational databases are horizontal in orientation or by row, wherein related data are on the same row divided by column. Data may also be organized so that objects are identified with their components. This would give you a table of cats and a related table of fur colors and a relationship model to tie the two together. This model allows you to reuse the same table of colors for dogs, and so on. This is an object-oriented model, wherein you may have cat with properties of color, size, sex, hair length, and so on.

With this model it is easier to express house cat as one class of cat and lion as another, but harder to relate this to other objects.

Data may be structured hierarchically, such as in a binary tree. Data may also be structured by columns, which is often offered as a superior approach to row-oriented designs. There are a number of approaches to the columnar approach, some where they partition the row store, some where data concurrency is allowed, and others with cells instead of fields.

The data in both a row-oriented design and a column-oriented design are often small discrete units; the data that organizations need to work with is not always small and discrete. Thus, there are databases designed to handle data at the document level, almost as if the database is presumed to be a file system but organized for rapid search. Then there are databases based on key values, which often overlap with hierarchical structures or object-oriented models. There are also graph databases with their support for semantics that are like natural language. There are grid databases, multidimensional databases (think of a five-dimensional grid), and multivalue databases. Finally, there are databases that provide multiple data models.

All data architects will be somewhat limited in what they can do for a data architecture based on the databases available to them. As an example, if all they have available to them is a database designed to be accessed using SQL, then they are limited to data models that are either row or column oriented, even where this is not the most effective way to organize the data. Even then, twisting the organization of a database designed for SQL toward columnar orientation with heavy indexing will not provide the same speed of data access that is available in a system designed to store data in such a fashion.

The data architects may be able to leverage multiple data stores within their application. A common example of just such an approach is to use a key value data store accessed via LDAP for user account management because of its fast read response times and an SQL-oriented data store for application data because of its ability to provide transaction rollbacks. This hybrid approach may allow the data architects to leverage the best of all worlds if they segment data based on use thus using a columnar approach where vast volumes of information must be stored so that the relationships within the information is retained, using a row-oriented approach where transactional rollback is a vital requirement, and using a key value data store for security information required for authentication and authorizations.

All of this is just in support of the need to relate data to data and to establish how best to organize, gain access to, and reference information. That is the work of the data architect. Data architects will take into account requirements for storing a transaction history and being able to roll back changes. They will look at requirements for search syntax, if the application needs to support parameters off of a form or a natural language string, or if the search needs to be able to match characteristics of an image. They will look at the manipulation of the data to derive information and consider requirements for statistical analysis. In other words, a data architecture puts data into an organization that optimizes requirement for storage, access, manipulation, and change tracking while leveraging the specifics of the languages and syntax used in the queries.

The application architect needs to understand this architecture and how to most effectively query and write into it. Few things have a more unintentional adverse impact on an application than a poorly considered data query string. The security architect needs to understand this architecture both to advise the application architect on how to implement the principles of least privilege in the authorization of access to read, write, and leverage the data and information derived from it. Regardless of data architecture, a key factor to the success of any SOA is that the data architecture is abstracted and invisible to the users of the application and that the security layers prevent it from ever becoming either directly accessible or visible.

# 3

# IMPLEMENTING AND SECURING SOA

To design the architecture of an application, you must understand the challenges of a successful implementation. This next section of this volume will address implementation challenges of the different kinds of service-oriented architectures (SOAs) and the challenges to secure them.

There are many kinds of applications that can be built with an SOA. While the classic SOA is the web application built on web services, there is also enterprise application integration and business-to-business applications. These applications may be designed around a "fat client", web client, or mobile client or even be multichannel.

Many modern applications are hybrids of these, and the modular nature of an SOA readily supports such diversity. Thus, it is possible for web services to be exposed to an application also supporting Web 2.0, both of which could expose to modern mobile clients the robust legacy application hosted on a mainframe.

First, I will review implementing a classic web services application, then a Web 2.0 application, and then I will examine the challenges of enterprise application integration. Client side issues will be considered for all back-end implementations.

## 3.1 Web Services

Web services are somewhat synonymous with SOAs in the minds of many individuals. They allow the dynamic sharing of capability across corporate boundaries in the service of business need in a secure and scalable manner unlike any other technology. The key behind web services is the use of SOAP to transport extensible markup language (XML) using publicly available schemas to describe both data and communications or the use of HTTP to transport XML.

Web services classically involve a Universal Description, Discovery and Integration (UDDI) layer, which allows discovery, a Web Services Description Language (WSDL) layer, which communicates the service contract and helps negotiate the communication, and the service interface itself. All web services communication depends upon XML.

## 3.2 Extensible Markup Language

XML was invented as a language to provide self-describing data. It is an open standard, managed by the World Wide Web Consortium (W3C), and uses Unicode as its character set. As a data description language, it has many rules for validating data structure, syntax, internal link checking, and data typing, all of which reflect a capacity for integrity management.

While the name indicates that XML is a markup language, it is not exactly a markup language but rather a set of rules for building markups of data sets. Markup is information added to a document that enhances the meaning of the content, identifying the parts and how they relate to each other.

Because working with a document as a basic unit is unwieldy for information exchange, the markup provides the patterns, which enable applications to parse the information contained in the document. Markup is represented in the document, much like in HTML, with tags. The tags have various roles. Boundaries identify the start and end of a collection of data. Roles identify the function of the data within the document. Some tags operate on the principle of containment, thus only on the information within a tag, and others by the relationship between objects. Also important to keep in mind when examining an XML document is that the position of objects also determines the relationship between items.

As XML is not a markup language but a set of rules for creating a markup language, an important component of any XML document is the modeling of data to be contained. The most common way to model data is with document type definitions (DTDs), which are a set of rules or data declarations, which specify what tags may be used and the nature of the information contained.

It is important to note, especially regarding security implications, that any deviation from the defined format of the document within its contents will produce a parsing error that must be reported by the

XML parser. While this guarantees that the XML will be read and processed the same no matter where it is received, it also can provide a mechanism for attack.

This declaration is located in the prolog. Declarations are expressed as follows:

`<name1 = "val1" name2 = "val2"?>` where name1 and name2 are property definitions where the variable called name1 or name2 are assigned the values of val1 and val2, respectively.

An element can have as many attributes as needed, as long as each has a unique name. `<music = "rock" band = "Beatles" song = "Yesterday">`.

If you use a DTD, you can restrict the use of handling of data types by specifying allowed sets. In the example I used above, I could specify an allowed set of all Beatles songs, with the results that the parser would reject the value of `<music = "rock" band = "Beatles" song = "Today">`, which is a Jefferson Airplane song.

DTDs are optional but have definite security implications. Their presence enforces data utility, integrity, and parser behavior. Security architects should ask that software and data architects collaborate in defining DTD standards and that these are enforced during code design and review.

There are rules regarding well-formed DTDs. These are more than just good style; they influence the performance and responsiveness of the parsers. Poorly formatted DTDs can actually cause an unintentional denial of service. A security review of an SOA should include an examination of the DTD for well-formed instructions.

Well-formed elements must have both start and end tags. An empty element's tag must have a slash "/" before the end bracket. All attribute values must be in quotes. Elements should not overlap. Isolated markup characters should not appear in parsed content. Element names should begin within either letters or numbers and only contain letters, numbers, hyphens, periods, and underscores.

Another element of concern for the security architect is the ability of an XML document to include links to external content. As external, there is no method to guarantee the integrity or authenticity of the returned data. This process of linking is especially vulnerable to Domain Name System (DNS) hijacking and other methods of name redirection. Hard coding IP addresses is not sufficient to eliminate the risk, as vulnerabilities in Border Gateway Protocol (BGP) allow for IP routing to be temporarily redirected.

It was partly to control the authenticity of the data returned that led to the development of the ID and IDREF element markers, which are guaranteed to match only specified elements in the referenced document. Specifically, the IDREF element marker guarantees unbroken links to deliberate components of linked documents.

When the external linked document is another XML document, the XPointer element marker may be used with the same results as IDREF: to link to a deliberate and specific part of an XML document. The use of XPointers and IDREFs within an SOA can reduce the risk of the source data not being authentic.

DTDs do not offer one key feature desired in data manipulation: the ability to restrict the data to particular patterns. XML schemas provide the ability to define data types and data patterns. This is invaluable when writing an XML document that needs to be able to work with data from a database. It also can address other security concerns regarding data validation. At revision 1.1, the XML schema specification is still rather immature; however, the use of data types and structures should increase both the security and functionality of applications, which leverage XML.

I am only going to explore the use of XML in a services-oriented application and only dive into the schema of particular elements where there is a specific concern with security. Thus, very important topics of application functionality will be neglected, while SAML, the security assertions markup language, will be expounded upon at length.

*3.2.1  Signing XML*

*3.2.1.1  XML Digital Signature*   XML digital signature provides the use of digital signatures in the signing of the whole or part of XML documents or attachments to XML documents. XML digital signatures can leverage certificates issued by a Public Key Infrastructure, which allows them to be globally understood and validated. More importantly for the security architect is that XML signatures are XML. In fact, digital signatures are XML documents and carry all the characteristics of a well-formed XML document.

XML signatures are generated from a hash taken of the canonical form of a signature manifest. Manifest here has the connotation of a collection of resources, which in this case are signed. These may be contained within the document or referenced by the document through links.

As a hash function is very sensitive to changes in content, the application of the concept of a hash function inside of the XML where syntactic variations are permitted over logically equivalent documents. Thus, two or more XML documents may differ in size but are semantically the same. Thus, the hash of an XML document is not a reduction of the contents through a hashing algorithm designed to uniquely identify the entirety of the signed object. Rather, the hashing of an XML document hashes the content, but only the syntactically significant content. Changing the white space, recording the objects will not break the hash, unlike with a traditional hash function applied to a traditional document.

The hash function is used twice in the digital signature process. First, all the objects to be signed within the document are hashed, and these hashes are collected as a manifest. Then, once the manifest is complete, it is hashed and signed. When the digital signature is tied to public key cryptography, then a mechanism exists to tie this digital signature to a person or a corporate entity; however, there is nothing in the signature itself that accomplishes this. That is done with the XML Key Management Specification (XKMS).

With these differences in mind, even those who are experts in the use of public key cryptography may wish to familiarize themselves with the other differences of how digital signatures work in XML, so I am going to go into this in some detail. XML digital signature's parent element is the <Signature> element, which contains two primary objects: <SignedInfo> and <SignatureValue>. Like in many representations of digital signatures, the value in <SignatureValue> will be represented in Base64 encoding. The contents of this field will be the hash of the contents of the <SignedInfo>, which in essence contains the manifest.

The <SignedInfo> may also contain the <CanonicalizationMethod>, <SignatureMethod>, and <Reference> methods. The <CanonicalizationMethod> element is a required element that specifies the algorithm applied to the <SignedInfo> element for canonicalization before applying signature calculations. The mandatory algorithms must be supported, and support of non-XML algorithms may result in security vulnerabilities. As canonicalization is a well-understood property that is implemented differently in XML, it is worth spending a moment to explore the concept.

Generally, canonicalization is the process of choosing the best option from a list of available options. However, in XML, it is narrowly a process allowing for simple comparison for basic equivalence. This permits two documents to be identical in results, while differing in nonmeaningful content. XML-based canonicalization implementations must be provided with an XPath node-set formed from the document containing the `<SignedInfo>`. XPath is a syntax for defining parts of an XML document and has elements similar to expressions seen in a traditional file system. This allows for the XML to refer to and include elements that are external to the document and allows the signing of those objects' inclusion.

A common use of this functionality is to use the XML as a mechanism to present to an individual a form, where the contents of the form are signed but the data as input by the end user is not. In this way the form may be validated for its integrity and important control against many attacks. Those who are concerned with integrity may also wish to sign the schema or DTD or both. The `<transforms>` element is used to govern what is signed and what is not.

To use the digital signature to validate the contents of the XML in what was signed, a method of verification of the digital signature is provided. The AlgorithmIdentifier object is used to provide the reader of the signature (the parser) the method to understand how the signature was generated. Also sent is a plain copy of the text that is signed. To validate the signature, the parser will take the plain text and reapply the same hash algorithm to the plain text. If the results match the hash that was provided in the `<SignatureValue>` object, then the document has not been modified from the document that was hashed.

There are two techniques for applying the signatures in XML, leading to two different kinds of signatures. Enveloped signatures are parent objects to the data they sign. Detached signatures place the signature elsewhere and without regard to the signed object. Such detached signatures may even be external to the XML, referenced through a link or reference uniform resource identifier (URI).

Such references are constructed using the <Reference> method. References are used extensively within XML to refer to external documents. They can also be used to refer to definitions and properties maintained by the XML standards organization, W3.org.

The <Signature> element can have two optional elements, the <KeyInfo> element and the <object> element. <KeyInfo> is the object that can contain an X.509 certificate either directly as a Base64-encoded object or as a link to an external object. This allows for signature verification without the parser having to find the verification key. However, this moves the problem of trust from the signature syntax to the application logic, which is not always a wise decision. If this object is included, then the application must know how to process and make the appropriate trust decisions on the basis of the contents of the elements inside of the <KeyInfo> element. This will be explored further in the chapter on key management.

We have already discussed how the manifest is a list of hashes, which describe different objects within the XML. Elements of the <manifest> that fail the validation may not cause a failure to validate the entire XML, though it could. It is important to note that though all references within the <manifest> are hashes, not all the hashes are checked by the core signature validation—only those referenced by the <SignedInfo> element. Other digests within the <manifest> may not be checked.

The <object> element provides additional information about the signature and how it can be used. The <object> element is the parent element of the much-discussed <manifest> element. It also contains the <Signature-Properties> element, which can contain vital information such as timestamping. Other elements that may be contained by the <object> element are <Id>, <MimeType>, and <Encoding>. XML has no defined use of these elements, allowing the application architects freedom in their choice of how, if at all, these elements are to be used by the application. One common use of timestamping is to prevent reuse of the specific signed instance of the data.

All of these properties can be seen in operation in this example of XMLDsig in use from www.w3.org, the organization responsible for the XML specification:

```
<Signature Id="MyFirstSignature"
xsi:schemaLocation="http://www.w3.org/2000/09/xmldsig#
xmldsig-core-schema.xsd">
<SignedInfo>
  <CanonicalizationMethod Algorithm="http://www.w3.org/
TR/2000/WD-xml-c14n-20000710">
  </CanonicalizationMethod>
  <SignatureMethod Algorithm="http://www.
w3.org/2000/09/xmldsig#dsa">
  </SignatureMethod>
  <Reference URI="http://www.w3.org/TR/xml-stylesheet/">
    <Transforms>
      <Transform Algorithm="http://www.w3.org/2000/09/
xmldsig#base64"/>
      <Transform Algorithm="http://www.w3.org/2000/09/
xmldsig#null"/>
    </Transforms>
    <DigestMethod Algorithm="http://www.
w3.org/2000/09/xmldsig#sha1">
  </DigestMethod><DigestValue>j6lwx3rvEPO0vKtMup4NbeVu
8nk=</DigestValue>
  </Reference><Reference URI="http://www.w3.org/TR/
REC-xml-names/">
    <Transforms>
      <Transform Algorithm="http://www.w3.org/2000/09/
xmldsig#base64"/>
    </Transforms>
    <DigestMethod Algorithm="http://www.
w3.org/2000/09/xmldsig#sha1">
  </DigestMethod><DigestValue>UrXLDLBIta6skoV5/
A8Q38GEw44=</DigestValue>
    </Reference>
  </SignedInfo>
<SignatureValue>MC0CFFrVLtRlkMc3Daon4BqqnkhCOlEaAhUAk8
pH1iRNK+q1I+sisDTz2TFEALE=</SignatureValue>
  <KeyInfo>
    <KeyValue>
      <DSAKeyValue>
```

```
    <P>...</P><Q>...</Q><G>...</G><Y>...</Y></
DSAKeyValue>
    </KeyValue>
  </KeyInfo>
<Object>
  <SignatureProperties>
    <SignatureProperty Target="#MyFirstSignature">
    <ts:timestamp>
  this is a test of the mixed content model
    </ts:timestamp>
    </SignatureProperty>
  </SignatureProperties>
</Object>
</Signature>
```

As with any other security technology, if it is poorly implemented it could do worse than fail to offer the security desired; it could actually create new vulnerabilities within an organization. Recognizing this shortfall, the W3 recently made certain best practices available. Primary in all practices is that the order of operations is important.

1. Fetch the verification key and establish trust in that key.
   - Most Internet-facing applications fail to validate the key, which may result in a revoked certificate being accepted post compromise. Key verification should include checking certificate revocation lists, expiration dates, authorized uses, trusted signers, and other checks as needed. RFC 5280 can be used as a guide to the options available for key validation.
   - Validate all <SignedInfo> with that key.
   - Validate the references.
2. Do not allow Extensible Stylesheet Language Transformations (XSLT) transforms. XLST transforms may easily cause a denial-of-service attack and may also be used to execute arbitrary code.
3. If you must do XPath Filter Transforms, use the second version of XPath Filter, as these are evaluated once, not for each iteration of the transform.

4. If you must use XPath streaming, avoid using the "descendant", "descendant-or-self", "following-sibling" and "following" axes when using streaming XPaths.
5. The retrieval method can point back to itself, setting up an infinite loop. These should be reviewed carefully.
6. Too many transforms can overwhelm a parser. You should limit the number of transforms supported.
7. It is not the worst idea to provide a clear text copy of what was signed so that signature validation can be performed manually. There are issues with this, of course, and this practice should be used where confidentiality is not an issue.
8. Care must be taken with the content that is externally referenced in that it should not contain malicious code.
9. Sign everything that matters to prevent injection attacks.

W3 has other recommendations, many of which are appropriate for sound application design.

### 3.2.2 XML Encryption

XML encryption provides XML with the structure to encrypt the whole of a separate XML document, part of an XML document, or the attachment to an XML document.

This provides the potential to provide end-to-end encryption. As there are some who would argue that existing encrypted transports are sufficient, let us take a few minutes to examine the existing use of encryption. Throughout the Internet, point-to-point encryption has been effectively deployed using Secure Sockets Layer/Transport Layer Security (SSL/TLS), but SSL/TLS is vulnerable to a variety of man-in-the-middle attacks due to flawed assumptions and incomplete implementations. The first flaw is embedded in the protocol: There is no method to enforce authenticity, not even through providing nonrepudiation. The inability to enforce authenticity means that users of SSL/TLS-encrypted tunnels have no mechanism to verify where they have connected, allowing successful man-in-the-middle attacks.

The one mechanism native to this, which could remediate this risk, is the use of strong authentication and key verification by the client. These technologies are generally considered to be too expensive to support and are commonly perceived as negatively impacting both performance and client satisfaction. Often, there is no evidence to back up these claims, beyond studies performed years ago when technology was slower and people were less used to complex technology.

Another factor limiting the effectiveness of SSL/TLS is that it only extends to the interface. Most implementations do not re-encrypt the transport after the interface, claiming that as it is now on private networks is sufficient security, especially considering potential performance impacts of re-encrypting.

This failure to enforce encryption on private networks allows the sensitive data to be visible to the malicious insider.

Traditionally, file encryption has been used to solve this problem. There are two issues with the use of file encryption. First, file encryption is an external process to business logic; second, the entire file is encrypted, which is often more than what is required. There is also the issue that many of the file encryption technologies have problems with key management. Finally, for many organizations, file encryption is not a very granular solution. What they require is data encryption of some data, while other data remains in the clear.

XML encryption can be used to solve these problems. It can use the same key management capabilities of a public key infrastructure and can encrypt the whole or any part of the document. XML encryption defines a process for encrypting data and representing the results using XML syntax.

There are two use cases for using XML encryption: encrypting an element and encrypting many elements. Many electronic commerce applications have the requirement to only encrypt data that is considered more sensitive than other data, such as credit card numbers, relying on transport layer encryption to preserve the privacy of the remaining data set. The sensitive elements are encrypted and replaced in the XML with two elements, the <EncryptedData> element and the <CipherData> element.

The <CipherData> element references the raw encrypted data, where the subordinate elements of <CipherValue> is the actual ciphertext. Where the ciphertext needs to be externally stored, you can use the `<CipherReference>` element instead.

```
<Name>John Doe</Name>
<CreditCard Number = '5555444433332222' Limit = '5,000'
Currency = 'USD'>
<ExpirationDate>0915</ExpirationDate>
<Issuer>Mega Bank</Issuer>
</CreditCard>
```

Is replaced by

```
<Name>John Doe</Name>
<EncryptedData Type = 'http://www.w3.org/2001/04/
xmlenc#Element'
xmlns = 'http://www.w3.org/2001/04/xmlenc#'>
<CipherData>
<CipherValue>ITORJJVTRHAIFHTU4HAPREJH</CipherValue>
</CipherData>
<EncryptedData>
```

You can encrypt any set, or subset of the data, allowing the expiration date, credit limit, and so on to be in the clear while the credit card number alone remains encrypted. However, in the event that an organization's data security policy requires that the entire XML document remain encrypted until needed, then you might have a document that looks like this:

```
<?xml version = '1.0'?>
<EncryptedData xmlns = 'http://www.w3.org/2001/04/
xmlenc#'
MimeType = 'text/xml'>
<CipherData>
  <CipherValue>ITHEAPHREIHTIAFAHFIJRHEAIVMAHGTIEHJRAFKNA
RUOPTHEIAJFKCAHTOIEAJFNCVHAOTHESLKDNFCVHBAPOTIHJAEKSFNUV
AHTIKLEASNFNVUPHAOILTJNEASNFOUVHAILNTRAJESNFCUVHNAIKLRTN
FJCVHOIUJARKFNCJNAIKLRSNTJFBSEACOIUJNZMGBEUASHF
</CipherValue>
</CipherData>
</EncryptedData>
```

There are situations where the business requires that sensitive data must be sent over unencrypted transports, thus necessitating the encryption of a significant portion of if not the entire document, but within which resides data that is more sensitive than other data sets, wherein on a need to know/see basis the decryption of the encrypted data should not expose this more sensitive data.

XML supports a concept called superencryption, or the encryption of encrypted data. When this is applied, you need to encrypt the entire element.

There is less need to worry about the syntax of the encryption than there is about digital signatures. A key architectural consideration is that encrypted data that is not signed can easily be replaced by a malicious actor without application knowledge; so, it is best if any encrypted content is signed.

Another consideration is the nature of the processing of the encrypted content. For each item to be encrypted, the encryptor must:

1. Select the algorithm and parameters, if any, to be used in encrypting the data.
2. Obtain and represent the key used in the encryption. They key may be external to the content and may be identified through the KeyInfo element, often with the subelements of KeyName, KeyValue, and perhaps RetrievalMethod where the encryption key is external to the document.
3. Encrypt the data. This is also a multistage process.
   a. If the data is an element or content of an element, it must be serialized. This may be done by either the encryptor or the application.
   b. If the data type is not already an octet, it must be serialized as octets.
   c. Encrypt the octets using the algorithm and key from steps 1 and 2 above.
   d. Provide the type of the data, which has been encrypted. This definition is bound to an identifier, which specifies how to interpret the plaintext octets after the decryption. Where appropriate, MimeType may be used, as in (MimeType = "text/plain") or more often (MimeType = "text/xml").
4. Build the EncryptedType structure. This is a representation of the algorithm, key, type of encrypted data, parameters,

and so on. If the data is to be stored within the XML in the CipherData element, it will be represented with base64 encoding within the CipherValue element. Where it will be stored externally, the URI will be placed within the CipherReference element.

5. Process the EncryptedData. If the type of the encrypted data is "element" or "element content", then the encryptor must be able to return this to the application. If the type is "content", the document resulting from the decryption will not be well formed and will thus represent a vulnerability within the application. If the type is not "element" or element "content", then the encryptor must be able to return the encrypted data to the application.

In any event, the handling of the encrypted data is up to the application and may be handled as per the business requirements for the application's behavior. Decryption is much the same process in reverse, however, and most important, the destination must be able to support the given data type if it is to decrypt the data successfully.

All encryption and decryption operations are transforms on octets. The application is responsible for making certain that XML is properly serialized. Another item to consider in application design is that the application must be able to provide the necessary information to permit a successful application of a digital signature, signature validation, or XSLT transform.

If an encrypted element contains a signature, that signature does not necessarily protect the authenticity or integrity of the ciphertext. Signatures only cover the material that is signed, and the recipients of encrypted messages must presume nothing of the integrity or authenticity of unsigned data.

Other concerns that must be considered include the need for a good random initialization vector or seed. The same plain text will always produce the same ciphertext if such a random element is not introduced. Because a significant part of an XML document is redundant and regular, it is possible for a knowledgeable attacker to use this to form the basis for an attack on the ciphertext if the random factor is not properly implemented. It is for this reason more than any that the architect is best served making certain that the algorithms in use are well-known and standard algorithms and that they are called using the appropriate business logic.

Great care must be practiced in the logic of the XML. If Encryptedkey "A" requires Encryptedkey "B", which in turn requires Encryptedkey "A", the application will fall into an infinite loop, causing a denial-of-service attack. This can be introduced into an XML application by a malicious actor where encrypted data is not signed and therefore vulnerable to injection attacks.

Finally, encrypted content may contain unsafe content such as malicious code. The encrypted content must be inspected before being acted upon by application logic.

### 3.2.3 Key Management

First, and importantly, all key management requests have the potential to be either synchronous or asynchronous. One potential use of this is to allow an administrator approval of key registration requests before they are processed. If a service responds asynchronously, then the ResponseMechanism code Pending must be sent in the request. If sent, then the initial response will be MajorResult code Pending.

Second, XML key management requests may employ a two-phase request protocol. This is often implemented to prevent a denial-of-service attack. The two-phase request protocol allows a lightweight authentication of the source of the XML key management request, and once authenticated through this light mechanism, the service prompts for a full authentication with the nonce that was returned with the light authentication. This allows validation that the request has authorization to read messages sent to the source address before providing full authentication.

*3.2.3.1 Key Information*  Because the XML signature specification allows the signer to optionally include information about the signing key within the signature block, the signer can communicate to the recipient which of the available public keys to use.

*3.2.3.2 Location*  One of the values available within the signature block `<ds:Keyinfo>` element is location. Key location may be queried using the `<LocateRequest>` element, specifying the different key properties, such as KeyName, KeyValue, X509Cert, X509Chain, and so on. The response will be within the `<LocateResult>` element.

*3.2.3.3 Validation*  Perhaps the most important part of retrieving key information would be the validation of the key being retrieved. Sadly, this is a step that is often omitted in applications which leverage SSL/TLS. To perform a key validation, the XML request must contain a <ValidateRequest> coupled with a request for the <KeyUsage> to validate that the key is permitted to perform the required function.

*3.2.3.4 Binding*  A key binding asserts a binding among the data elements which relate to a public key, such as <ds:KeyName>, <ds:KeyValue>, and so on, as contained within a specific <ds:KeyInfo> element. This allows the service to represent to the client and only to that client that the binding between the data elements is valid under the trust policy which the service offers to that client.

*3.2.3.5 Key Registration*  The registration request may be used to assert a binding to a public key pair. The generation of the key pair may be performed by either the client or the registration service. If generated by the client, the registration service may require the client to provide proof of possession of the private key. The choice of which way to proceed depends upon the application and the type of key. Keys used for code signing are generally best generated from a client so that access to the private key can be controlled; in the case of a key used for encryption, the risk of key loss is a higher risk than key compromise, and thus, this is often generated at the service with the private key delivered to the client. Where a key is used for both signing and encryption, the key point in making a decision regarding the source of the key generation is if there is a requirement for key recovery.

Some registration services provide support for key reissuance, but most registration services will provide support for key revocation. Security architects would be best advised to avoid using registration services that do not support this key functionality.

*3.2.3.5.1 Considerations for Security in Application Designs That Leverage XML Key Management*  Attacks against XML Key Management, if successful, could allow full access into the application. As such, in the design of a service that supports Key Management, the architect should consider the following threats when profiling the application.

Replay: Replay attacks can be prevented through the placement of a unique token in each message, such as a message origination time, a nonce, or perhaps a message serial number (if non-incremental). In all cases, these need to be properly verified.

Denial of Service (DoS): Because signature verifications, key exchanges, and URL resolution are all CPU intensive, they should not be performed unless the request comes from an authenticated device. Care should be taken with signature verifications especially, as these are a critical component of authentication. Use of two-phase key validation should be considered.

Recovery policy: Key recovery may invalidate a security architecture, resulting in the loss of confidence in the security of a signed document or component. While key recovery of keys used exclusively for encryption may be a desirable option, key recovery of a key used for signing should only be an available option where non-repudiation is not a requirement.

Limited-use shared secret: Care must be taken in the use of limited-use shared secrets to set sufficient entropy to ensure that the key cannot be guessed. While the standard recommends a minimum of 128 bits of entropy for limited-use shared secrets used for more secure operations, with modern computing power, this is no longer a significant hurdle. As keys of even as many as 512 bits of entropy can be brute forced quickly with modern computing power, I would recommend that the shared secret have 1024 bits of entropy wherever actual security is desired.

Security of Not Bound Authentication data: If the service must support authentication using the <NotBoundAuthentication> element, then controls must be put into place to ensure the confidentiality of the authentication, and, ironically, to ensure that the <NotBoundAuthentication> element is bound to the request.

Privacy: Sometimes key management requests may require data that is considered private, such as requesting addresses for an X.509 key pair in the European Union. A privacy notification mechanism such as the Platform for Privacy Preferences Project (P3P) should be considered in the event that such data is collected.

Message length disclosure: Where the message length is different between accepted and refused transactions, this can provide an attacker sufficient information to isolate a valid credential. Unifying message lengths with random data can prevent this information disclosure.

Checking for signature value of a signed SOAP message: When a SOAP message is signed, the XML Key Management Service must check for a signature value reference in the to-be-signed data. Implementations must ensure all the bytes of the messages are part of the hash and therefore in the resulting signature value.

### 3.2.4 XML and Databases

There are two approaches to databases and XML: using XML as a database query language and building a database in XML. As application architects often design applications with one or the other as a core component of the design, it is worth spending enough time for the security architect to understand how each work and to provide the application architect with security considerations useful for threat profiling.

### 3.2.4.1 A Database Query Language for XML

Database query languages, both object oriented or relational in nature, exist to solve problems of data extraction, transformation, and integration. XML was designed with transformations in mind; so it is no stretch to leverage it for data extraction and integration. As both relational queries and object-oriented queries depend on an ordered underlying data model which is fundamental to the understanding and use of the language (relational vs. object oriented), it is important to begin with XML's data model.

XML data is loosely structured, allowing flexibility in design not approached in traditional relational database (RDB) or open database (ODB). Joins between objects or tables can be accomplished through matching two or more elements with the same value.

XQuery is the most commonly used XML language to access databases. Instead of operating under the syntax of yet another language, it uses the logical structure of an XML document. Unlike most languages, XQuery does not allow variable substitution if the variable declaration contains construction of new nodes. XQuery is case sensitive and allows expressions that are spelling equivalents to its keywords to be used as normal expressions. This could readily lead to misunderstanding of the function of the code by a code reviewer, and therefore, vulnerabilities may be readily missed.

Before a query can be processed, it must be represented as an XML Document markup (XDM) instance. XDM is composed of a string of arguments: <what>, <who>, <where>, <when>, and <why>. Preserving this information will provide auditors a good part of what they need, once date/timestamps have been added. These are built on named events .

*3.2.4.2 XML Databases*   Though all XML documents are database documents, there is no need to spend much time on that issue in this volume. It is important to point out that where a uniform structure and schema are imposed upon a repeated set of documents, you create a record set of common structures that can be queried. The data is easily expressed as a set of tables, which consists of records, which consists of fields. The tables correspond to element nodes, which contains other element nodes nested therein, which then contains fields, which are element nodes with a data node as its only child.

As every external reference needs to be tracked for threats to confidentiality, integrity, and availability, this conceptual treatment of XML data as that of a distributed database does not alter the approach of a security architect to integrate an XML database which fits in an SOA into a larger security architecture. Rather, it should heighten the imperative to be thorough in that integration.

### 3.2.5 UDDI

UDDI is a security nightmare. It provides a standard method for publishing and discovering the exposed software components of an SOA, or in security terminology, it is an information disclosure vulnerability.

The UDDI's registry provides a representation of the data and metadata about web services. The data model exposes a description of the service's business function, information about the service publisher, technical details on how to call the service, and other metadata. UDDI nodes support one or more of the functions of the data to which it has access. A registry is a collection of one or more UDDI nodes, and affiliated registries are individual registries that implement policy-based sharing of information.

The idea is that instead of needing to write applications with specific calls to a specific application-programing interface (API), the UDDI would provide to the application a dynamic code base which would allow the application to continue to function even as the underlying service changes. The idea, initially, was that this would be registered in public repositories, much in the same way that DNS has become the public repository of host names to IP address mappings.

Anyone needing a service would query the repository for an appropriate service to meet their business requirements, and their applications would automatically know how to engage with the service as the UDDI provides to the service the instructions on how to use the chosen service.

While hackers loved UDDI, enterprises did not, at least for externally facing services. Three of the big UDDI-affiliated registries closed their public UDDI registries in 2006, and by 2010, Microsoft announced that UDDI would not be supported in future versions of their operating systems.

The working group that was maintaining the UDDI standard has closed the standard, and the wiki for the working group is so poorly maintained that it is covered with postings for illegal pharmaceuticals and other items normally found only in SPAM.

UDDI may still be found deployed internally within an organization, behind a security perimeter that would prevent external malicious use of the information that UDDI so readily exposes.

*3.2.6 WSDL*

WSDL, currently in its second revision, serves to define web service-to-service discoverers. It does this in two ways, one abstract, and the other concrete. In the abstract, a WDSL will describe the messages the service sends and receives, typically using XML schema. It defines operations associating message exchange patterns with one or more messages. Message exchange patterns are the sequence and cardinality of messages sent and received. At the concrete level, a WDSL will specify bindings of transport and wire format details for an interface and associate a network address with a binding.

Like UDDIs, WSDLs are publicly available and often can be queried through the appending of a ?WSDL to the end of a URL. Like UDDI, WSDL can often provide malicious individuals with a road map to attacking a web service, but for the most part, they simply define and publicize the application programing interface for all web services applications which need to leverage the published service. As long as all sensitive functionality and data requires authentication and authorization, there should be nothing in the WSDL that provides an attacker with anything useful.

WSDLs define services as collections of network endpoints. These are called ports, not in the traditional sense of Transmission Control Protocol (TCP) or User Datagram Protocol (UDP) ports but a binding of the data being exchanged and the operations on the data. WSDL documents use the following elements to describe and define how to interface with network services:

Types: A container for data-type definitions.

Message: Abstract, typed definition of data to be communicated.

Operation: Abstract description of the action supported by the service.

Port Type: Abstract set of operations supported by one or more of the endpoints.

Binding: A concrete protocol and data format for a particular port. Binding types do not need to be common among multiple services and may be unique to the specific service; however, use of common binding types where appropriate allows ease of implementation and use.

Port: A single endpoint defined as a binding and a network address. Unlike with TCP or UDP ports, these are not numbered by service type nor are they global; they are local and specific to the service. Ports can support four primitives as operations: one way, request-response, solicit message, and notification.

Service: A collection of related endpoints. Within the WSDL, a service groups a set of related ports together in a preferably logical manner. While grouped together, none of the ports communicates with each other (necessarily). Ports within a service that share a port type but with different bindings or addresses are alternatives. Care must be taken that all alternatives are equally secure.

WSDL can use XML schema specifications for its type language, but this can be extended where insufficient. The binding mechanism is most often used to provide the public definition for how to call SOAP, as well as how to perform an HTTP GET or POST, and how to leverage Multipurpose Internet Mail Extensions (MIME) within the specific service.

WSDL documents are simply a set of definitions, with a definitions element at the root, with definitions inside. WSDL documents can be assigned an optional name of attribute NCNAME that serves as a lightweight form of documentation. Within the document, each definition requires its own name scope. Names within a name scope must always be unique. Where URI are used, they must never be relative.

While the WSDL can be read, as can all XML by humans with a fair amount of clarity, WSDLs benefit from the use of the wsdl:document element as a container for documentation targeted at people.

XML uses XML Schema Definition (XSD) as the type system, though it does not require the resulting data to be XML. XSD can be used to specify multiple bindings for the same message and to specify bindings that are not in widespread use.

Messages consist of one or more logical parts, each part associated from some type system using a message-typing attribute. As with everything, the set of message-typing attributes is extensible, with WSDL predefining "element" and "type" for use with the XSD. The WSDL may have as many parts as it needs to logically convey the means to the interface with the service it describes.

A WSDL binding defines the message format and protocol details for operations and messages for a particular port. A port may have any number of bindings, using the name attribute to provide a unique name within all the bindings within the WSDL. Bindings must specify just one protocol and may not specify address information.

WSDL includes a binding for SOAP endpoints, with default support for URI addressing. While the SOAP:binding will ensure binding to the envelope, header, and body of the SOAP message, the WSDL will do nothing to ensure that the SOAP is encoded or formatted properly.

WSDL also includes support for SOAP:operation and SOAP:body. SOAP:operation specifies if the object is remote procedure call (RPC) oriented, accepting and returning parameters, or if it is a document. SOAP:body provides information on how to assemble the different message parts of the SOAP message and is used in both RPC and documented-oriented SOAP bodies.

WSDL supports the fault, headerfault, and header functions of SOAP messages with SOAP:fault, SOAP:headerfault, and SOAP:header elements. The address function of SOAP is also supported, where the address must be a URI.

WSDL supports HTTP GET and POST bindings. This allows support of Representational State Transfer (REST) as well as SOAP-oriented SOA. It does not need to be written that any support for POST should be accompanied by authentication over secure protocols. To permit these elements to function with URI, WSDL provides the http:address, http:binding, and http:operation elements that duplicate the function of similar SOAP elements. WSDL also supports http:urlEncoded and http:urlReplacement to permit the encoding of URI with standard URI encoding rules to specify a form post and to provide a replacement algorithm for URI operations.

Less often used but nevertheless equally capable is WSDL's support for MIME bindings. These are often used to transfer and leverage static content to be represented at the display layer by the service as an extension of SOAP- or REST-provided content, such as sending a corporate logo along with the data needed to process a hotel reservation.

The elements associated with MIME in WSDL are mime:content, mime:multipartRelated, mime:mimeXml, and SOAP:body.

## 3.3 SOAP

SOAP is probably the most commonly used protocol within an SOA because of its versatility. It has a very simple structure to it, being composed of an envelope, header, and body.

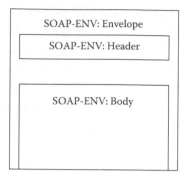

**Exhibit 3.1**   SOAP structure.

The envelope is a construct, which defines the overall framework for interpreting a SOAP message, in essence defining the vocabulary, who should deal with it in whole or part, and what parts if any are mandatory.

The header carries a representation of a resource, which is needed to process the SOAP message but which cannot be obtained through the URI for the resource carried within the message.

The header and the envelope allow SOAP to provide a flexible and custom workflow implementation for the SOA. However, this flexibility comes at a cost of lower performance as each SOAP message must be parsed so that the vocabulary may be learned and its instructions followed appropriately by the service.

Fundamentally, SOAP is a protocol for transporting XML documents. It is intended to be a lightweight protocol, though often in implementation it is not so lightweight, but it is ideal for exchanging information in a distributed decentralized environment.

In the efforts to make SOAP lightweight, the designers of the protocol left out any controls around reliability, security, correlation, and routing. Thus, and unlike most XML processing, SOAP does not require the processing of the schema. Rather, SOAP presumes that its elements and attributes as defined by the specification are strictly adhered to.

The protocol has certain key concepts, many of which we will explore in detail. These concepts are:

- SOAP node
- SOAP role

- SOAP binding
- SOAP feature
- SOAP message exchange pattern
- SOAP application

As SOAP is a messaging protocol, there are also key concepts regarding these roles. Most of these roles are self-evident from the naming convention:

- SOAP sender
- SOAP receiver
- SOAP message path
- Initial SOAP sender
- SOAP intermediary
- Ultimate SOAP receiver

### 3.3.1 SOAP Roles and Nodes

In the processing of a SOAP message, a node will act in one or more SOAP roles, each of which will be identified by the URI which corresponds to the SOAP role name. There are three roles, which have special significance in a SOAP message. These are:

| SHORT-NAME | NAME | DESCRIPTION |
|---|---|---|
| next | http://www.w3.org/2003/05/ soap-envelope/role/next | Each SOAP intermediary and the ultimate SOAP receiver must act in this role. |
| none | http://www.w3.org/2003/05/ soap-envelope/role/none | SOAP nodes must not act in this role. |
| ultimateReceiver | http://www.w3.org/2003/05/ soap-envelope/role/ ultimateReceiver | The ultimate receiver must act in this role. |

Other roles may be defined as is necessary for the specific application. The best practice is to define the name of the role based upon its function. SOAP Header blocks may be used to carry role attribute information. It should be noted that SOAP Header blocks targeted at http://www.w3.org/2003/05/soap-envelope/role/none are never processed. Often an application will use these header blocks to carry data that is required for the processing of other SOAP Header blocks and are usually relayed to the ultimate receiver unless explicitly removed by the action of an intermediary.

### 3.3.2  SOAP Header Blocks

A SOAP Header block can carry extensions to SOAP, or SOAP modules, which are not mandatory for the targeted node to process. These modules must identify themselves with a URI, must declare their function, clearly and completely specify the content and semantics necessary to implement the behavior in question, and must clearly specify any known interactions with or changes to the interpretation of the SOAP body. SOAP Header blocks may utilize property conventions, which, if followed, must clearly describe the relationship between the abstract properties and their representations in the SOAP envelope.

A SOAP Header block may carry a mustUnderstand attribute information item, which, if true, makes that particular SOAP Header block mandatory. These mandatory header blocks are presumed to modify the semantics of other SOAP Header blocks or body elements. If a node does not process a mandatory SOAP Header block that is targeted at it, it must not process the message at all and instead generate a Fault.

If the receiver node, even the ultimate receiving node, receives such a mandatory header block that is not targeted at it, it simply does not process it.

### 3.3.3  SOAP Fault

The SOAP Fault is used to carry error information within a SOAP message. The Fault element must have the local name of Fault, with the URI of http://www.w3.org/2003/05/soap-envelope. It must contain at least two child elements in order as follows:

* A mandatory Code element
* A mandatory Reason element
* An optional Node element
* An optional Role element
* An optional Detail element

SOAP Faults will only have the Fault element in the body when properly generated. It is also common to have within the SOAP envelope a SOAP Reason element that contains a human readable reason for the Fault. This will usually have a Text element contained therein with that reason. Other items that may be placed in the envelope would be the Node element, as a reference to which node generated the Fault and a Code element that would indicate the code that generated the Fault. It may also be useful to have the envelope contain the Role element to indicate the role the node has, though this will often be evident. The SOAP detail element in the SOAP envelope may be used to convey details regarding the error. Where present, it is common practice to refer to the specific detail in the SOAP Fault code.

### 3.3.4 SOAP Data Model

The SOAP data model is optional and not needed for applications, which use XML. It is a subset of the Directed Labeled Graph class of data models. More specifically, the SOAP data model is application-defined data structures and values as a directed edge-labeled graph of nodes. Edges in the graph originate at a graph node and terminate at a graph node. An edge label is an XML qualified name. The SOAP data model abstracts the details of the referencing mechanism, allowing merging of the encoding by folding together the abstract edge-labeled data.

A graph node may be single reference or multireference, where the single reference has only a single inbound edge. Values on the graph are represented as graph nodes with lexical values. Each graph edge is encoded as an element information item. Both simple and complex values can be encoded. As is typical, the type property of a graph is a pairing of a namespace name and local name, using QNames.

### 3.3.5 SOAP Encoding

SOAP encoding provides a way to encode instances of data that conform to the SOAP data model. This may be used to transmit data in SOAP Header blocks or bodies. However, this is not required, and other encoding and unencoded data may be used in both the header blocks or bodies or both.

While XML rules for data encoding are very flexible, SOAP is less so. I am not going to review the intricate details of SOAP encoding, as this is not a guide to programming SOAP, but intend to review it at a high level to provide architects with sufficient information needed for sound design.

As one of the design goals of SOAP was to enable the exchange of information, mapping conveniently definitions and invocations of the methods and procedures of various applications and programming languages, SOAP encoding allows the mapping between XML and the SOAP data model. More than one encoding can be used for any graph. Each graph is encoded as an element information item, where if the element information item representing an edge does not have a ref attribute among its attributes, then the element information item is said to represent a node in the graph and the edge terminates at that node. If it does have a ref attribute, then the value of that item must be identical to the value of exactly one id attribute in the same envelope. The outbound edge is encoded as an element information item child of the element information item that represents a node. When these are distinguished by labels, the local name and namespace value properties determine the value of the edge label. When these are distinguished by position, the ordinal position corresponds to the position of the child element information relative to its siblings, and the local name and namespace name properties of that child element are not significant. When the graph node represents an array, the element information item representing an array node may have an itemType attribute information item or an arraySize attribute.

### 3.3.6 Bindings

SOAP allows the exchange of SOAP messages using a variety of protocols. The formal rules which govern this relationship are called bindings. The binding specification declares the features provided by a binding and describes how the services of the protocol are used to transmit SOAP, honor the contract, handle all potential failures, and define the requirements for constructing a conforming implementation.

Where multiple features are specified in the binding specification, the specification must define the information necessary for the successful use of these features in combination, detailing dependencies where they exist.

The binding framework does not provide a fixed naming or typing; however, where consistency is desired for a commonly used feature, conventions may be added to the specification such as the HTTP binding in SOAP 1.2 part 2.

Bindings may depend upon information outside of the SOAP message, such as URLs, and may transmit this information to other nodes. There is a rather large security risk from doing so, however, as the behavior of the application becomes dependent upon externally provided information.

A common technique in the development of SOAP protocol bindings is to leverage the same endpoint identification as the underlying protocol that SOAP is being bound to. This is done to reuse the existing infrastructure associated with that underlying protocol, such as the TCP port numbers (UDP is rarely if ever used with SOAP due to its "best effort" delivery paradigm). This can have unintended consequences, especially with security controls regarding protocol flow. A common web proxy could thus derail a SOAP binding to TCP port 80, and ISP SPAM filtering could derail a SOAP binding to a TCP 25.

Of course, security vulnerabilities can readily be introduced into the application by not following the specification regarding "MUST", "SHOULD", "MUST NOT", and "SHOULD NOT" instructions. Unfortunately, the documentation regarding the protocol binding is often unclear, and until there is sufficient experience in the implementation of a protocol binding, a misunderstanding could result in an exploitable framework. This is why any good development life cycle includes static and dynamic code analysis as well as credentialed penetration testing of application logic.

### 3.3.7 Documents and RPC

There are many debates in developer circles on the relative merits of which approach within SOAP is a better messaging style to use. RPC messaging provides tightly coupled integrations; the other allows loosely coupled application interoperability. Both approaches offer attractions to software architects, with the RPC solution offering elegance and simplicity and the Documents solution offering flexibility.

SOAP RPC is an encoding style that offers tremendous simplicity; you make a call to a remote object with the appropriate parameters and receive the results. SOAP RPC manages the encoding, decoding, and binding to the remote objects automatically. If the data is in XML format, SOAP RPC allows literal encoding of the XML as a serialized single parameter.

When a client invokes SOAP RPC, it actually is invoking a proxy stub that provides the presentation layer for the actual procedure or method. This proxy stub collects the parameters into a SOAP message, encodes them, and then serializes them across the TCP/IP connection where the recipient deserializes the stream, decodes, and binds the parameters to the appropriate internal variables within the invoked procedure or method.

This is a standards-based process, rigorous and reliable. However, it does not always meet an organization's needs and not all service providers can support it. Even worse, it is not very flexible. If you change the number, order, or data types of the parameters the service accepts, all clients must adjust their settings. While SOAP RPC is synchronous, most web services applications are asynchronous, primarily due to the latency associated with distributed applications. Organizations, as an example, that use Axis 2.0 cannot support SOAP RPC, while organizations that leverage Axis 1.0 can.

SOAP Document style messaging offers the development team full control over how to convert data from internal variables into XML. There is full control over the content and its format. You can pass complex business documents and invoke complex distributed workflows, ignoring extraneous parameters. However, with Document style messaging, the client and server must agree on a service identification mechanism. Some organizations choose to use SOAP Header entries; others use name elements in the body of the message. Another option is to put in place a service that performs structure or content analysis to identify the services needed to process the document. The first approach has been standardized in the web service (WS)-Routing proposal.

Neither approach has more or less merit for the security architect who should stand back and let the software architect choose the best approach for the application design and lifecycle. That person is likely to choose the RPC approach if the code is likely to be relatively static over a long period of time as the RPC approach makes managing application changes more onerous, especially where the distributed software architecture involves extensive use of third parties. Where application change and growth is anticipated, the Document style will be the more likely choice as changes can be rolled out without adversely impacting other components of the distributed application. However, the RPC approach does permit more ready integration with existing .net or J2EE applications, which were not designed with service interfaces, and is often found as custom-designed middleware to existing applications where a business decision has been made to extend the functionality of an application as a service.

While RPC may offer a simpler and more elegant application design, this simplicity does not translate in this case to greater security. There are no specific security controls unique to the RPC implementation and both approaches are liable to the same design mistakes. Nor does the Document approach offer greater security. Both require the same rigor in threat profiling and data protection.

### 3.3.8 Messaging

SOAP messages are XML. The comments, elements, attributes, namespaces, and character information items are able to be serialized as XML 1.0, though this does not require the use of XML 1.0 to perform the serialization. It consists of a document information item with exactly one member in its children property, which must be the SOAP envelope information item. This element information item is also the value of the document element property.

SOAP messages must not be sent with processing instruction information items, and they must not be inserted by any SOAP intermediaries. When such a message is received, SOAP receivers should generate a SOAP Fault with the ValueOfCode set to "env:Sender". However, there is no requirement for intermediaries to strip processing information items out of any messages to be relayed.

The SOAP Envelope element information item will have:

The local name of envelope.
The namespace name of "http://www.w3.org/2003/05/
    soap-envelope."

Zero or more namespace qualified attribute information items in its properties.

A Body element information item.

Perhaps, a Header element information item.

The encoding rules used to serialize parts of a SOAP message are defined using the SOAP encodingStyle attribute information item. This will have:

A local name of encodingStyle

A namespace name of "http://www.w3.org/2005/05/ soap-envelope"

The encodingStyle attribute information item is of type xs:anyURI, where the value specifies a set of serialization rules which can be used to deserialize the SOAP message. This attribute may appear in:

The SOAP Header block.

A child element information item of the SOAP body element information item.

A child element information item of the SOAP detail element information item.

Or the descendants of any of the above.

Where SOAP Header blocks are used, they must contain a namespace property that has a value. They may also contain any number of character information item children, which may be namespace qualified. They may also contain attribute information items in the attributes property; this, in turn, may contain as required any or none of the following:

An encodingStyle attributes information item

A role attribute information item

A mustUnderstand attribute information item

A relay attribute information item

We have already discussed the purpose of the encodingStyle attribute information item. The SOAP role attribute is used to indicate the SOAP node to which a particular SOAP Header block is targeted. This will have the following properties:

A local name of role

A namespace name of "http://www.w3.org/2003/05/
   soap-envelope"
A specified property with the value of "true"

The type of the role attribute is xs:anyURI. If this is omitted, then the default value of "http://www.w3.org/2003/05/soap-envelope/role/ ultimateReceiver" is assumed.

The SOAP mustUnderstand attribute information item is used to indicate if processing the SOAP Header block is mandatory or optional. Considering this, it is not surprising that the value is of type: xs:boolean, with false being 0 and true being 1. It contains the following properties:

A local name of mustUnderstand
A namespace name of "http://www.w3.org/2003/05/
   soap-envelope"

The SOAP relay attribute is a similar attribute structurally, with the function of defining if the header block is to be relayed. The following properties make up the attributes:

A local name of relay
A namespace name of "http://www.w3.org/2003/05/
   soap-envelope"
A specified property with the value of "true"

The SOAP body is where the actual information is transmitted to the SOAP receiver. The body element information has:

A local name of body
A namespace name of "http://www.w3.org/2003/05/soap-envelope"

In addition, it may also have attribute information items in its attributes properties and element information items in its children property. All child elements should have a namespace property or be namespace qualified, to use the technical term. These elements are less ambiguous.

As things go wrong, SOAP has the Fault element. This element has:

A local name of Fault
A namespace name of "http://www.w3.org/2003/05/soap-envelope"

Mandatory elements called Code and Reason, with the optional elements of Node, Role, and Detail. The aim of the Fault codes is to provide a means by which Faults are classified. Each SOAP message provides a hierarchical list of the SOAP codes and associated supporting information in each SOAP Fault message. A SOAP node must understand all SOAP Fault codes to interpret the Detail element information contained in the SOAP Fault.

Because it is not mandatory that SOAP receivers understand all Faults, there is the capability to place NotUnderstood in the SOAP Header blocks. This element information item must not have an encodingStyle attribute information item, just the local name of NotUnderstood, the namespace name of "http://www.w3.org/2003/05/soap-envelope", and a qname attribute information item in the attributes property. This qname will have a local value of qname, but no namespace name and will have the specified property with a value of true that matches to the Fault that was not understood.

There is nothing in SOAP to provide even the most basic of security controls. Fortunately, there have been many extensions to SOAP, and where SOAP is sent as part of a web services call, the service layer can provide sufficient protection. Simply sending over encrypted protocols can guarantee a level of confidentiality and integrity, but as most implementations of encrypted protocols are not strongly authenticated, that may not be sufficient for the business application. Even worse, all the calls SOAP makes internally to http://www.w3.org are not encrypted. While these calls are not regarding sensitive information and so encryption may seem to be unnecessary, the basic encryption provided by SSL/TLS also provides a level of transport integrity, which will be missing as the application leverages http://www.w3.org for its namespace.

A key SOAP extension to provide integrity is the SOAP Security Extensions: Digital Signatures.

As noted frequently in earlier chapters, digital signatures provide verifiable integrity to the signed content. Ironically, the namespace which is mandatory for the header entry syntax for the SOAP-DSig is "http://schemas.xmlsoap.org/soap/security/2000-12", which as a clear text link lacks any controls around integrity, and as of this writing, W3.org has not signed its DNS domain, leaving them vulnerable to DNS hijacking, which would subvert the entire namespace system.

SOAP-DSig conforms to the XML Signature specification we discussed earlier in this volume. The ds:Reference element refers to the signed part of the SOAP envelope. To help applications identify which attributes are of type ID, the SOAP-Dsig specification defines the SOAP-SEC:id global attribute.

## 3.4 WS-Security

WS-Security is a suite of standards, which provide the security layer of a web-facing or Internet-facing SOA. The suite consists of WS-Policy, SAML, XML Signature, and XML Encryption; though WS-Trust, WS-Authorization, WS-SecureConversation, and WS-Privacy also exist, they are less common.

More specifically, the WS-Security stack was developed to protect SOAP messages against the following threat models:

- Message modification
- Message disclosure
- Flooding message queues with well-formed but content-free messages

To protect against the threats of message modification or disclosure, a Message Security Model was proposed where security tokens combined with digital signatures would be used to protect the confidentiality, integrity, and authenticity of the message. Security tokens assert claims that can be used to create bindings between authentication keys and application identities. A trusted authority can authorize or endorse the claims made by a security token, such as that provided by a certification authority's (CA) signing of a certificate and its entitlements. These digital certificates can be used not only to encrypt but

| WS-DigitalSignature | WS-Encryption | XMLKMS (Key Management Service) |
|---|---|---|
| WS-SecureConversation | WS-Federation (SAML, .Net Passport) | WS-Authorization |
| WS-Policy | WS-Trust | WS-Privacy |
| WS-Security | | |
| SOAP | | |
| SSL/TLS | | |

**Exhibit 3.2**  WS-Security Stack. *Abbreviations:* SOAP, Simple object access protocol; SSL, Secure Sockets Layer; TLS, Transport Layer Security.

also to sign objects, either entire messages or components within the messages, such as just the body or just the header, or just specific elements within the body.

Admittedly, all of this can be accomplished by just using XMLDsig and XMLEncrypt but each implementation would be unique and specific, creating interoperability problems and a need to negotiate the technical details of key exchange for each service partner. What WS-Security enables is a uniform method of implementation.

There are some unique elements to the WS-Security stack that provides the application architect with options that afford scalability and flexibility to the security model. The first is the `<wsu:Id>` element, which allows the reference of other (even external) message elements as extensions to the identity or identification/authentication/authorization logic chain. This allows the processing of security elements without a need for the understanding of the entire schema or the processing of the entire message. As neither XMLSig nor XMLEncrypt allow attribute extensibility, WS-Security allows the use of local ID attributes, the wsu:Id and xml:id attributes. These are checks in no particular order:

- Local ID elements of XML Signatures
- Local ID elements of XML Encryption
- Profile-specific defined identifiers
- Global xml:id attributes
- Global wsu:Id attributes

WS-Security recommends that an ID reference is used instead of the XPath when a security token is used to sign part of or the whole of the body. For frameworks which support WS-Security, this will simplify processing. However, if needed, xml:id may be used for signing elements.

WS-Security provides a `<wsse:Security>` header block targeted at a specific recipient. If a message is targeted at multiple recipients, then it may have multiple `<wsse:Security>` header blocks. To differentiate, all except the first must have either the S11:actor or S12:role attribute. Where elements are added to the `<wsse:Security>` header, they should be ordered by usage, so that no element depends upon anything after it. However, it must be noted that this is not mandated, and the receiving application can process the headers in whatever order is required.

I have made references to the S11:actor and S12:role attributes. They are both optional subordinate elements of the wsse:Security element, which is a header block for passing security-related information to the recipient of a SOAP message. Other optional attributes include @S11:mustUnderstand, which is ironically used to indicate if a header entry is mandatory or optional for the recipient to process. This attribute has a binary value, with 1 being true and 0 false. Almost identical is the @S12:mustUnderstand attribute, also binary in nature with the values having the same meaning. All that is different is the context. Where these attributes are present, a Fault must be generated by the recipient in the event that it is not understood.

To permit mapping of security tokens to usernames or personal identifiers, the <wsse:UsernameToken> supports the attributes of @wsu:Id, wsse:Username, the associated wsse:Username/@{any} to extend wsse:Username. wsse:UsernameToken also supports both the wsse:UsernameToken/{any} and wsse:UsernameToken/@{any}.

Binary security tokens may be attached using the <wsse:binarySecurityToken> element. This allows both x.509 certificates and Kerberos tickets to be used as credentials. The @wsu:Id attribute is used to map these to the specific identity (which can be different but should not be different from the subject of the x.509 certificate). @ValueType is used to indicate the value space of the encoded binary data such as the certificate. If the binary data is encoded, such as with base64 as is common when representing x509 certificates, the @EncodingType attribute is used to specify the encoding mechanism. As with other WS-Security elements, the wsse:BinarySecurityToken can be extended with a @{any}.

When it is a requirement that the token passed in the header be encrypted, then <xenc:EncryptedData> may be used to encrypt the token. When it is processed at the receiving end, it is replaced logically with the decrypted form. To refer to such a token, the <wsse:SecurityTokenReference> element is provided. This can be done through the subelements available.

wsse:SecurityTokenReference/@wsu:Id is a string label for the reference, not the ID of what is being referenced. That ID should be referenced using the <wsse:Reference> element within the <wsse:SecurityTokenReference>.

wsse:SecurityTokenReference/@wsse11:TokenType is used to identify the type of the referenced token by URI. When specified with a wsse:KeyIdentifier/@ValueType attribute or wsse:Reference/@ ValueType attribute that is used to indicate the type of the referenced token, the token type must be consistent with the security token type in the wsse:ValueType attribute.

wsse:SecurityTokenReference/@wsse:Usage specifies the usage of the <wsse:SecurityTokenReference> using URIs. Multiple usages may be specified using XML list semantics.

wsse:SecurityTokenReference/{any} allows extensibility, as does wsse:SecurityTokenReference/@{any}. wsse:SecurityTokenReference/ {any} allows different extensible schema references, while wsse:SecurityTokenReference/@{any} just allows additional attributes.

It is a good idea, when using <ds:KeyInfo> to add <wsse:SecurityTokenReference> elements to reference the key used for the signature or encryption.

Within the wsse:SecurityTokenReference, the <wsse:Reference> element provides a specific and extensible mechanism for referencing security tokens by URI. This contains the attributes of @URI which specifies an abstract URI for a security token, @ValueType which specifies a URI used to identify the type of token, and wsse:Reference/ {any} and wsse/@{any} providing extensibility to both different types of security references or attributes, respectively.

If the application architect does not wish to use a direct reference, the use of a <wsse:KeyIdentifier> instead of a <ds:KeyName> is recommended. This allows the values and algorithms to be specified in token-specific profiles, rather than a specification. This allows for both greater flexibility and supportability, replacing algorithms as they prove no longer viable. This element only has a few attributes: wsse:KeyIdentifier/@wsu:Id, a string label for the identifier and @ValueType, used to indicate the type of KeyIdentifier being used. @EncodingType can be used when needed to identify an encoding type in use, and @{any} allows additional values as needed.

Sometimes, the application architect needs to have the token embedded within the element, instead of located elsewhere and referenced by a URI. In such cases, the <wsse:SecurityTokenReference> element will use the attribute <wsse:Embedded>, which has the attributes of @wsu:Id, wsse:Embedded/{any}, and wsse:Embedded/@{any}.

The use of <wsse:BinarySecurityToken> is recommended to specify the key information, using the <wsse:KeyIdentifier> to specify the actual key.

I have stressed repeatedly throughout the volume the role of signatures in guaranteeing both integrity and authenticity. SOAP Headers can be rather mutable; so the specification highly recommends against using the Enveloped Signature Transform defined in XML Signature but explicitly defining those elements that are to be signed. For similar reasons, producers should not use the Enveloping Signature as defined in XML Signature. Still, WS-Security is based on XML Signature and uses the same requirements for algorithms. WS-Security has the same issues with Inclusive and Exclusive Canonicalization, and these are not worth reiterating here other than to point out that Exclusive Canonicalization is very useful when you have a signed XML document that you might want to insert into other documents, such as signed SAML assertions inserted in the security header of a SOAP message. By using Exclusive Canonicalization, you ensure that the SAML will always verify.

To add a signature to a <wsse:Security> header block, a <ds:Signature> element conforming to the XML Signature specification must be prepended to the existing content. This allows the indication of the correct order of operations to the recipient. Because of the ease of modification by intermediaries, the validity of the digital signature is rather fragile, which is why Exclusive Canonicalization is the preferred canonicalization method.

Where URIs, IDs, and XPaths are not viable mechanisms to refer to a token, internal or external to the message, WS-Security has extensions to the <wsse:SecurityTokenReference> element that provide tremendous flexibility. This is done through a new reference option for XML Signature called STR Transform, or #STR-Transform. The transform is specified by a URI. When applied to a <wsse:SecurityTokenReference>, the output is a token referenced by the element, not the element itself. The transform leverages the following attributes:

/wsse:TransformationParameters is used to wrap parameters for a transformation. It allows elements even from the XML Signature namespace.

/wsse:TransformationParameters/ds:Canonicalization specifies the canonicalization algorithm which is to be applied to the selected data.

/wsse:TransformationParameters/{any} allows extensible parameters.

/wsse:TransformationParameters/@{any} allows additional attributes.

The actual algorithm is identified by #STR-Transform, which takes a single mandatory parameter, `<ds:CanonicalizationMethod>`, which is used to serialize the output. This parameter must be wrapped in a `<wsse:TransformationalParameters>` element.

The signature will fail validation checks under the following conditions:

- The syntax of the content does not conform to the specification.
- The validation of the signature contained in the element fails.
- The application rejects the message because of its own valida-tion policy (see "WS-Policy").
- There is no guarantee that a Fault code will be reported. Where the application architect has a requirement to get confirmation of the signature, WS-Security provides a model for signature con-firmation in `<wsse11:SignatureConfimation>`. When a confirmation is sent, a `<wsse11:SignatureConfimation>` must be sent for each signature or each `<ds:Signature>` ele-ment. The `<wsse11:SignatureConfimation>` must con-tain the corresponding signature value in the Value attribute. Those implementations that support this must include it inside of the `<wsse:Security>` header of the associated response message for every `<ds:Signature>` element that is a direct child of the `<wsse:Security>` header block from the origi-nating message. The responder must also include the contents of the `<ds:SignatureValue>` and the @Value attribute of the `<wsse11:SignatureConfirmation>` element. If the originating signature is encrypted, the returned confirmation should also be encrypted.

The supported attributes are:

- /wsse11:SignatureConfirmation/@wsu:ID is a mandatory attribute used to provide an unambiguous reference to the signature in the `<ds:SignedInfo>` reference list.

- /wsse11:SignatureConfirmation/@Value is an optional value used to convey the contents of the `<ds:Signature-Value>` from the original request.
- WS-Security allows the encryption of any combination of blocks or substructures by either an out-of-band symmetric key or a key carried in the message. To permit this, WS-Security leverages the already discussed `<xenc:ReferenceList>` and `<xenc:EncryptedKey>` from XML Encryption. Whenever an object is encrypted, a subelement must be prepended to the `<wsse:Security>` header block. Where SOAP Header blocks are encrypted, WS-Security provides the `<wsse11:EncryptedHeader>` to store these values. It does not matter that `<wsse11:EncryptedHeader>` is a custom element; the encrypted parts must still be in compliance with the XML Encryption specification, so the `<S11:Header>`, `<S12:Header>`, `<S11:Envelope>`, `<S12:Envelope>`, `<S11:Body>`, and `<S12:Body>` must not be encrypted, but child elements of the header or body constructions may be as needed. Encrypted objects must be replaced by `<xenc:EncryptedData>` objects and should be referenced in the `<xenc:ReferenceList>`.
- In the event that the entire SOAP Header block must be encrypted, the original header block should be replaced with a `<wsse11:EncryptedHeader>` element containing the `<xenc:EncryptedData>`. It is a good idea to include a wsu:Id attribute. Where required, this encrypted header block may be then recrypted and replaced with a second `<wsse11:EncryptedHeader>` containing the original encrypted header.
- Not all of WS-Security deals with signing and encryption. As time tracking is an important element in many security transactions, WS-Security provides the `<wsu:Timestamp>` element. `<Wsu:Timestamp>` should be compliant with the xsd:dateTime type defined in the XML schema. This places the timestamp in Coordinated Universal Time (UTC) time, which is very desirable for event correlation across geographic boundaries. There must not be more than one

<wsu:Timestamp> per SOAP Header. It has a number of attributes designed to indicate time boundaries and state.

- wsu:Timestamp/wsu:Created is an optional element indicating the creation time of the security semantics in scope.

- wsu:Timestamp/wsu:Expires represents the moment that the security elements referenced by the timestamp are no longer valid. The application architect, where security timestamps are chosen as a variable, should design the logic so that when the timestamp expires, the referenced semantics cease to provide access or authorization. The use of this attribute in a digital signature goes a long way to prevent replay attacks.

- wsu:Timestamp/{any} allows full flexibility to add new elements.

- wsu:Timestamp/@{any} specifies a schema ID that can be used to reference this timestamp.

- wsu:Timestamp/@wsu:Id specifies an XML schema ID which can be used to reference the element.

- An important item to consider as we move forward into the WS-Security suite of standards is that WS-Security provides token independence. It does not matter to the underlying application if the client presents one kind of token or another; WS-Security can through WS-Trust and WS-Policy define how to use all supported tokens so that a binding can be established and SOAP messages exchanged securely.

- However, that does not preclude the real issue that some tokens are intrinsically more secure and scalable than others. So while WS-Security can be token agnostic, that does not imply that using it this way is architecturally sound. This depends somewhat upon what is being protected and why. If all that is being protected is a service that provides a unification of hotel reservations, airline reservations, and other travel services, there is no need to impose any security controls at all until it is time to finalize a selection and make a purchase. Basic tokens that guarantee data integrity would be more than sufficient up to that point. WS-Security provides just such a set of tokens and will provide them in a unified systematic way that allows everything to work together smoothly. This can all be accomplished without WS-Security but not nearly as effortlessly when it comes to third-party service integration.

- Use the appropriate token to protect data in an appropriate fashion. While this author will push using certain signing techniques, there are some cases where that approach is over-kill. Select what is appropriate and know that WS-Security will allow you to implement it.

### 3.4.1 WS-Trust

Web Services Trust (WS-Trust) is part of the WS-Security specification that exists to define both the implementation of web service security per service and the engagement with supporting web services so that security is maintained. As part of a suite of standards, it is not self-contained and makes explicit reference to other WS standards and has dependencies with them.

WS-Trust is a standard which defines how to exchange trusted SOAP messages in a protocol agnostic way. It provides a mechanism to define how to request and obtain security tokens and how to establish, maintain, and assess trust relationships. This is accomplished through requiring that incoming messages prove a set of claims defined for the application. It leverages WS-Policy, another part of the WS-Security standard to communicate these requirements programmatically to service consumers.

The key driving requirements for the specification are:

Requesting and obtaining security tokens
Establishing, maintaining, and assessing trust relationships

The WS-Trust model is based upon the assumptions that the processes used by the web service requiring incoming messages to present a set of claims defined by the application owner is sufficient to establish trust between business partners and that all applications which conform to the defined specifications can be trusted. WS-Trust defines how to verify that the claims in the incoming message are sufficient to comply with the defined policy, ensuring message compliance (and assumed trust). It provides a defined mechanism to verify that the attributes of the incoming message are proven by any provided signatures, either directly or through an identity broker. WS-Trust also provides a mechanism to verify that the issuers of any security tokens are trusted to issue the claims they have made and, if necessary, to externally verify these tokens.

While it is not necessary to use WS-Trust to define and maintain web services trust relationships, WS-Trust provides a predefined framework for doing so, one that when conformed to ensures interoperability with the trust models of other service providers who support the standard. While conformance to the standard may or may not be sufficient to meet business requirements for trust relationships on the application layer, it provides a foundation upon which additional capabilities can be layered.

Before we explore the mechanisms of WS-Trust, I wish to point out some architectural assumptions that are made by the specification. The first is that trust is specific and exclusive to the requirements for engaging and using the service and does not extend past the capabilities of the service. Establishing a trust relationship within WS-Trust for making hotel reservations does not extend to being trusted to perform banking transactions. In other words, trust, as defined within WS-Trust is specific and narrowly bound to trust to engage the specific service.

The second architectural assumption made by the specification is that trust relationships may depend upon the need to trust other services or third parties not bound by the WS-Trust specifications or policies for the applications but necessary to enforce those policies. As an example, WS-Trust will often require that the transactions be transacted over a TLS or SSL encrypted tunnel, but WS-Trust does not define the properties of the x.509v3 certificate used to encrypt this tunnel; those are defined by the third-party CA which has been trusted by the business to both sign its private keys and manage the signing authority so that it remains an uncompromised and verifiable signing authority. In 2011, business that held certificates signed by both Verisign and Comodo suffered from the reduced trust associated with both CAs as they both suffered security breaches which impacted the ability to validate certificates signed by their signing authorities.

With those assumptions made explicit, let us now explore the internal mechanisms of the WS-Trust standard. WS-Trust supports different modes for obtaining tokens and brokering trust based upon either token acquisition (explicit requests) or out-of-band token management.

Where the application architect opts for explicit token requests, the process uses `<wst:RequestSecurityToken>` to request the token, with `<wst:RequestSecurityTokenResponse>` containing the response to the specific WSDL port. If the response token contains values that are not supported by the recipient, then the recipient may fault with either a `<wst:InvalidRequest>` or a more specific fault. The token may also be returned with the requesters choosing to disregard because it does not meet their needs. The application architect will wish to use bindings to define the specifics of the responses and how they are handled by their service.

By now the reader will have anticipated that both the request and the response should be signed, and if signed, that these signatures must be validated. The `<wst:RequestSecurityToken>` element contains the following mandatory and optional attributes:

Mandatory:
   wst:RequestType: This is a URI which indicates the class of function that is being requested. The allowed values are defined by specific bindings and profiles of WS-Trust, and the URI should correspond to the WS-Addressing Action URI.

Optional:
   wst:TokenType: This element describes an identifier for the request. If included, all subsequent responses to the request for security token must carry this attribute. This allows the token and the response to be correlated.
   wst:@Context: This provides a URI which specifies the identifier for the request. Where included in the request, it must be included in the response, allowing for request–response correlation.
   wst:SecondaryParameters: This very optional attribute is a holding place for adding parameters needed by the application for trust processing. Obviously, these may be parameters that the other party may choose not to process, especially if the risk of processing is deemed to be great. Similar is the "any" and "@any" which also allow

additional schema elements to be added; however, in these cases, they may be used in bindings.

wst:TokenType: This is used when the token type cannot be inferred. To add clarity, this element is often used with the WS-Policy element `<wsp:AppliesTo>` to define the specific target scope for the token. When the `<wst:TokenType>` element is not present, using `<wsp:AppliesTo>` functions like the Kerberos target service model in ensuring the token is properly applied.

wst:Claims is an optional but rather useful element to request that a specific set of claims be asserted in the response. These should be met in the response or fail the trust. The syntax for this can be specified and clarified by using a wst:claims@Dialect element. While the specifications and URI would be defined elsewhere (such as in WS-Policy), this element is used to represent which specific claims are in scope to maintain the trust.

wst:Entropy is used to specify that keys provided must use the entropy required by the application. While either an `<enc:EncryptedKey>` or `<wst:BinarySecret>` can be used for the value, I strongly recommend only using the `<enc:EncryptedKey>` element even where the transport of the application is encrypted.

wst:BinarySecret is used to convey either a symmetric or public key of an asymmetric key in base64 encoding within the message. A good use for this is to convey the public key used with the signing private key.

The optional but highly recommended element of wst:Lifetime specifies the window of use wherein the token requested will be available for validity to maintain the trust. It is not uncommon for this optional element to leverage the wsu:Created and wsu:Expires elements to convey additional information about the token's viability.

When the application architect has specific business requirements to meet regarding the nature of the authentication paradigms that can be accepted, the wst:AuthenticationType allows a very flexible way to indicate the nature of the authentication required. No specific classifications are called out, allowing the application architect complete flexibility. Thus, WS-Trust has the capacity to call for a specific government authentication level, a specific private enterprise authentication level (such as executive team vs. audit team vs. staff), and so on.

Associated with the AuthenticationType, but distinct is the wst:KeyType. This element allows specification of public key, bearer token, or symmetric key. While some of these formats have fixed token formats, new algorithms can be inserted by defining URI in other specifications and profiles. The subelement most frequently associated with AuthenticaitonType is wst:SignatureAlgorithm, which uses the XML Signature for signing algorithms. If the architects wish to allow key reuse, they may choose to associate the AuthenticationType with the subelement of wst:RequestSecurityToken called wst:UseKey and the associated subelement wst:UseKey/@Sig or wst:SignWith, either of which can be used to sign the message.

WS-Trust supports the following authentication types:

- Sign-in with Smart Card
- Sign-in over SSL using a strong password with expiration
- Sign-in over SSL using a strong password
- Sign-in over SSL using a digital certificate or key
- Sign-in over SSL
- WS-Trust allows for the establishment of a default sign-in mechanism for mechanisms like WS-Federation that can leverage this, as well as support for an unknown authentication level

Not frequently associated with the need for authentication but related to the KeyType is wst:EncryptionAlgorithm, wst:CanonicalizationAlgorithm,        wst:ComputedKeyAlgorithm, wst:Encryption, wst:ProofEncryption, wst:KeyWrapAlgorithm, and of course, wst:EncryptWith. The use case for these subelements is to permit the encryption of the token, something to be encouraged as the best means to ensure authenticity of the token.

On a similar basis, the wst:RequestSecurityTokenResponse has many attributes, though none of them mandatory. The wst@Context is somewhat of an exception as it must be in the response if it was in the request, but otherwise it is optional.

The ws:TokenType does nothing more than specify the type of token returned. More useful is wst:RequestedSecurityToken that is used to return the actual requested security token, except when a security token reference is used instead. The wst:RequestedSecurityToken can be placed into the <wsse:Security> header to secure the actual message itself, in which case the <wsse:SecurityTokenReference> element is placed in the wst:RequestedSecurityToken, pointing to its location in the header.

Similar with the request element, there are "any" and "@any" elements to provide extensions. If any of these are not understood, they should cause a fault to be generated.

To facilitate bindings, Organization for the Advancement of Structured Information Standards (OASIS) has predefined some URI using WS-Addressing. The <wst:RequestType> element uses http://docs.oasis-open.org/ws-sx/wstrust/200512/Issue. This allows for the use of both symmetric and asymmetric keys, allowing use of Kerberos or of public key authentication.

Some application designs will require the request of many tokens. To allow for operational efficiency, WS-Trust supports batch token requests. This is accomplished by embedding the wst:RequestSecurityTokens within a <wst:RequestSecurityTok enCollection> element. Each request must use an action URI in the RequestType element, which corresponds to the batch version of normal action URI, such as BatchIssue or BatchValidate, BatchRenew, or BatchCancel. Signatures must reference the entire collection, and every request must be handled by a single endpoint. The responses are returned in a wst:RequestSecurityTokenResponse embedded within a wst:RequestSecurityTokenResponseCollection.

There are certain situations where an identity may wish to delegate authority to a trusted individual, such as when the identity holder is on vacation and an urgent task arises. WS-Trust supports identity delegation as part of the wst:RequestSecurityToken element through the following subelements: wst:DelegateTo, wst:Forwardable, and wst:Delegatable. The application architect should carefully consider which application functions are delegatable and which can only be performed by the designated individual. Where delegation is supported, the architect must ensure that the audit trail of actions taken under delegated authority include both the authority and the identity item to which authority has been delegated.

To ensure that policy has been clearly and effectively communicated, the following extensions to the wst:RequestSecurityToken have been defined: wsp:Policy and wsp:PolicyReference. While the use of the policy reference instead of the policy allows for a smaller message size, it is more prone to failure as you now rely upon the availability and utility of the URI, and, as it is technologically possible albeit unlikely to change the policy between the request issuance and the receipt of the request, providing policy within the message is more resilient and legally binding.

As sometimes the business needs to allow multiple people to use a token, wst:RequestSecurityToken supports defining authorized token participants through the use of the wst:participants, wst:Primary, wst:Participant, and wst:Participants subelements.

To preserve both confidentiality and authenticity, the token request framework is often used. The request type establishes a binding using http://docs.oasis-open.org/ws-sx/ws-trust/200512/KET. The desired token type can be specified using the wst:TokenType attribute and the scope of the token's authority established using wsp:AppliesTo. As always, the response should be signed.

Where key exchange is used as part of the token request, care must be taken to ensure that private keys are never sent, and that where symmetric keys are used, they are only sent to trusted parties. The simplest mechanism for doing this ad hoc is to generate a temporary key, which is then encrypted using the <xenc:EncryptedKey> element. While this will ensure confidentiality, it will not ensure authenticity, so while this is simple, it is far from the best practice that would have the application architect use asymmetric encryption, with the private key signing the encrypted ciphertext.

Where public CA-signed keys are not used, composite keys allow symmetric keys to be formed from two shared secrets. Both the requester and the respondent contribute, and they are combined to create a secret. This is best used to create new keys which are then used to encrypt the data. Again, this provides some protection for confidentiality, but does not ensure authenticity.

WS-Trust not only permits composite key generation but also permits key transfer, brokered key distribution, and delegated key transfer. Delegated key transfer grants the right to use a key but does not transfer the key. Thus, the delegated agent does not ever know the key, preserving confidentiality of the key while permitting utilization of the application's functionality by the delegated party.

Encryption is used not only to protect data but also to provide a mechanism for authentication. Many application architects need to require that both the service and the client authenticate each other. While this can be done readily using CA-signed public–private key pairs on both, it can also be done using any generated key for encryption and any other generated key for the signature by following the procedures for key generation, response, signing, and transference as specified in WS-Security.

It is recommended that if the application architect decides to use a custom-generated key to perform mutual authentication instead of mandating using keys issued by a mutually trusted certification audit, the application architect enforces the property of perfect forward secrecy. This may be achieved by specifying a `<wst:entropy>` element that contains a `<xenc:EncryptedKey>` that is encrypted by a public key pair used for a single key agreement. Think of it as a custom-generated one-time pad using both asymmetric and symmetric cryptography. As the public key is only used to provide additional entropy, it does not require authentication, eliminating the need for it to be signed by a third-party trusted CA.

Generating this one-time pad using public key cryptography is effective but slow. Where speed is of the essence, use of the Diffie–Hellman key exchange can speed things up without significant reduction in security. This will provide a random integer and single modular exponent that can be used as the one-time pad.

Authenticity is preserved when using perfect forward security to create cryptographic one-time pads but only if the entropy is kept secret. If the entropy used in the key generation is ever made public, an unauthorized third party could generate their own one-time key using the same techniques and successfully authenticate. Thus, it is imperative that this element be kept under strict control to ensure confidentiality. Also, such authentication methods do not ensure that no tampering of the message has occurred; so the security of the authentication still needs to depend upon the signing of the message to ensure message integrity and authenticity.

The easiest way to ensure authentication and integrity while maintaining confidentiality is to leverage keys signed by a trusted third-party CA. The public keys can be exchanged for mutual authentication, and the message can be signed by the private key. While this is slower than other methods, it is comprehensive. Using this technique, the public keys are pre-exchanged between the parties. The messages are encrypted and signed using the public keys of the other party. They cannot be decrypted without the private key. If a one-time pad is required, the public key can be used to generate the one-time pad using the perfect forward security mechanism. Only the recipient with the associated private key can decrypt and access the token to authenticate it.

The public key can be and should be validated, both cryptographically and with the signing authority. The application architect should look for a CA that supports not only a frequently updated certificate revocation list (CRL) but also an Online Certificate Status Protocol (OCSP) so that the current status of the key pair's validity can be checked programmatically. Signature validation is key to detect attacks against the integrity of the message and the authenticity of the authentication, key elements to maintain the trust.

Errors in handling WS-Trust elements are processed using the SOAP Fault mechanism. Defined Fault codes should be used but with minimal information, lest the error-reporting mechanism be used as a mechanism for attack analysis by a malicious party.

The following is a list of all valid Fault codes:

- wst:InvalidRequest
- wst:FailedAuthentication
- wst:RequestFailed
- wst:InvalidSecurityToken
- wst:AuthenticationBadelements
- wst:BadRequest
- wst:ExpiredData
- wst:InvalidTimeRange
- wst:InvalidScope
- wst:RenewNeeded
- wst:UnableToRenew

A common attack against a security token request is to flood it with requests. If external controls are put in place so as to accept requests only from authorized parties, this risk is effectively transferred to other layers of the application and network stack.

### 3.4.2 WS-Policy

WS-Policy is often considered to be a component of WS-Security as it is used to communicate the various policies including the security policies of the web service much like the WSDL is used to communicate the rules of engagement for the service. Like the WSDL, it defines those rules that must be followed and those that are optional but in a hierarchical manner wherein some or all of the child objects must be satisfied to comply with the defined policy. The primary purpose of the specification is to define a consistent policy for establishing secure communication that is used by SOAP Message Security, WS-Trust, WS-SecureConversation, WSS10, and WSS11.

The goal is to leverage the framework's intersection algorithm for selecting from the specific defined policy alternatives and associate them with web service artifacts. Thus, wherever possible, WS-Policy does not define specific parameters or attributes and relies upon QName assertion matching. Where attributes are added, policy matching will not leverage those attributes as they will be treated as informational properties.

Policies, however, should never be accepted unless they are signed.

To accomplish this, the assertions defined must be organized into simple and clear patterns, such as protection assertions, conditional assertions, security-binding assertions, supporting assertions, trust assertions, and so on.

These assertions must then identify specific message parts to be protected and define the specifics of the protection, such as confidentiality or integrity. These assertions may be nested within each other, providing qualification on the behavior of the application.

As the assertions are designed to be used in multiple combinations, the bindings are specified in a way as to represent common usage patterns. These bindings may describe the minimum set of tokens permitted and how they are bound to messages, key transport mechanisms, required message elements, the content and ordering of elements in the wsse:Security header, and various parameters related to the use of cryptographic algorithms. When placed into the context of the conditions and scope of the assertion, they provide the defined mechanisms for securing messages between initiator and recipient. Nowhere, however, is there a mechanism for providing the initiator the ability to evaluate if the use of the service is desirous. However, the use of WS-Policy can be extended by the evaluating service to look for specific contexts and make a determination regarding information exchange based upon the policy as communicated.

WS-Policy supports the following bindings:

- TransportBinding
- SymmetricBinding
- AsymmetricBinding

Those bindings not only provide confidentiality but can also be used to provide message integrity.

There are two methods used to define the parts of a SOAP message which require integrity protecting: XPath expressions referring to any part of the message or QNames specifying message headers or parts of the body. The binding-specific token properties detail the means by which this protection is provided. These are specified in the SignedParts assertion, and digital signatures are used to protect the integrity of the message contents. If a SignedParts assertion is made without children, then all message headers and the message body must be signed.

The SignedParts assertion contains the following elements and attributes:

/sp:Body: This optional empty element indicates the need to protect the integrity of the entire SOAP message body.

/sp:Header: This specifies that the SOAP Header elements targeted to the same actor/role as the security header must be signed. Which header to protect is defined using the /@Name attribute or the @Namespace attribute. @Namespace is required but @Name is not.

/sp:Attachments: This optional element indicates that all SOAP messages with attachments are to be signed. If SOAP Message Security is used to enforce this, then all the message parts other than the primary SOAP envelope are to be signed. If needed, the optional empty elements of /sp13:contentSignatureTransform and/sp13:AttachmentCompleteSignatureTransform indicate the requirement to perform the AttachmentContentSignatureTransform or the AttachmentCompleteSignatureTransform as part of the attachment process.

There are also two methods used to specify the elements to protect the confidentiality of encrypting at the element level or at the header/body. The SOAP Message Security mechanism may be required, or an out-of-band mechanism may be required. The binding-specific token properties detail the exact mechanism by which protection is provided. Many security professionals like to debate that the protections provided by SOAP Message Security that make use of out-of-band mechanisms like SSL/TLS are no longer important, and that encrypted SOAP may be sent in the clear over the Internet. I would encourage architects to leverage every protection available to them. While SOAP Message Security provides excellent enforcement of controls for confidentiality, SSL/TLS keeps the communication private on public networks. Otherwise, the entire message can be copied in transit, and the encryption broken off line, with the targets of the attack completely unaware that their reliance on message security was insufficient to protect the sensitive content.

However, there are attacks against SSL/TLS that, in the absence of strong authentication, make it desirable to use SOAP Message Security. It is hard to convince companies to invest in strong authentication for SSL/TLS. Where content is sensitive, it is best to encrypt it using SOAP Message Security AND send it over a SSL/TLS encrypted tunnel.

To require that parts of the message be encrypted by SOAP Message Security, WS-Trust uses the EncryptedParts assertion. There is no benefit in having multiple assertions; multiple EncryptedParts assertions are the logical equivalent of having all the message parts mentioned in a single assertion. Remember, the policy does NOT encrypt the message parts; it simply requires that they be encrypted.

The assertion uses the following elements and attributes to indicate which message parts are to be encrypted:

/sp:Body: This optional empty element indicates that the entire body must be encrypted.

/sp:Header: This optional element indicates that the specific SOAP Header or set of headers requires protection. However, as this uses the WSS 1.1 Encrypted Headers to encrypt the SOAP Headers, if this is not supported, then this element cannot be used to require the protection. If you have multiple SOAP Headers with the same local name but different namespaces, each requiring encryption, you must use multiple assertions.

/sp:Header/@Name: Optional attribute; indicates the local name of the SOAP Header requiring encryption. You can use this where you only need to require that certain headers in a common namespace be protected.

/sp:Header/@Namespace: This is a "required" attribute indicating the namespace of the header elements requiring encryption. It is only required, however, in the event that the EncryptedParts assertion is made at all.

/sp:Attachments: This optional element indicates that all the SOAP messages with attachments are to be encrypted.

Where you desire only elements within the message header or body to be encrypted, the EncryptedElements assertion should be leveraged. Much like with the EncryptedParts assertion, if you specify multiple EncryptedElements assertions, they are logically treated as a single EncryptedElements assertion with all the specified XPath expressions unified underneath.

The XPath elements can be specified with the /sp:XPath element, which specifies a string that identifies the nodes requiring encryption. If needed, you can specify the /@XPathVersion attribute to indicate the version of XPath to use. If not provided, then version 1.0 is assumed.

The ContentEncryptedElements assertion is used to require encryption of the element contents instead of the elements. Like the EncryptedElements assertion, XPath elements can be specified with the /sp:XPath element, which specifies a string that identifies the nodes requiring encryption. If needed, you can specify the /@ XPathVersion attribute to indicate the version of XPath to use. If not provided, then version 1.0 is assumed.

Beyond requiring confidentiality and integrity protection for SOAP message parts, elements, or element contents, WS-Trust can also require a set of header elements that the message must contain. This is done through the RequiredElements assertion. Like the EncryptedElements assertion and ContentEncryptedElements assertion, XPath elements can be specified with the /sp:XPath element, which specifies a string. However, this string identifies those header elements the message must contain. If needed, you can specify the /@XPathVersion attribute to indicate the version of XPath to use. If not provided, then version 1.0 is assumed. This capacity can be used to enforce P3P-like controls regarding required data for application functionality.

As RequiredElements is based on XPath, which not all applications can or will support, WS-Trust provides RequiredParts assertions, which are based on QNames. Otherwise, the assertion works the same, with elements of sp:Header, specifying the header elements that must be present, sp:Header/@Name, the required local name of the SOAP Header which must be present to comply with your policy, and the sp:Header/@Namespace attribute indicating the required namespace of the SOAP Header you require.

Where the application or security architects require that tokens be presented with SOAP messages, they should use a token assertion. These define the kinds of tokens accepted to protect messages and bindings. Token assertions may optionally carry an sp:IncludeToken attribute, forcing a copy of the token to be included with the message. This should only be done when a local copy of the token is necessary for decryption or signature validation. Otherwise, the transaction will be less efficient, and the unnecessary exposure of the token could result in token compromise.

There are some times, however, when you need to require a token. One kind of token that is frequently required is a username token, which is required through the UserNameToken assertion. This is often done, ironically, to protect the username, preserving the privacy of the actual user of the service. It is also often done when there is a lack of encryption of the message or transport, thus providing privacy without encryption.

This assertion may have the following attributes:

/sp:IncludeToken, an optional attribute identifying the need to include the token.

/sp:Issuer, an optional attribute containing a reference to the issuer of the required token.

/sp:IssuerName, an optional element containing an xs:anyURI which is the logical name of the issuer of the token.

/wsp:Claims, an optional element, which, when present, specifies required claims that the token must contain to satisfy the requirements for the username.

/wsp:Policy, a required element identifying additional requirements for the UsernameToken assertion.

/wsp:Policy/sp:NoPassword, an optional element forbidding the password element.

/wsp:Policy/sp:HashPassword, an optional element not only requiring a password but also specifying that it must be hashed with the timestamp and nonce as defined in the www:UsernameTokenProfile. Sending hashes, even hashes salted as these will be with a timestamp and a nonce, over unencrypted protocols is a very bad idea. The speed of modern password cracking routines will break even complex passwords hashed with sophisticated salts rather quickly. If your business requirements specify that you must transmit a password, simply hashing it is not enough. The transit must be over an encrypted tunnel, preferably with controls in place to detect a man-in-the-middle attack.

/wsp:Policy/sp13:Created, an optional element, required in the event that the default clear text password case is used. There are no valid business cases for using the default clear text password case with modern computing, not with the high incidence of successful man-in-the-middle attacks.

/wsp:Policy/sp13:Nonce, an optional element, required in the event that the default clear text password case is used.

/wsp:Policy/sp:RequireDerivedKeys, an optional element which sets the Derived Keys, Explicit Derived Keys, and Implied Derived Keys properties for the token to be true.

/wsp:Policy/sp:RequireExplicitDerivedKeys, an optional element which sets the Derived Keys and Explicit Derived Keys properties for the token to be true and Implied Derived Keys to be false.

/wsp:Policy/sp:RequireImpliedDerivedKeys, an optional element which sets the Derived Keys and Implied Derived Keys properties for the token to be true and Explicit Derived Keys to be false.

/wsp:Policy/sp:WssUsernameToken10, an optional element forcing the use of the older version of the standard, www:UserNameTokenProfile1.0.

/wsp:Policy/sp:WssUsernameToken11, an optional element forcing the use of the newer version of the standard, www:UserNameTokenProfile1.1.

Sometimes the business requirements are that a token is created and issued for the purpose of securing the message. The CreatedIssuedToken assertion voices that requirement, with the following optional and mandatory attributes for the /sp:/IssuedToken element:

/@sp:IncludeToken, an optional value to identify the inclusion value for the token assertion being mandated.

/sp:Issuer, an optional attribute containing a reference to the issuer of the token. Where this is a third party, this should be a required part of any WS-Policy assertion for tokens, as should be the related /sp:IssuerName which requires the logical name of the issuer as an xs:anyURI.

/wsp:Claims, an optional element, which, when present, specifies required claims that the token must contain to satisfy the requirements for the token.

/Sp:RequestSecurityTokenTemplate is a required element containing those elements that must be placed into the request security token wst:SecondaryParameters to the issuer.

Now, the issued token security model involves a three-party setup, with a target server, a client, and a trusted third party called a Security Token Service (STS). The policy you mandate flows from server to client, which is obvious, and then again from the STS to the client. The policy may be embedded in the issued token assertion (recommended) or provided out of band (not recommended as it is not a method that scales when policy changes, and policies will change). Parts of the assertion are therefore to be processed by the client and other parts by the STS provider. These are passed in the wst:SecondaryParameters, mandated in the policy by the RequestSecurityTokenTemplate.

There is one optional attribute for this element, the /@TrustVersion which refers to the version of the WS-Trust specification using a namespace URI.

Wsp:Policy is a required element used to identify additional requirements. This has the optional sub-elements of RequireDerived-Keys, RequireExplicitDerivedKeys, ReqireImpliedDerivedKeys, RequireInternalReference, and RequireExternalReference, all of which should be self-apparent by now.

The token may be of multiple types, but it is desirable to specify those types that would be acceptable to meet the requirements of the application and business. Supported assertions are X509Token, KerboerosToken, SpnegoContextToken, SamlToken, RelToken, HttpsToken, KeyValueToken, SecurityContextToken, and SecureConversationToken. While each business will have their own requirements and those requirements should drive token acceptance, there are some distinct advantages in using either X509Token or SamlToken over any other token choice available. Both are cryptographically sound methods of carrying identity information safely across public networks and represent identity federation, or in other words, the client organization is responsible for maintaining the credential and provides to you easy and scalable means to validate the current status of that identity and its authorization. When properly configured, either will withstand any attack against identity.

The X509Token has some elements and attributes that are common to all tokens and have been already discussed, but there are some elements and attributes that are unique to this token type. They include:

/Sp:WssX509V3Token10 which requires that an x.509 v3 token should be used as defined in the WSS:X509TokenProfile1.0.

/Sp:WssX509Pkcs7Token10 requires that the x.509 token must be in the public-key cryptography standards #7 (PKCS7) format as defined in the WSS:X509TokenProfile1.0.

/Sp:WssX509V3Token11 which requires that an x.509 v3 token should be used as defined in the WSS:X509TokenProfile1.1.

/Sp:WssX509Pkcs7Token11 requires that the x.509 token must be in the PKCS7 format as defined in the WSS:X509TokenProfile1.1.

/Sp:WssX509V3Token10 which requires that an x.509 v3 token should be used as defined in the WSS:X509TokenProfile1.0.

/Sp:WssX509PkiPathV1Token11 requires that the x.509 token must be in the public key infrastructure (PKI) Path format as defined in the WSS:X509TokenProfile1.1.

KerberosTokens come from the very well-respected Kerberos security model. Kerberos is best served as an internal authentication engine and is most often used in that capacity. It requires that a central server be present and available at all times and that time clocks are strongly synchronized, things which are hard to mandate in a multiorganization-distributed application like most service-oriented applications. However, as the Microsoft Windows operating system makes strong use of Kerberos in the more modern versions of the platform, internally focused service providers encourage the use of Kerberos as it provides ease of use, ease of support, and a single reliable scalable credential for common authentication and authorization. Unfortunately, Microsoft's implementation has not only expanded the Kerberos specification but it often is also vulnerable to the very attacks against the credential that Kerberos was designed to be immune to in a strictly compliant implementation of the authentication protocol.

The elements that are unique to the KerberosToken assertion are sp:WssKerberosV5ApReqToken11, which requires a Kerberos Version 5 Ap-REQ token as defined in the WSS:KerberosTokenProfile1.1 and sp:WssGssKerberosV5ApReqToken11, which requires a Generic Security service (GSS) Kerberos Version 5 Ap-REQ token as defined in the WSS:KerberosTokenProfile1.1.

Simple and Protected GSSAPI Negotiation Mechanism (Spnego) is supported in the SpnegoContextToken Assertion. Spnego is an authentication mechanism that permits negotiation of the authentication mechanism between two parties which know nothing of each other's capabilities, allowing them to find a commonly supported mechanism. Support for this in WS-Trust is more than a little ironic considering that WS-Trust is a means to provide instructions on what security mechanisms are supported. Support for this mechanism permits Spnego-enabled clients to transparently supply an authentication without having to be rewritten to support a more robust security protocol. I highly recommend against the use of this token except for SOAs that are not only internally focused but also have a poorly trained or understaffed support organization. The unique elements in it are:

/sp:MustNotSendCancel, an optional element that indicates that the STS does not support the cancel RST messages. I would encourage application architects to always design support of RST cancel messages into their platform.

/sp:MustNotSendAmend, an optional element that indicates that the Security Context Token (SCT) does not support RST amend messages.

/Sp:MustNotSendRenew, an optional element that indicates a lack of support for token renewal.

With the support of the SecurityContextToken assertion, WS-Trust does not provide a mechanism for these context tokens to be requested or to be issued. This has to be constructed out of band, and if this cannot be assumed, then the SecureConversationToken should be used instead. There are no attributes or elements unique to this assertion other than /sp:SC13SecurityContextToken, which is an optional element indicating that these tokens should be used as defined in WS-SecureConversation.

The SecureConversationToken assertion in WS-Trust is a requirement that the indicated issuer address supply the Secure-ConversationToken either from an indicated issuer (with the Issuer attribute specifying the issuer) or from the same address as the service endpoint if that attribute is empty or null. It provides mechanisms for defining support for amending, renewing, and canceling the tokens all in compliance with the WS-SecureConversation specification discussed separately.

Much like with the SecureContextToken, WS-Trust does not define how to get an SAML assertion. The only unique elements to this WS-Trust assertion are those related to the requirement of versions of SAML-supported WSS:SamlIV11Token10, WSS:SamlIV11Token11, and WSS:SamlIV20Token11 for versions 1.0, 1.1, and 2.0, respectively.

WS-Trust does not also define how Rights Expression Language (REL) tokens must be issued; the assertion, when present, just requires an REL token. The REL token supported is specific to the version of the WS-Trust specification, the number within the name specifying the appropriate version: sp:WssRelV10Token10, sp:WssRelV20Token10, sp:WssRelV10Token11, or sp:WssRelV20Token11.

WS-Trust can, and should, mandate the use of Hypertext Transfer Protocol Secure (HTTPS) using the HttpsToken Assertion. Along with this, WS-Trust can mandate the use of Basic, Digest, or strong client certificate authentication through the use of sp:HttpBasicAuthentication, sp:HttpDigestAuthentication, or sp:RequireClientCertificate. I would recommend that where the sp:RequireClientCertificate element is used, the X509Token assertion is also used to define the specifics for the certificates, and specific CAs (issuers) are supported.

WS-Trust can allow reference to an arbitrary key pair using a KeyValueToken assertion with a KeyValue token. The policy can specify the algorithm used to generate the key pair, using the sp:RsaKeyValue optional element. The presence of this element enforces the use of the Rivest, Shamir, and Adelman (RSA) algorithm instead of other cryptographic public key algorithms such as Digital Signature Algorithm (DSA) or Diffie–Hellman. The associated KeyValue token allows the application to specify an arbitrary key pair to be used to sign or encrypt XML elements. As CA-signed x509V3 certificates are now available rather cheaply, the incentive to use such privately generated but unvalidatable public key pairs is significantly less than it was when the WS-Trust specification was written.

When constructing security bindings, the defined properties (often specified in a WS-Policy assertion) are used much like variables. The assertions populate the properties and the bindings use these properties to control their behavior.

WS-Policy is used to define the defaults used when creating the security bindings. It does this through presenting the available options as common primitives to allow reuse and then placing these into patterns to facilitate logical use. Some common assertions that are made to facilitate bindings are:

AlgorithmSuite defines the properties of the algorithms that are supported and often the strength of the algorithm (such as SHA 256).

AsymmetricBinding is used when wss:SOAPMessageSecurity is used. This assertion specifies the use of public key cryptography, allowing the public key to be shared openly and the private key kept secure and confidential. This assertion allows the requirement that the data be encrypted before signing and that the signature itself is encrypted.

Layout specifies a requirement for a particular security header layout, using elements such as sp:Strict, sp:Lax, sp:LaxTsFirst, and sp:LaxTsLast.

TransportBinding specifies the requirement to specify a means to securely transport SOAP messages other than wss:SoapMessageSecurity. One example is enforcing the use of HTTPS. Embedded within the TransportBinding element might be an optional wsp:Policy element that applies to the transport only, with subelements of TransportToken, AlgorithmSuite, Layout, and Timestamp.

SymmetricBinding, like AsymmetricBinding, is used when wss:SOAPMessageSecurity is used. It defines the requirements for both the encryption and signature tokens. Like the asymmetric binding, it has some properties that make it an attractive binding set to use, such as the ability to encrypt the signature and force signing the entire header set as well as the body. Because both the signature and encryption algorithm are symmetric, encryption–decryption options are fast but the keys must be protected from unauthorized users.

The tokens we have discussed up to this point have been mandated by policy to secure the authentication, authorization, and confidentiality and integrity of the transport. The bindings mandated by those policy assertions have the entire message as their scope of authority. WS-Policy can be used to specify requirements for bindings for elements within the message as well. This is done through the use of supporting tokens.

Without supporting tokens, the signature in the security header will be used to sign the timestamp, the SOAP body, and all SOAP Headers. However, sometimes, the business requirements call for the signing of the message signature. This can be accomplished by adding a supporting token, an additional signature in the security header. Thus:

Signature A signs the Timestamp, SOAP Headers, and SOAP body.
Signature B signs signature A.

This is mandated in WS-Policy using the sp:Endorsing-SupportingTokens element. An alternative is the sp:PSignedEndorsingSupportingTokens assertion that requires that the second signature used to sign the first must itself be signed. Where you wish to mandate both signing and encrypting the signature used to sign and encrypt the SOAP Headers and body, the WS-Policy should use the sp:SignedEncryptedSupportingTokens assertion or the sp:SignedEndorsingEncrypted SupportingTokens assertion if the supporting token also needs to be an endorsing token.

While it is possible to have more than two signing tokens or two encrypting tokens, it is not recommended as that would actually make you vulnerable to XML substitution attacks that would be undetectable even with the signed messages. In fact, I recommend that the only policy an organization supports is the OnlySignEntireHeadersAndBody assertion, and that only independently signed x509V3 certificates are used for the signature token as that architecture provides an out-of-band signature validation mechanism.

There are some elements of SOAP Message Security independent of trust and tokens, which apply to the endpoint. WS-Policy has assertions related to governance of these functions. There are two issues which need careful handling on the part of the application related to the capabilities of WS SOAP Message Security. One issue is that SOAP Message Security allows for multiple equivalent reference mechanisms to be used in a single reference. Another is that in a multimessage exchange, the same token may be referenced using different mechanisms. Because of these issues, the policy must define controls that both the recipient and the issuer must be able to handle; otherwise either may send a fault.

These requirements are handled through the Wss10 Assertion or the Wss11 Assertion depending upon if you need to support the WSS:Soap Message Security version 1 or 1.1.

They are:

WSS:SOAP Message Security 1.0
- Direct References
- Key Identifier References
- Issuer Serial References
- External URI references
- Embedded Token References

WSS:SOAP Message Security 1.1
- Thumbprint References
- Encrypted Key References
- Signature Confirmation

On a similar basis, the sp:Trust assertion is used to assert which of WS-Trust's controls are being set by policy. The available options are:

- Client Challenge
- Server Challenge
- Client Entropy

- Server Entropy
- Issued Tokens
- Collection
- Scope Policy 1.5
- Interactive Challenge

### 3.4.3 WS-SecureConversation

The conventions of SOAP and WS-Security are all geared around messages and message authentication. The trouble is that many applications need to be designed to support multiple messages or a stream of messages. In such contexts, the WS-SecureConversation standard is more useful as a mechanism for exchanging tokens than WS-Security or WS-Trust. The security context is established using the `<wsc:SecurityContextToken>` element. This element does not support references to it using key identifiers or key names, but references to it with a `<wus:Id>` or `<wse:Reference>` to the `<wsc:Identifier>` element are supported. Once trust is established through the authentication and authorization of the token, multiple messages may be exchanged.

The element has the following attributes:

wsc:SecurityContextToken/wsc:Identifier is a required element that uses an absolute URI that is unique to both sender and recipient. Ideally, this is globally unique in time and space or at least to the application context. This will involve URI tracking to ensure an inability to reuse that is logged across all services. I would recommend that the URI have strings in them to indicate context as a partial means to enforce global uniqueness, similar in nature to an object identifier (OID) as found in American National Standards Institute (ANSI)-based standards such as a media access control (MAC) address or x509 serial number.

wsc:SecurityContextToken/wsc:Instance allows the ability to reveal the context without revealing the actual key. While this is not required for the initial instance (though I would recommend it), all subsequent issuances with different keys must have a wsc:Instance element with a unique URI.

wsc:SecurityContextToken/@wsc:Id is optional and provides a
string label for the element that can be used to make reference
to the token.

wsc:SecurityContextToken/@{any} allows additional attributes.

wsc:SecurityContextToken/{any} allows additional elements.

Obviously, the wsc:SecurityContextToken must be preserved from
source to intended destination; however, the consumer may append tags
to it. This does mean that signing the entire wsc:SecurityContextToken
is problematic, though the consumer may sign the additions.

SCTs may be created by the STS, wherein when a
request security token is received, the response includes
both a SecurityContextTokenResponse containing the
RequestedSecurityToken and perhaps a wst:RequestedProofToken
pointing to the secret of the returned control.

The SCT may be created by one of the communicating parties and
sent forward with the message. This only works when the sender is
trusted by all parties. It also may be created through a negotiation
among the participants. In both cases, it is best if the constraints
imposed by WS-Trust be utilized to enforce constraints.

SCTs are not required to have lifetime semantics and are limited to
a specific set of algorithms and parameters as expressed in the policy.
Bindings may be established with or without a target scope.

When the request contains no information regarding the web
service with which the requester wants to communicate, then it is a
request without a target scope. This information must be known from
an out-of-band communication.

When the request has the <wsp:AppliesTo> with an endpoint
reference as described in WS-Trust, then this will be the target scope.
SCTs can be altered, allowing them to carry additional claims. This
is done using the sct:Amend binding. To accomplish this, proof of
possession of the key associated with the binding must be provided.
The most reliable and scalable means to do this is to create a signature
on the message body and key headers associated with the security
context.

SCTs may be renewed as needed using the renew binding. In a way,
renewing is a specialized form of an alteration, and thus, proof of possession of the key material is critical. However, during the renewal,

new key material may be extended, especially if the timestamp indicates that the existing token has expired.

When there is no further need for the security context, it can be canceled readily using the Cancel request from WS-Trust. Once canceled, it must be permitted no further interaction with the service.

When the Security Context Token contains a common shared secret, keys may be derived from this, which can be used to sign and encrypt by all parties in question. These keys can be readily expired and replaced to prevent a third party from attacking the key space. The <wsc:DerivedKeyToken> is used as the mechanism for indicating which derivation is used and to derive keys from the shared secret. The P_SHA-1 algorithm is used with three parameters: secret, label, and seed. It should not need to be said that the secret is the shared secret.

The supported attributes of the <wsc:DerivedKeyToken> are:

wsc:DerivedKeyToken>/@wsu:Id, the XML ID which can be used locally to reference the element.

wsc:DerivedKeyToken>/@Algorithm, when not specified, P_SHA-1 is assumed.

wsc:DerivedKeyToken>/wsse:SecurityTokenReference is used to specify a specific context token, security token, or shared secret used in the derivation of the new keys.

wsc:DerivedKeyToken>/wsc:Properties allows metadata to be associated with the derived key.

wsc:DerivedKeyToken>/wsc:Properties/wsc:Name provides the derived key a URI name that can be used as a source for other derived keys.

wsc:DerivedKeyToken>/wsc:Properties/wsc:Label defines a label for all keys derived from the specific derived key.

wsc:DerivedKeyToken>/wsc:Properties/wsc:Nonce defines a nonce used for all derived keys from this key.

wsc:DerivedKeyToken>/wsc:Properties/{any} extends the key with attributes as needed.

wsc:DerivedKeyToken/wsc:Generation is used when the application architect needs to specify which generation (fixed size) key to use.

wsc:DerivedKeyToken/wsc:Offset is used when fixed size keys are not used but rather the <wsc:Offset> and

<wsc:Length> elements are used to indicate where in the byte stream the generated key may be found. Offset starts at 0 for the first position, and length is specified in bytes.

wsc:DerivedKeyToken/wsc:Label is an attribute that can be specified using the wsc:Label element. If this is not specified, a default value of "WS-SecureConversationWS-SecureConversation" is used.

wsc:DerivedKeyToken/wsc:Nonce is an optional base64-encoded nonce used in the key derivation function for the derived key. If a nonce is used for a derivation sequence, it should be used for all subsequent derivations.

The @wsc:Nonce attribute can be added to the security token reference. When present, it is an indication that the key is not in the referenced token but is derived from that referenced token's secret key, implying a derived key. The @wsc:Length can be used to indicate key length, and if desired, the @wsc:Offset can be used to indicate where in the secret key the derived key begins. If @wsc:Length is not specified, the default length is 32, and if the @wsc:Offset is not specified, the default is 0. Cryptographic experts would recognize that in essence what is being done here is generating a Caesar cipher from the key. This is not very secure if the secret key is known. If you are going to be generating such derived keys as part of your security model, the secret key must be kept confidential and authentic, it must always be under your control while remaining useful and available for deriving keys, and it must not be permitted to change. A failure on any one of the six elements of the Parkerian hexad is a distinct failure of the security model.

The SCT can be referred to both from within the <wsse:Security> element and from without. In neither case does the SCT support references to it using key identifiers or key names. To refer to it from an external source, you must use a <wsc:Identifier> element value. Internally, you can use either the <wsu:Id> or <wsse:Reference> to the <wsc:Identifier>; however, I highly recommend that the <wsc:Identifier> is the only mechanism used to provide consistency across environments.

When an error occurs, the default fault codes are as follows:

- Wsc:BadContextToken
- Wsc:UnsupportedContextToken

- Wsc:UnknownDerivationSource
- Wsc:RenewNeeded
- Wsc:UnableToRenew

Those fault codes can carry the default or a custom fault string. The application architect has to be careful in the customization of fault strings that attackers are not provided with information that can lead to providing an attack path or hint to an attack method.

### 3.4.4 WS-Privacy and the P3P Framework

Before I get into the standards, I need to take a few moments to discuss privacy. Privacy goals fall outside of the traditional goals of information confidentiality. Confidentiality always presumes that the service or application knows the individual using it and provides services tailored for that individual. As an example, you may shop anonymously, but when it is time to make a purchase, you must provide key information (name, address, credit card number, etc.) to receive the purchase. The service provider, once it has the data, has the obligation to prevent unauthorized access, even from itself. However, there is tremendous business value in some of that information, and the business entity will wish to reuse it where possible and permissible. This reuse can take many forms, from directed marketing to cross-selling attempts to actually selling the list of customers to other companies.

Individuals are not always happy to have the information they have provided to be used for other purposes, especially not when they are unaware of the reuse. Privacy controls grew out of a need to communicate to the client the intended uses, both necessary to use the service and extraneous uses, and provide to the client the opportunity to express their preferences regarding the use of this information. In effect, privacy controls may keep the information provided to the service provider confidential from the service provider.

WS-Privacy as an OASIS standard never took off. This has a lot to do with an immaturity of understanding of privacy and the success of a competing standard from W3C called the P3P. While never formally advanced to a standard by W3C, which has more to do with how W3C views standards rather than the maturity and adaptation of the specification within the industry, P3P has become accepted within the industry as the means to communicate privacy policy to systems.

P3P is independent of web services or a service oriented architecture, though it can be used by them. As it is a mechanism for conveying information on a key control, privacy, it is worth covering in this volume. I will also discuss the use of WS-Policy along with other components of the WS-Security stack to perform the same or similar role; however, they perform different functions by design. WS-Policy is designed to enforce policy; P3P is designed to communicate policy so that a decision on use can be made by the client. However, where multiple service providers have established support for identity federation for single sign-on using WS-Federation, WS-Federation allows the definition of data elements and metadata considered to be confidential in nature and usable only by defined members of the federation rather than the entire federation. I will cover that in the section on WS-Federation as it only applies to service providers who support federated identity using WS-Federation, which is a subset of service providers that support identity federation.

Much like web services depend upon XML to convey information, so does P3P, and much like web services are designed to facilitate application-to-application communication and transactions, P3P is designed to facilitate client-to-application communications so that the client understands the policy regarding the handling of personal and private data by the application. In this case, the client can readily be a web browser as well as any other application configured to parse, interpret, and act on the information conveyed in the P3P document.

P3P policies may be designed to reflect usage within an application that spans multiple servers, reflect a single site, or just the specific components of a web site. P3P uses XML with the namespaces syntax, or XML and XML-Name.

Privacy data concerns data that can be used to identify a person in some real and tangible manner. While an address may identify any person who lives there or has lived there, an address combined with a phone number identifies all the people at that address for the duration of that phone number being active, narrowing down the people referred to. Other identifying information, such as government identifiers and cell phone numbers directly refer to a specific individual. Privacy policies reflect the treatment and handling of all of this information within the application and by the company. They convey if any data is collected in cookies, how data is used, and how, if at all, data is shared. A key consideration in any privacy policy is how to contact the company regarding removing one's data from their system, and how to engage a third-party arbiter (if any) for dispute resolution in the event that the company is not responsive to requests for removal.

Not all the data collected by the application or platform are identifiable. For example, if the web site collects the IP address but does not store the entire address, just the fourth octet, then this information cannot be traced back to an individual and is nonidentifiable. This anonymization of data needs to be called out by the privacy policy.

P3P policy files are expected by P3P-aware clients to be found at /w3c/p3p.xml on the web site or application home. Where the application architect has a need to support multiple P3P files, action URI can be used to point the client to the specific location. If the site is using P3P headers, then it can use the policyref directive to provide a URI to the specific P3P policy. P3p-link-tags can be used within HTML to provide the same functionality within the body of the HTML.

P3P conveys the state of the current privacy policy, but as that changes, the P3P should provide a reference to the past policy and must provide appropriate notice to clients of a change in policy.

P3P 1.1 may be integrated into a service-based application that uses web services through the WSDL. P3P 1.1 provides a new binding mechanism to allow for policies to apply to content not associated with a URI. This is accomplished through the use of the generic attribute, p3pattr, which takes a URI of a valid P3P policy as its value. Unfortunately, you cannot use this to refer to a P3P policy reference file. A common implementation technique would be to place the reference in the definitions part of the WSDL, establishing it as a bindings endpoint.

P3P supports the following elements and subelements:

*3.4.4.1 POLICIES* The POLICIES element allows one or more P3P policies to be located in a single file. It is the root element of the policy file, present even if there is just a single policy. It can be inside of a policy reference file, in the META element, allowing the client to fetch only a single file which contains both the reference file and the policies; however, this technique only works for web-based clients and is not appropriate for representing policies in a service-oriented application.

The POLICIES element usually contains an xml:lang attribute and an EXPIRY element to indicate when the policy expires and a DATASCHEMA element to contain an embedded data schema. It must contain an ENTITY element, which is the legal entity asserting the policy and an ACCESS element as well as one or more STATEMENT elements. A well-formed policy will contain a DISPUTES-GROUP element; however, technically this is optional for the standard. Architects should know that no policy that does not contain this attribute will be accepted for Safe Harbor nor will it conform to the European Union (EU) privacy regulations and should work with their chief privacy officer to ensure that both a DISPUTES-GROUP element is present and refers properly to the privacy dispute mechanisms both internally to the organization and the selected third-party arbiter.

A POLICY must also contain the following mandatory elements:

name: The name of the policy, used as a fragment identifier
discuri: The URI of the natural language privacy statement

A POLICY may contain the following optional elements:

xml:lang: The language the policy is written in
opturi: A URI providing instructions that clients can use to opt
    in or out of a particular use of their data

The STATEMENT-GROUP-DEF element allows policy authors to specify different policies for different sections of the application, such as a policy, which applies to casual use versus one that applies to authenticated use and is only available post authentication. I must note that this may seem at first a valid means to segregate one's privacy policy to ensure compliance with both Safe Harbor and EU privacy regulations, a single policy with no internal segregation. However, the same privacy policy must apply for all services and applications maintained by the corporation.

Another use is to offer groups of usages allowed based upon the consent attribute, opting in or out of the functionality. However, application behavior cannot be based upon statement groups, just the collection of the client's preferences and the presentation of them to the client.

STATEMENT-GROUP-DEF contains the following optional attributes:

id: A string that uniquely identifies the statement group. While it must be unique, this constraint is enforced only for the policy.

short-description: A short human readable description of the statement group.

consent: Used to allow or prevent the simultaneous consent to a variety of opt-ins.

The ENTITY element describes the legal entity that asserts the privacy policy. It must contain the name, address, phone number, email address, URL, and other information as required by applicable law. It is commonly extended with the fields of the business data set.

The ACCESS element indicates what information is provided by the site to the user. It must contain at least one of the following elements:

nonident: No identified data is collected.

all: Access is given to all identified data.

contact-and-other: Access is given to identified data online, and physical contact data, and certain other identified data

ident-contact: Access is given to identified online and physical contact information.

other-ident: Access is given to certain other identified data.

none: No access to identified data is given.

The DISPUTES element is optional for the standard, but in practice, this is a required element for both Safe Harbor and EU compliance. There should be at least two DISPUTES elements, one for internal dispute resolution, the other for the third-party arbiter.

Each DISPUTES elements must have a resolution-type attribute with one of four values: [service] customer service, [independent] authorized third-party arbiter, [court] legally mandated in certain jurisdictions, and [law] the relevant laws and their enforced remedies for disputes.

The DISPUTES element must also contain the following attribute:

service: The URL of the customer service web page, independent organization, court, or law

The DISPUTES element may contain:

verification: The URI or certificate used for verification. Third-party arbiters often will provide a seal using this attribute to verify arbitration. This may also be used for the Safe Harbor seal.

short-description: A short human readable description regarding the dispute mechanism. This is to be no more than 255 characters. If more is needed, then use the LONG-DESCRIPTION.

LONG-DESCRIPTION: A long human readable description regarding the dispute mechanism.

IMG: Used for an image logo of the independent organization or perhaps the court.

src: the URI of the image logo (mandatory when using an IMG).

width: Width of the logo in pixels.

height: Height of the logo in pixels.

alt: A short textual alternative to the logo which is mandatory when using an IMG.

The DISPUTES element should also contain a REMEDIES element that specifies what the legal entity will do in the event of a breach of privacy. Much like the DISPUTES element, while optional to the P3P standard, it is mandatory for both Safe Harbor and EU compliance. This must contain one or more of the following remedies:

correct: The policy the legal entity has enacted to respond to a breach or disputes

money: The compensation plan the legal entity has put in place for either breaches or disputes

law: Specific legal obligations regarding the response of either a breach or a dispute

The STATEMENT element is used to describe data practices that are applied to particular types of data. A statement may or may not be associated with other statements in STATEMENT-GROUP. It will group together a PURPOSE, RECIPIENT, RETENTION, and

DATA-GROUP elements, and optionally a CONSEQUENCES element. It is up to the service provider to specify the actions they will take regarding the data collected from the client and represent it to the client using these elements.

The CONSEQUENCES element is a short human readable summary of the data practices. This may include language to indicate the desirability of the client allowing the functionality as a positive consequence.

The NON-IDENTIFIABLE element is used to indicate that all data collected will be anonymized. Where data is replaced by unique values, this must be done with a nonreservable algorithm such as a hash but only if the set of possible values is sufficiently large to prevent reversing the hash.

The PURPOSE element is provided for those statements that do not include a NON-IDENTIFIABLE element to permit the description of the purpose for collecting the information collected. This element must contain one or more of the following elements:

current: Provides support of the completion of current activities for which the information was collected.

admin: The information may be used in support of the web site and the underlying programs. This includes authentication and authorization activities.

develop: The information is to be used to enhance the service rendered and is not to include personal or private information specific to a client.

tailoring: The information collected may be used to customize the look or style of the application's presentation layer. Sometimes this is used to advertise items, such as "others who purchased this item also purchase these" functions of e-commerce services.

psuedo-analysis: Despite the name, this allows for analysis of usage patterns without tying that usage to a particular identity. This information is used for research, analysis, and reporting.

psuedo-decision: This is trickier as it identifies information used to build a record of a particular person that is anonymous but tied to an existing and ongoing session to that the application's behavior and may be altered by the character-istics of that client but not in a way that is traceable to the actual identity.

individual-analysis: This is similar to the psuedo-analysis, as it is information collected for the purpose of analysis and report-ing. This information may be combined with that of other individuals to be examined in the aggregate but the informa-tion is not anonymized. However, that does not mean that the goal is to track individual behavior but rather to address ques-tions such as what the usage habits for all males of age 44–50 are in New England and why they are so different from those of all males of age 44–50 from the Midwest.

individual-decision: This describes how the specific informa-tion collected about the specific person is used to make deci-sions on the operation of the service or application, such as "based upon your purchase history we present the following recommendations."

contact: The information collected here may be used to contact the person. This does not impact the current operation of the service or application; the current element would be used to track that information.

historical: The information collected may be archived for the pur-pose of preserving usage under an existing law of policy. The law or policy or both must be referenced in the DISPUTES element and must include information on who can access this information for what purpose, where it will be stored, and how the collection of this data is specifically used.

telemarketing: The information provided may be used to con-tact the client via telephone for the promotion of a product or service. This is not related to the current ongoing session or any requests for customer service; otherwise current would be used.

The following optional attributes are available to the PURPOSE element:

required: Indicates if the purpose indicated is a required one for use of the site. This has the optional attributes of always, opt-in, and opt-out. I have already discussed opt-in and opt-out.

This always can be thought of as a mandatory opt-in and is increasingly becoming a problem with clients especially in applications where there is an expectation of privacy.

The PURPOSE element is an extension element allowing client agents to determine the use of recipient-collected information. The client may specify multiple usages from the available options. This element must contain one or more of the following attributes:

account: The information collected may be used to update an account or subscription, including creating or termination of the said account.

arts: The information may be used for delivering any of the visual, literary, or performing arts.

browsing: Information may be exchanged for the purpose of web browsing.

charity: The information collected may be used for a charitable donation.

communicate: The information provided may be used to facilitate communication between users.

custom: The information collected may be used to customize the application, such as changing the language used to render the presentation layer.

delivery: The information collected may be used to deliver a product.

downloads: The information collected (e.g., platform) is for the purpose of facilitating the download of executable software.

education: The information collected may be used for educational purposes.

feedback: The information collected may be used to provide customized feedback to the user, such as using the client's name in application messages and other communications.

finmgt: The information collected may be used for banking and financial management. It should not need to be stated that clients will be very concerned about the handling of such information.

gambling: Information may be used for online gambling. It should not need to be stated that clients will be very concerned about the handling of such information.

gaming: Information may be used for online gaming that does not involve gambling.

government: The information collected may be used to provide government services.

health: The information collected may be used to offer products or services related to physical or mental health. It should not need to be stated that clients will be very concerned about the handling of such information.

login: The information collected may be used for authentication and authorization services. It should not need to be stated that clients will be very concerned about the handling of such information.

marketing: The information collected may be used for marketing and promotional purposes.

news: Information may be used to deliver news or news media.

payment: The information collected may be used to facilitate a financial transaction with a third party. It should not need to be stated that clients will be very concerned about the handling of such information.

sales: The information provided may be used as part of a business transaction with the client to complete a sale. It should not need to be stated that clients will be very concerned about the handling of such information.

search: The information provided may be used by any third-party search engine.

state: The information collected may be used to maintain a session state.

surveys: The information collected may be used to conduct surveys and questionnaires.

The RECIPIENT element is provided for statements that do not include a NON-IDENTIFIABLE element. The recipient itself is the legal entity for whom the privacy policy exists. Sites or applications or both must classify their recipients into one or more of the six possibilities.

ours: This would be the service provider and any agent acting on behalf of that organization under their authorization.

delivery: Legal entities performing delivery services which may use the provided data for purposes other than the stated purpose.

same: Legal entities other than the service provider who follow the practices of the service provider in the collection, use, and handling of privacy data.

other-recipient: This is a legal entity or entities who are accountable to the service provider but may use the data collected in a way not specified in the service provider's practices.

unrelated: Legal entity or entities whose data-usage patterns are not known by the original service provider.

public: Public forums such as bulletin boards.

The JURISDICTION element allows the service provider to specify the legal jurisdiction of the legal entity with the goal of enhancing trust in the adherence to privacy regulations. As an example of usage, an organization may refer to http://europa.eu.int/eur-lex/lex/LexUriServ/LexUriServ.do?uri = CELEX:31995L0046:EN:HTML, which is the URI of the specific EU data protection law.

The RETENTION element must be used in every statement not containing a NON-IDENTIFIABLE element. This indicates the data retention policy that applies to the data referenced in the statement. This element must contain one of the following attributes: no-retention, stated-purpose, legal-requirement, and business-practices, indefinitely. The business-practices attribute may be a URI to a data retention policy.

The DATA-GROUP element must be present in any STATEMENT that does not include a NON-IDENTIFIABLE, and it must contain datatype extension attributes. The DATA-GROUP element may also identify a datatype as optional or not, if the data is required to complete a transaction.

Within these, the categories elements may be used to make the use of data clear to the client. Standard categories are physical, online, uniqueid, purchase, financial, computer, navigation, interactive, demographic, content, state, political, health, preference, location, government, and other-category.

The EXTENSION element is used to extend the syntax of the P3P specification. It will contain the attribute "optional" to indicate if an attribute within the EXTENSION is mandatory or optional.

While the P3P standard provides a mechanism to convert the privacy policy to a compact policy represented in a cookie, this is less than useful for a service-oriented application as this cannot be provided in a WSDL.

### 3.4.5 WS-Federation

In many ways, WS-Federation is where application architecture, identity architecture, and security architecture collide. This facilitates seamless communication and transactions between divergent applications, companies, and user communities in ways that few other technologies can. While other technologies allow authentication and authorization to such a degree, they lack the mechanisms to communicate and enforce policy embedded in WS-Federation, with the possible exception of SAML.

It was developed precisely because SAML was not being adopted at the time by all vendors, and the business community desired a framework that would permit single sign-on (SSO) and mutual authentication and authorization that was token-neutral, permitting certificates, Kerberos, cookies, passwords, and other tokens so that regardless of the token supported, interoperability could be ensured.

The reader of this volume has by now come to the conclusion that there are many ways to leverage the standards in the development of their application, and they would be right. WS-Federation when combined with WS-Trust and WS-Policy allows you to perform identity federation or allow your customers to manage the credentials that they will use in your application. However, SAML can do this all by itself. To complicate things, WS-Federation, WS-Trust, and WS-Policy all support SAML assertions, and there is no explicit need for WS-Federation. However, WS-Federation was added to provide a systematic and standards-based means to establish federated relationships.

There are many debates on the part of application architects and developers on which approach is better, but because the standards support each other, each application architect should choose the approach that is better for his/her own application and business requirements.

While I have voiced my opinion on other architectural choices (such as use of X509V3 certificates in preference to other tokens for signing), I have no opinion on the merits of SAML over WS-Federation. Somethings to note: WS-Federation can be a key component to enabling WS-Trust and WS-Policy to be understood by a browser; so when your SOA has a presentation layer that needs to be accessed through a web browser, WS-Federation can be a tremendous tool. More to the point, not all service providers support SAML, and there are others that do not support WS-Federation. A good application architect will make sound decisions in the design of their application based upon the business context. If, instead of choosing sides in the debate and only designing it to support one approach and you design your application so that it can use SAML, WS-Federation, and SAML within WS-Federation, then you will have the flexibility to meet the business requirements of the next client who does not support what you would have chosen to require.

WS-Federation was created to allow the following:

- Sharing of identity, authentication, and authorization data
- Use of different types of tokens, trust topologies, and infrastructures
- Facilitating the brokering of trust for both SOAP requesters and web browsers
- Sharing of federation metadata to facilitate communication
- Allowing for identity mapping, even if local identities are maintained
- Allowing for different levels of privacy for different identities
- Allowing for authenticated but anonymous sessions

Federations can be ad hoc collections of systems and individuals within a community or they can be organized relationships within or between companies. The identity can be either universally accepted or brokered into a trust relationship, most often by using identity mapping.

A digital ID can be represented in different forms requiring different kinds of mapping. If the ID is fixed, or cannot be changed across domains, then the only time mapping that is likely to be needed is if local accounts must be used. While fixed identities make for easy tracking of the use of an identity, it can be problematic for privacy concerns, especially in the light of the "right to be forgotten" legislation. Where an individual has multiple identities within a system, they can choose which identity they use in the leverage of a service. This can lessen privacy issues as it is mildly harder to track use to a person, but only marginally, and the service provider still has to account for the "right to be forgotten" where the credential of concern is immutable.

A more flexible approach is to use pairwise mapping, where a unique digital ID is used for each principle at the target service. This simplifies service tracking as each service is given a unique ID for each requester. As the source-unique ID may be different for each session for the individual, the "right to be forgotten" can be more readily adhered to. However, there is a risk of identity collision. A more privacy-friendly approach is to require the service to be responsible for the identity mapping. The service is provided with an object or string provided in the credential that is used to map to an identity it understands. This may be random or fixed, but is not traceable back to an individual. This inability to track a session back to an individual is problematic for security investigations or forensics in the event of a breach of security.

Information security architects will almost universally require the ability to trace a session back to an individual in the event of a security breach. This does not have to be in conflict with a right to be forgotten. If the actual digital identity is captured with a hashing algorithm, session-specific information can be tracked in the logs, where a mapping is maintained in a hash table that would be access restricted save in the event of a breach.

There is a need to exchange metadata regarding policies of the participants of the federation governing access for a particular use of the service regardless of how tightly coupled the identities are. The target service allows the metadata regarding its services to be queried by the requesting service by providing a metadata endpoint reference (MEPR). The MEPR can point to a location where metadata can be obtained, which then points to the actual service, or if the service provider leverages WS-MetadataExchange, the MEPR can point to an actual service containing the metadata, saving a step.

Metadata used for identity federation describes setting and information used within the federation and how a service participates within the federation. Federated metadata can be scoped to services, endpoints, or messages, and the nature of the metadata will vary depending upon the role of the service and the nature of the federation. Using the metadata, the requester can discover any related services needed to fully engage with the target service, a functionality overlap with WSDL and UDDI. WS-Federations are fully flexible, allowing for mixes of MEPRs, which point at metadata endpoints and MEPRs, which have the actual service references along with the metadata working together to provide the right mix of metadata and metadata descriptors and service endpoints to meet the architectural needs of the application's security infrastructure.

As the options are rather daunting, especially when you consider that you also need to communicate metadata within the communications policies through WS-Policy. One way to simplify this is to include both communications policies and federation metadata in the same WSDL using the mechanisms described in WS-PolicyAttachment. Federated metadata can also be referenced in a master MEPR that contains references to subordinate MEPRs. This allows, as an example, a service to participate in multiple federations with metadata downloaded as applies only to each specific federated relationship.

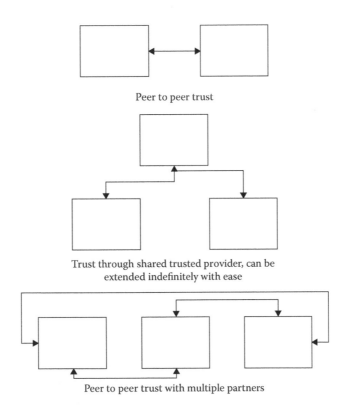

Peer to peer trust

Trust through shared trusted provider, can be extended indefinitely with ease

Peer to peer trust with multiple partners

It is most common to have the services of identity provider be coresident with the services of security token provider. One common trust architecture is to have a requestor trust such an identity provider/ security token provider, which has an established federated relationship with a similar identity provider/security token provider trusted by the desired resource.

One of the more powerful federated identity architectures is one in which there is a single trusted identity provider common to both the requestor and the resource. This single trusted provider may or may not be an STS or may in turn trust a third-party STS. Either way, both the requestor and resource in this model trust the same identity provider/security token provider.

Where there is a need for identity mapping for either the requestor or resource or both, these architectures may be combined so that a central identity provider/security token provider is trusted by the provider's and requester's respective identity provider/security token provider.

It is not necessary, though convenient, to have such a central identity provider/security token provider to established federated relationships among multiple service providers. A network of trust relationships can be established among the various service providers' identity providers/security token providers. This does not scale well. A more scalable solution for multiple trusts is to establish a common centralized identity provider/security token provider trusted by all service providers. Some companies offer this as their entire product line, as this is a viable and flexible architecture, which mimics that of a public key infrastructure.

Protecting privacy in a federated system will often require special controls. If, as an example, you use an external identity provider, you may need to make certain that certain attributes regarding the identity and system usage are not shared with the identity provider without crippling its ability to issue authoritative tokens. One approach is to establish a pseudonym service. A pseudonym service allows the individual to maintain different identities in different realms, perhaps using a different one for each login. In this case, a pseudonym service functions as a trusted identity provider/STS for both the requestor and resource service, which in turn trust each other. This allows records to be kept in the resource service regarding session usage without regard to the identity of the individual. If the mapping between the requester identity and the pseudo-identity established by the pseudonym service

provider is a temporary one, then all bindings between person and action can be immediately lost upon closing the session.

While this allows for privacy of transaction, it does present challenges for security forensic investigations in the event of a data breach. While a complete record can be retained of all that was done, there is no record of who performed what actions. This is why most pseudonym service providers retain a mapping of identity to pseudonym. This is not available to the resource service save in the event of a security breach, and even then only if there is legal access perhaps established by contract with the pseudonym provider.

Where the business model is to offer a service for which identity tracking would be problematic, the ability to offer anonymous yet secure access is very attractive. However, the very anonymity prevents the ability to offer a personalized service to the client. One common solution is to permit the client to map identities to a locally stored identity that is retained between sessions that is used for the personification of the service to the client. The privacy policy should be very explicit that if the client chooses to do this, they are forfeiting complete anonymity across sessions, or in other words, within the application, session activities can be tracked.

While federated relationships can be set up manually, and there is often business justification for this, especially if the service providers intend to openly federate their service with many requestors or many responders, they may wish to use the federated metadata document to exchange the necessary data to establish the federation automatically and then use metadata associated with each token to establish local identity and local identity mapping.

There are two formats for the federation metadata document. The distinction between them is based upon the namespace of the root element of this XML document. The first extends the core concept of the SAML metadata document (SAMLv2Meta) so that it can describe objects beyond SAML assertions and entities. This is done through the element md:EntitiesDescriptor and /md:EntityDescriptor which are used to express either the authoritative information about all the entities or a specific entity. The /md:EntityDescriptor element has an optional attribute of @fed:FederationID which is a string identifier of the federation to which the metadata applies.

There is an older (legacy) format for the federation metadata document which you may encounter using the fed:FederationMetadata element. This should not be used in new implementations. However, the fed: class of elements are still used, where there is no md: equivalent, such as fed:PseudonymServiceEndpoints. Where there are md: equivalents, they should be used. However, placing fed: elements inside of an md:EntityDescriptor is quite acceptable, where the value of the fed:FederationID attribute must be the same as the value of the md:Name attribute of the md:EntitiesDescriptor element.

Role descriptors are expressed in terms of SAML profiles and protocols, often using an extension of md:RoleDescriptor. Not all metadata statements will apply to all roles.

| ROLE | METADATA |
| --- | --- |
| Any | mex:MetadataReference |
| | fed:AttributeServiceEndpoints |
| STS | md:KeyDescriptor |
| | Fed:PseudoymServiceEndpoints |
| | fed:SingleSignOutSubscriptionEndpoints |
| | fed:ToekTypesOffered |
| | fed:ClaimTypesOffered |
| | fed:AutomaticPseudonyms |
| | fed:LogicalServiceNamesOffered |
| Service Provider | fed:TokenIssuerName |
| (includes STS) | md:KeyDescriptor |
| | fed:SingleSignoutNotificationEndpoints |

*Abbreviation:*   STS, Security Token Service.

The metadata statements must define if they are optional or mandatory, and unknown elements should be ignored if not required. If required, obviously a Fault should be generated.

To express role definitions, the md:RoleDescriptor has been extended by the fed:WebServicesDescriptorType. This provides the following elements and attributes:

/fed:WebServiceDescriptor/@ServiceDisplayName: This is an optional string attribute providing a friendly name for the service instance that can be shown in the presentation layer. It can also be used to index metadata.

/fed:WebServiceDescriptor/@ServiceDescription: This is an optional string attribute used to contain a human readable

description of the service that can be shown in the presentation layer.

/fed:WebServiceDescriptor/fed:LogicalServiceNamesOffered: This is an optional element used to provide the federation metadata provider's logical name associated with the specific service. Sometimes token issuers need to be referred to by a logical name representing an equivalence class of issuers, such as accepting Visa regardless of the issuing bank. This element allows such logical names to be added to tokens. The element can also be used as a correlation mechanism.

/fed:WebServiceDescriptor/fed:TokenTypeOffered: An optional element with an obvious purpose specific to the service. It has the following attributes and subelements:

fed:TokenTypesOffered: Used to express the token types an STS can issue.

fed:TokenTypesOffered/@{any}: This allows attributes to be added.

fed:TokenTypesOffered/{any}: This is undefined.

fed:TokenTypesOffered/fed:TokenType: Lists an individual token type that an STS can issue.

fed:TokenTypesOffered/fed:TokenType/@Uri: This is undefined.

fed:TokenTypesOffered/fed:TokenType/{any}: This is undefined.

fed:TokenTypesOffered/fed:TokenType/@{any}: This allows attributes to be added.


/fed:WebServiceDescriptor/fed:ClaimTypesOffered: An optional element which allows the federation metadata provider to offer claim types. Claim types are something we have not yet come across; so please permit me a moment to explore them. Claims are information made regarding an identity or specifically the credential representing the identity most often used to provide personalization of service. An example of a claim would be that the credential represents an individual who provided proof of frequent flyer membership to the identity provider, which is claiming to the service provider that the credential is authorized to receive customizations and discounts (if any) associated with that membership. Again, this is an area where a privacy policy would inform the service requester on how this information is used by the provider. Other associated optional elements dealing with claims are:

/fed:WebServiceDescriptor/fed:ClaimDialectsOffered
/fed:WebServiceDescriptor/fed:ClaimTypeRequested

The/fed:WebServiceDescriptor/fed:AutomaticPseudonyms is an optional element informing if the service provider automatically maps pseudonyms.

/fed:WebServiceDescriptor/fed:TargetScope is used to indicate the endpoint references associated with the token scopes of the STS or relying party.

Where an organization wishes to establish an STS, WS-Federation provides the SecurityTokenServiceType. This has the following required and optional attributes and elements:

fed:SecurityTokenServiceType/fed:SecurityServiceEndpoint: A required element in support of the WS-Federation and WS-Trust interfaces. It must contain a valid endpoint reference that provides the transport address for the STS.

fed:SecurityTokenServiceType/fed:SingleSignOutSubscription ServiceEndpoint: This is an optional element providing an endpoint that can subscribe to SSO sign-out messages. This is typically specified by token issuers and STSs.

fed:SecurityTokenServiceType/fed:SingleSignOutNotification ServiceEndpoint: This optional element, if present, defines the endpoint where SSO push notifications are sent. This is typically specified by token issuers and STSs.

fed:SecurityTokenServiceType/fed:PassiveRequestorEndpoint: This optional element provides the endpoint address for the WS-Federation Web Passive Requestor Protocol.

While it is rare for an attribute service to be spun up as a distinct service, an attribute service related to WS-Federation makes a world of sense as it can provide a central place for the generation and processing of the attributes needed in identity federation and mapping and allows the extension of other elements in WS-Federation. WS-Federation defines an attributeServiceType, which contains a required fed:AttributeServiceEndpoint providing the endpoint for the attribute service and an optional fed:SingleSignOutNotificationServ iceEndpoint.

Where attribute services provide value is when they provide multiple service providers information about identities that they reference in common, such as the Automobile Association of America (AAA) may provide an attribute service related to its membership that is accessible to its business partners as AAA members user these partners' services. When the privacy concerns for such information sharing are well understood and accepted by the individuals in question, this can provide tremendous value. The key will be an effective privacy policy.

As the users of a web service are just as likely to be other applications as they are to be individuals, attribute services must be able to provide attributes regarding these applications with the same flexibility as they provide attributes to individuals.

By placing an attribute service behind a WS-Security-protected interface, with WS-Policy-defining requirements for access and WS-Trust-enforcing policy, an attribute service can be made secure. Using WS-Federation would permit transparent access to it from the rest of the service architecture.

*3.4.5.1 Pseudonyms*  The pseudonym service is a specific type of attribute service that is used to provide an alternative identity to an individual. Key questions to consider when spinning up support for a pseudonym service or launching one are the degrees to which anonymity will be maintained. Will associated memberships be identified, such as when the client's name and so on are unknown, but their active membership in a group or employment in a company is known and tracked? Service providers that accept pseudonyms are likely to want to allow for pseudonym-specific and selected privacy policies, allowing the principle to decide to what degree any attributes added to the pseudo-ID are tracked.

Pseudonyms are retrieved using the WS-Transfer "GET" method with the WS-ResourceTransfer extensions. The elements and attributes available are:

/fed:Psuedonym
/fed:Psuedonym/fed:PseudonymBasis: Provides the security token as per WS-Security. Often this is the same as the basis in the request but may be different if multiple pseudonyms are returned.

/fed:Psuedonym/fed:PseudonymBasis/@{any}
/fed:Psuedonym/fed:PseudonymBasis/{any}
/fed:Psuedonym/fed:RelativeTo
/fed:Psuedonym/fed:RelativeTo/@{any}
/fed:Psuedonym/wsu:Expires
/fed:Psuedonym/fed:SecurityToken
/fed:Psuedonym/fed:SecurityToken/@{any}
/fed:Psuedonym/fed:SecurityToken/{any}
/fed:Psuedonym/fed:ProofToken
/fed:Psuedonym/fed:ProofToken/@{any}
/fed:Psuedonym/fed:ProofToken/{any}
/fed:Psuedonym/@{any}
/fed:Psuedonym/{any}

The PseudonymServiceType is provided for those service providers, which desire to offer pseudonym tokens. This type does not support many elements:

fed:PseudonymServiceType/fed:PseudonymServiceEndpoint specifies the endpoint address of the pseudonym service in support of WS-Federation and WS-Trust. When this is present, it indicates that the service should use the pseudonym service to map identities to local names. This is desirable not just to preserve the privacy of the agents or clients but also because the names of the identities may vary across uses in the preservation of that privacy. Typically this is used, if at all, by token issuers and STSs.

fed:PseudonymServiceType/fed:SingleSignOutNotificationServiceEndpoint serves the same functionality for pseudonym services as it does for the STS, which makes sense.

Pseudonym service providers must support certain interfaces defined in the standard for retrieving, setting, and deleting pseudonyms.

A bit more common and useful to separate out as a service is the ApplicationServiceType, which provides a definition for a WS-Federation-based application service. There are three basic elements which are available to support this:

fed:ApplicationServiceType/fed:ApplicationServiceEndpoint
fed:ApplicationServiceType/fed:SingleSignOutNotificationServiceEndpoint

fed:ApplicationServiceType/fed:PassiveRequestorEndpoint

The WS-Federation specification defines a number of filtering mechanisms that can be used to improve the handling of searches on the metadata associated with a pseudonym. This can be accomplished by using the pseudonym dialect with the WS-ResourceTransfer extension to WS-Transfer, or by applying the `<fed:FilterPseudonyms>` within the header as per WS-Tranfer. When using the `<fed:FilterPseudonyms>` within the header, the specification recommends the use of the SOAP mustUnderstand attribute be set to TRUE. One item of note is that if the `<fed:FilterPseudonyms>` is specified within the header, no other filters may be present. The following elements and attributes are available to the `<fed:FilterPseudonyms>` element:

/fed:filterPseudonyms: This element is used to filter a pseudonym operation based on provided metadata.

/fed:filterPseudonyms/fed:PseudonymBasis: This is used to specify the security token or token reference identifying the known identity information. This may be omitted if the context is known.

/fed:filterPseudonyms/fed:PseudonymBasis/@{any}: This allows the extension with new attributes.

/fed:filterPseudonyms/fed:PseudonymBasis/{any}: This extension allows the inclusion of the relevant security token.

/fed:filterPseudonyms/fed:RelativeTo: This indicates the scope for which the pseudonym is requested. The specification recommends its usage.

/fed:filterPseudonyms/fed:RelativeTo/@{any}: This allows the extension with new attributes.

/fed:filterPseudonyms/@{any}: This allows the extension with new attributes.

/fed:filterPseudonyms/{any}: This extensibility point allows content elements to be specified.

Pseudonyms are updated using a WS-Transfer "PUT" using the specification defined by the `<fed:FilterPseudonyms>` in the header. This allows you to specify multiple pseudonyms. Pseudonyms can also be deleted using the WS-Transfer "PUT" syntax. Careful filtering can prevent the wrong pseudonym from being deleted. The WS-Resource "Create" operation using WS-ResourceTransfer extensions are used to create pseudonyms.

One more thing about pseudonyms. Some application architects have to meet a business requirement to support what are called client-based pseudonyms. These are requested by the client using the `<fed:ClientPseudonym>` element with specific attributes and subelements. If these requests are accepted, then the entirety of the request must be accepted and processed, not just some of it. The/ fed:ClientPseudonym element supports the following optional elements:

/fed:ClientPseudonym/fed:PPID: Any form of personal private identifier in a string. This may be used as a seed to create the issued token.

/fed:ClientPseudonym/fed:PPID/@{any}: As always, this allows additional attributes.

/fed:ClientPseudonym/fed:DisplayName: This provides the desired subject name or display name for the issued security token.

/fed:ClientPseudonym/fed:DisplayName/@{any}: As always,this allows additional attributes.

/fed:ClientPseudonym/fed:EMail: The string value of the email address.

/fed:ClientPseudonym/fed:EMail/@{any}

/fed:ClientPseudonym/{any}: Atypical of the ability to extend this element with other elements is that if the STS does not understand the extensions, it must either ignore the `<fed:ClientPseudonym>` or Fault.

/fed:ClientPseudonym/@{any}: As always, this allows additional attributes.

*3.4.5.1.1 Requesting Information from Metadata*   Much of the information needed to map identities using WS-Federation is often stored in the federation metadata document. The client may request this in a variety of ways, but not all service providers will support all mechanisms. The specification recommends that the client try the following methods in order:

A well-known HTTPS address with the federation ID
A well-known HTTPS address for the default federation

A well-known HTTP address with the federation ID

A well-known HTTP address for the default federation

*3.4.5.1.2 DNS SRV Records Indicating Federation Metadata Locations*    If the service provider is using technology provided by Microsoft internally within an organization, they may wish to explore using the Domain Name System Service Record (DNS SRV) records first as Microsoft makes extensive use of DNS SRV records to identify services and service provider locations. In the event that multiple sources are found, the specification recommends using HTTPS and failing that, WS-Transfer, and failing that, HTTP as a method to download the information.

Where the protocols of either HTTP or HTTPS are to be used to download the metadata file, the default path may be provided as a mechanism to locate the document. This would have the syntax of protocol (HTTP,HTTPS)/Server-name/FederationMetadata/ spec-version/FederationMetadata.xml. The specification version for WS-Federation 1.2 is the string "2007-06"; this permits the document to be downloaded using a WS-Transfer "GET" or a HTTP "GET" and retrieve the information needed. As always, consider the sensitivity of the information found within the metadata. Even though the material is a prerequisite for using federated authentication and authorization services, you may wish to consider requiring an authentication to retrieve the information, because it provides a guidebook for how to use your authentication and authorization services that can be used maliciously.

In practice, it is most common for service providers to leverage WSDL documents to store the `<fed:FederationMetadata>` element in much the same way that the WS-PolicyAttachment is stored. This can be referenced for a service, port, or binding, which allows the flexibility to provide multiple metadata documents specific to each port, service, or binding as required by the service provider. WSDL, after all, will be present in almost all web services deployments and will be inspected by the client to allow for service transactions to be called properly and effectively.

Just as important as considering using authentication to provide access to the metadata document, the service provider should consider signing the metadata document. I would encourage clients to make this a requirement in their use of service providers and to strongly consider not using service providers that do not sign their metadata documents. It would be too easy for a metadata document to be replaced maliciously, providing the client with a compromised mechanism to be used for authentication and authorization.

Equally important to the authentication and authorization process is the sign-out or log-out process. The sign-out mechanism allows requesters to send a message to the identity provider or security trust service that they are terminating their SSO session. The `<fed:SignOut>` element contains:

/fed:Signout/fed:Realm: This optional element specifies a realm as a URI; if none is specified, it presumes that the target uses a fixed realm. This allows the termination of session with only one component or the entire infrastructure. SSO sessions with realms not specified are not terminated.

/fed:Signout/fed:SignOutBasis is a required element specifying that the principle is signing out and may reference a specific token or multiple tokens, most often using the `<UsernameToken>`. The token signing out must be referenced.

/fed:Signout/fed:SignOutBasis/@{any} allows additional attributes to be added to the element.

/fed:Signout/fed:SignOutBasis/{any} allows the inclusion of the relevant security token reference or token.

/fed:Signout/fed:@wsu:Id is an optional attribute providing a string label for the element.

/fed:Signout/@{any} allows additional attributes to be added to the element.

/fed:Signout/{any}allows the inclusion of additional elements.

As with all other security elements, this should be signed, and architecturally the service should be designed to ignore unsigned sign-outs as unauthentic.

Much like authentication messages, sign-out messages often need to be distributed across the federation. There are two mechanisms for doing this, sequential and parallel, where in the first model, the recipient of the sign-out message sends to each member of the federation in sequence, and in the second, it sends the message to all token services and target services. It should not need to be said that the second model is both less prone to failure and more secure. In the first model, the session remains with some components of the architecture after it is terminated with others, and this can cause subsequent components to fail to terminate the session in the event of a Fault. However, and specifically where narrow realms are specified, the sequential method allows for easier termination of just some components of the session without impacting the others.

Where the architect desires to use WS-Eventing to create an SSO subscription model, SSO subscription filters may be specified using XPath filters as defined by WS-Eventing or using the SSO filter specified by WS-Federation. If using WS-Eventing, the elements and attributes which would be useful would be:

/Wse:Filter/fed:Realm

/Wse:Filter/ Each relevant security token specified through the `<wsse:UsernameToken>`. If multiple tokens are specified, they represent a logical OR.

As an individual/application uses its credentials to sign into multiple services, it may be more efficient to forward a reference to its authentication token than to forward the token itself. The recipients can then choose to retrieve the token, if they have a need, or trust that the token provides the authorization needed for the service using the proof information associated with the reference. The provided proof is used to sign such messages, providing protection of both token authenticity and integrity. Architects may also choose to have the service provider return a reference token instead of the actual token. This reference token is a security token and can be used the same way the original token can be used.

The elements and attributes that are available for reference tokens are:

/fed:ReferenceToken: This element specifies the actual reference token.

/fed:ReferenceToken/fed:ReferenceEPR: This provides the reference to which the WS-ResourceTransfer GET request is directed. There must be at least one of these present if using reference tokens.

/fed:ReferenceToken/fed:ReferenceDigest: An optional hash using Secure Hash Algorithm 1 (SHA1) of the token to be returned. While the standard does not specify that other algorithms may be used, implementations of WS-Federation and WS-Resource Transfer support more modern hashing algorithms. As of this writing, SHA1 is in the process of being replaced by the National Institute of Standards and Technology (NIST) and should no longer be used where security is the requirement of the hash. Use SHA256 instead. Most software, which provides support for these standards, will permit this hashing algorithm to be used as the digest of choice. This digest will be represented as a base64 string within the XML.

/fed:ReferenceToken/fed:ReferenceDigest/@{any}: As always, this permits the use of additional attributes.

/fed:ReferenceToken/fed:ReferenceType

/fed:ReferenceToken/fed:ReferenceType/@{any}: As always, this permits the use of additional attributes.

/fed:ReferenceToken/fed:SerialNo: This is an optional URI which uniquely identifies the reference token, such as the X.509v3 serial number where digital certificates are used.

/fed:ReferenceToken/fed:SerialNo/@{any}: As always, this permits the use of additional attributes.

/fed:ReferenceToken/{any}: As always, this permits the use of additional elements.

/fed:ReferenceToken/@{any}: As always, this permits the use of additional attributes.

Often reference tokens meet business requirements better than regular tokens. These can be required by using the/fed:RequireReferenceToken element. This element has the following subordinate elements and attributes:

/fed:RequireReferenceToken/sp:IncludeToken: Despite the name, this optional element does not actually include the token but rather identifies the token inclusion value for the token assertion.

/fed:RequireReferenceToken/wsp:Policy: This optional element identifies additional requirements for the use of the assertion.

/fed:RequireReferenceToken/wsp:Policy/
fed:RequireReferenceToken11: This optional element

indicates that the reference token should be used as defined in the standard.

/fed:RequireReferenceToken/wsp:Policy/
fed:RequireReferenceToken11/@{any}: This, as always, allows attributes to be added.

/fed:RequireReferenceToken/wsp:Policy/
fed:RequireReferenceToken11/{any}: This, as always, allows additional elements to be added.

/fed:RequireReferenceToken/@{any}: This, as always, allows attributes to be added.

/fed:RequireReferenceToken{any}: This, as always, allows additional elements to be added.

In the event that a service provider is a member of multiple federations, you can process token requests in the context of a particular federation by using the /fed:FederationID element along with/fed:FederationID/@ {any} to extend it with the attributes needed for service processing. When this is not specified, then a default is assumed.

Under such conditions, it is entirely desirable that the application architect develop the capability to handle situations where the service needs to process a security token where the application does not possess the ability to use and extract the session key. This is done by requesting proof keys from the identity provider or STS or both. The process works by the requester presenting a token, which cannot be directly processed by the service provider; the service provider requests proof that the token holder was authorized by a trusted member of the federation and properly authorized to use its service; this is then forwarded to the identity provider or STS which returns the proof token. The request is made with the /fed:RequestProofToken element as part of a validate request. This element can be extended using /fed:RequestProofToken/@{any} to specify additional attributes and with /fed:RequestProofToken{any} to specify additional elements.

Much like sessions are often set to expire after an idle time, and passwords expire after a determined use period, there are many benefits from using time to bound the usefulness of security credentials. When using identity federation, all one can do is force the token issued to expire. This is set using the <fed:Freshness> element. Ironically, this element can also be used to allow the use of cached credentials. This is done through the use of the /@AllowCache attribute, which has a default value of true. If the credentials are not fresh, then the fault fed:NeedFresherCredentials fault must be returned to allow the requester the opportunity to request a new security token.

*3.4.5.2 Authorization*   Too much security within application design is focused on authentication and not enough on authorization. Whether an individual has the need to know or the need to use a particular data element should be the evaluation for each request for access to data. Failure to validate authorization permits SQL injection attacks and cross-site scripting attacks to work. If the application is designed to check and deny access to data requested, even if requested through bypassing input controls by injecting an SQL statement or other attack on input validation, then the majority of security breaches through the application layer would be prevented.

One approach to the problem of authorization within a distributed application or when using a service architecture is to create an authorization service. An authorization service is simply an STS that operates as a decision broken. When it receives a request for a token, it evaluates business logic to determine if the request can be authorized. If so, then the token is issued allowing access. The authorization service must evaluate the claims provided, constructing a table of name/value pairs representing the claims required by the target service and map those against the claims provided by the authenticated party.

The WS-Trust protocol provides the framework for the service to specify the desired properties of the required token. Each property must be provided as a child element of the request for a security token. Where there is a need to convey additional content based upon the desired properties, the STS may need to leverage the <auth:AdditionalContext> element to provide the required information in the request for a security token. This element has the following subelements and attributes:

/auth:AdditionalContext
/auth:AdditionalContext/ContextItem: This element provides
   additional authorization context in simple name/value pairs.

/auth:AdditionalContext/ContextItem/@Name:   The   required URI attribute for the kind of context being provided.

/auth:AdditionalContext/ContextItem/@Scope:The optional URL attribute specifying the context item. There are three that are predefined:

http://docs.oasis-open.org/wsfed/authorization/200706/ctx/ requestor: On behalf of the requestor

http://docs.oasis-open.org/wsfed/authorization/200706/ctx/ target: To what it applies to

http://docs.oasis-open.org/wsfed/authorization/200706/ctx/ action: The intended action.

/auth:AdditionalContext/ContextItem/Value:   This   optional element specifies the simple string value of the context.

/auth:AdditionalContext/ContextItem/{any}: As always, this permits the use of additional elements.

/auth:AdditionalContext/ContextItem/@{any}: As always, this permits the use of additional attributes.

/auth:AdditionalContext/@{any}: As always, this permits the use of additional attributes.

/auth:AdditionalContext/{any}: As always, this permits the use of additional elements.

WS-Federation's largest challenge in providing seamless integration of the security model of many and divergent organizations is the manifold means to express the same thing. One of the mechanisms it provides to architects to weave into the security fabric of their distributed application is the Common Claims Dialect. This allows claims to be expressed in a format-neutral way using the <auth:ClaimType> element to represent a claim. This may be used within the <wst:Claims> when making token requests and may be used within WS-SecurityPolicy to detail the organization's requirements. The following elements and attributes are available for use:

/auth:ClaimType/@URI: The required URI of the specific kind of claim being indicated.

/auth:ClaimType/@Optional: An optional boolean attribute used to indicate if the claim is optional or required. If optional, the value is TRUE; if required, the value is FALSE.

/auth:ClaimType/auth:DisplayName: An optional friendly name for the presentation layer.

/auth:ClaimType/auth:DisplayName/@{any}: As always, this allows additional attributes to be added.

/auth:ClaimType/auth:Description: Provides a description of the semantics of the claim type.

/auth:ClaimType/auth:Description/@{any}: As always, this allows additional attributes to be added.

/auth:ClaimType/auth:DisplayValue: Provides a displayable value for the claim returned in the token.

/auth:ClaimType/auth:Display/@{any}: As always, this allows additional attributes to be added.

/auth:ClaimType/auth:Value: A specific string value specified for the claim

/auth:ClaimType/auth:EncryptedValue: This is used to convey the ciphertext of the value specific to a claim. Considering that the values convey information used for both authentication and authorization, there may be sensitive information that needs to be conveyed. Encrypting the values using this element allows that information to be protected from even someone who has access to other aspects of the XML.

/auth:ClaimType/auth:ClaimType/auth:EncryptedValue/xenc:EncryptedData: This is used to convey the KeyInfo for the encryptedValue. Ideally this is a signed key; else the entire encrypted value and the key can be replaced without notice or warning.

/auth:ClaimType/auth:ClaimType/auth:EncryptedValue/@DecryptionCondition: This attribute provides a URI indicating the conditions under which the claim should be decrypted. The decryption should not be undertaken except when these conditions have been satisfied.

/auth:ClaimType/auth:StructuredValue: This provides the value of a claim in well-formed XML. I would highly recommend that this be used whereever possible instead of/auth:ClaimType/auth:Value where the value can be expressed in plain text.

/auth:ClaimType/auth:ConstrainedValue: This optional but critical element allows the architect to enforce constraints on a claim, allowing you to specify claims that must be satisfied. This element has many predefined subelements and attributes. Most of the uses are self-evident; the only thing that must be specified is that all of the below are to be defined as string values, even where you are doing greater-than or less-than comparisons.

/auth:ClaimType/auth:ConstrainedValue@AssetConstraint: The important thing to remember as you are developing business logic is that this specifies that when the claim is asserted, the constraint itself is asserted, or a value adheres when the claim is not asserted, and thus the condition is false.

The following objects are self explanatory in function:

/auth:ClaimType/auth:ConstrainedValue/auth:ValueLessThan

/auth:ClaimType/auth:ConstrainedValue/auth::ValueLessThan/
auth:Value

/auth:ClaimType/auth:ConstrainedValue/auth::ValueLessThan/
auth:StructuredValue

/auth:ClaimType/auth:ConstrainedValue/
auth::ValueLessThanOrEqual

/auth:ClaimType/auth:ConstrainedValue/
auth::ValueLessThanOrEqual/auth:Value

/auth:ClaimType/auth:ConstrainedValue/
auth::ValueLessThanOrEqual/auth:StructuredValue

/auth:ClaimType/auth:ConstrainedValue/
auth::ValueGreaterThan

/auth:ClaimType/auth:ConstrainedValue/
auth::ValueGreaterThan/auth:Value

/auth:ClaimType/auth:ConstrainedValue/
auth::ValueGreaterThan/auth:StructuredValue

/auth:ClaimType/auth:ConstrainedValue/
auth::ValueGreaterThan/auth:Value

/auth:ClaimType/auth:ConstrainedValue/
auth::ValueGreaterThan/auth:StructuredValue

/auth:ClaimType/auth:ConstrainedValue/
auth::ValueGreaterThanOrEqual

/auth:ClaimType/auth:ConstrainedValue/
auth::ValueGreaterThanOrEqual/auth:Value

/auth:ClaimType/auth:ConstrainedValue/
auth::ValueGreaterThanOrEqual/auth:StructuredValue

/auth:ClaimType/auth:ConstrainedValue/
auth::ValueGreaterThan/auth:Value

/auth:ClaimType/auth:ConstrainedValue/
auth:ValueGreaterThanOrEqual/auth:StructuredValue

/auth:ClaimType/auth:ConstrainedValue/auth:ValueInRange

/auth:ClaimType/auth:ConstrainedValue/auth:ValueInRange/
auth:ValueUpperBound

/auth:ClaimType/auth:ConstrainedValue/auth:ValueInRange/
authValueLowerBound

/auth:ClaimType/auth:ConstrainedValue/auth:ValueOnOf

/auth:ClaimType/auth:ConstrainedValue/auth:ValueOneOf/
auth:Value

/auth:ClaimType/auth:ConstrainedValue/auth:ValueOneOf/
auth:StructuredValue

/auth:ClaimType/auth:ConstrainedValue/{any}: As always, this
permits the use of additional elements.

/auth:ClaimType/@{any}: As always, this allows additional
attributes to be added.

/auth:ClaimType/{any}: As always, this permits the use of
additional elements.

Because applications are distributed, claims often need to be
directed to a particular target within the federation. The /wst:Claims/
@fedClaimsTarget attribute allows you to specify the particular target
of a particular claim. This ensures that the authorization system has
the values it needs to properly evaluate the request for access.

Authorization requestors and service providers must abide by these
core behaviors:

An authorization service must:

- Accept a `<wsp:AppliesTo>` target in the request for security token.
- Accept the reference properties in the `<wsp:AppliesTo>`
target.
- The `<auth:AdditionalContext>` parameter must be
accepted, as well as any claims made regarding dialect. However,
it may ignore elements in the `<auth:AdditionalContext>`
which it doesn't understand. A well-formed response does not
need to fault on a lack of response here, as this simply means

that the authorization service does not need this extra information to authorize the request for access or to deny it.

- Specify a `<wsp:AppliesTo>` target in the request for security token response if requested. This should be encoded if the token format supports encoding. The `<wsp:AppliesTo>` response is not limited to a response that only applies to the scope, but can be broader.

While a fault is not required if the metadata cannot be understood, the logic of issuing a SOAP Fault can allow the service provider to request additional or new information if needed. As an example, if the purchase is made from a new computer, a Fault can be issued to allow ascertaining that the request is indeed from a cardholder, or if the purchase requires a large outlay of funds, a request for proof of ability to pay may be in order. The specification recommends that when a SOAP Fault is issued for this purpose, you use the WS-MetadataExchange format, using fed:SpecificMetadata to express the fault and the `<S:Detail>` to specify the required additional metadata using a mex:Metadata element.

Precisely because WS-Federation involves the systemization of access to and authorization to resources often of rather different organizations, WS-Federation extends WS-Trust and WS-Policy to cover concerns about privacy. This is accomplished through the `<priv:ProtectData>` element as an extension of `<wst:RequestSecurityToken>`. `<priv:ProtectData>` supports wst:Claims as an optional subordinate element to indicate which claims must be treated as confidential. The service provider must provide appropriate protections for these claims. The `<priv:ProtectData>` element supports being extended through the /{any} and /@{any} extension mechanisms.

Unlike the `<priv:ProtectData>`, the `<priv:Enumerate Parameters>` defines optional elements and attributes, which may be honored by the responder. A well-formed privacy policy should clearly spell out what is done with what data under what conditions, but unless this has been specified in P3P format, the requester may be ignorant of this and make requests that will not be honored. To allow the service to provide the requester with appropriate feedback on its willingness/ability to manage the request, a key subordinate element is /priv:EnumerateParameters/FaultOnUnacceptedRstParameters. This element supports being extended through the /{any} and /@{any} extension mechanisms. To permit the service provider to evaluate each and every claim for data privacy, `<priv:EnumerateParameters>` supports the subordinate element of /priv:EnumerateParameters/ EnumerateAllClaims.

To prevent service calls with unsupported claims, WS-Federation provides a mechanism for publishing the privacy policy for enumeration by a services client. This is done through the `<priv:PrivacyPolicyEndpoint>` element which provides an endpoint reference which allows the policy to be made available to service-based clients programatically. Unfortunately, this is a lost opportunity within the WS-Standards to provide a language for parsing and understanding policies like P3P provides. I hope that application architects use P3P instead of poorly thought-out solutions such as the `<priv:PrivacyPolicyEndpoint>` element.

As I specified early on in this chapter, WS-Federation has a secondary function of enabling browsers to understand WS-Trust and WS-Policy and participate in a SOAP-based federated single sign-on. As there is no easy way for a browser to easily make SOAP requests, the processing is limited to the use of the typical HTTP 1.1 verbs of GET, POST, and so on, and redirects, cookies, client-side certificates (where available) as well as HTTP redirects. This allows the application architect to have the power and capability of a SOAP-based web service available to a REST interface. There are REST service models, which we will discuss later in this volume, but those would not be able to participate in the WS-Federation-brokered identity federation.

As might be expected, when a browser client is authenticated, regardless of mechanism, a mechanism needs to be provided to not only maintain the session but also to permit other nodes in the identity federation to recognize the browser as an authenticated entity and process authorization requests.

This security token is often a cookie or string within the URL. It must be noted that other nodes within the federation may require secondary authentication independent of the token presented by the browser.

It is important to design a mechanism to track which nodes in the federation the browser client has authenticated to facilitate logout. This can be done by adding additional cookies, appending to a cookie, or tracking it off-line in the security trust service. Regardless, when a sign-out is requested, the identity provider must leverage the session tracking to terminate the sessions with all authenticated services.

All attributes, pseudonyms, and metadata are processed in the back-end service as they are for a SOAP-based client; the only difference is the storage location. WS-Federation supports artifact cookies to store this data, and it is strongly recommended that the information stored within these cookies is encrypted as well as configured to expire after a defined period of time. Parameters are passed using GET and POST URL parameters; so it is imperative that such sessions are over SSL/TLS to prevent session theft as well as data loss. WS-Federation defines standard parameters to be used. These are:

wa: This is a required parameter which is used to specify the action to be taken. Where sign-in is desired, the string must contain "wsignin1.0". Where this parameter is included in a URI, a URI can be overloaded to specify multiple functions. When it is time to sign out, the client will pass the value of "wsignout1.0". Where attributes are requested, this parameter will have the value of "wattr1.0". Where a pseudonym is requested, the parameter will have the value of "wpseudo1.0".

wreply: An optional parameter containing the URI to which responses are redirected. For sign-in processes, the architect often has this direct to the specific functionality that corresponds to a main page. For the sign-out process, this may return to the landing page or some other page such as one containing an advertisement of a specific enhancement of services. Where an attribute request is to be conveyed, this will contain the URL to return, once complete. It is the same when a pseudonym has been requested. This value is easily spoofed; so you would be best served to do explicit lookup and verification of the URLs provided. Unfortunately, most browsers do not do a good job of signature validation, and simply relying upon transport security such as SSL or TLS will only provide a guarantee of privacy, not of integrity.

wres: An optional legacy parameter for the URL for the resource accessed. Modern implementations will use wtrealm instead.

wctx: This optional parameter, having the same function as the WS-Trust RST @Context attribute, is used to provide a context which must be returned if the attribute is in the request.

wp: An optional parameter containing the URL for the policy related to the action specified in the wa attribute but may have a broader scope. It mostly serves the same function as the Policy element of WS-Trust RST.

wct: This optional parameter specifies the date/time of the sender. It is not only useful for maintaining freshness but can also be used for policy enforcement regarding use and availability hours. This has roughly the same function as WS-Security Timestamp.

wfed: Mapping to the FederationID of the RST message, this optional element provides the federation context of the request.

wencoding: This optional parameter is used to indicate the encoding style used for XML parameter context. base64URL is the only predefined encoding style; others can be defined using the WebBinding assertion.

The common means to support browser-based security token requests is to expose a GET. POSTs can also be supported but provide no specific benefit and come with the additional security risks associated with any data input. No matter what the method supported is, WS-Federation adds to the attributes we have already discussed the following:

wtrealm: A required parameter containing the URI of the requesting realm. This roughly corresponds to the WS-Trust AppliesTo element.

wfresh: This is an optional parameter used to define freshness requirements for token issuance. A value of "0" forces reauthentication before token issuance. This parameter is equivalent to the WS-Trust Freshness element.

wauth: This is an optional parameter used to indicate the required authentication level, much like WS-Trust's AuthenticationType element.

wreq: This is an optional parameter used to specify a token request. This may be using either the WS-Trust's RequestSecurityToken element or a full request as defined by

WS-Trust. If not specified, it is presumed that the responding service knows how to respond.

whr: This optional parameter is used to indicate the account partner realm of the client by referring to its identity provider by URL, uniform resource name (URN), or universally unique identifier (UUID).

wreqptr: This optional attribute is a URL that functions as a reference pointer to a wst:RequestSecurityToken element. It is for use in situations where wreq cannot be used, and they are mutually exclusive. If this parameter is used, then the service provider should authenticate the request.

Security tokens are returned in an HTTP form. This form may then be submitted in a post as the means to authenticate to service providers. This form may use any of the parameters defined above, as well as:

wresult: This is a required parameter that specifies the result of the token issuance. This is equivalent to the WS-Trust Request Security Token Response (RSTR) element. This can also be used when an attribute is requested to convey in the response the result of the action and the attributes or when a pseudonym has been requested.

wctx: This optional parameter can be used to provide the context passed with the request.

wresulptr: This allows you to pass a pointer to the security token in the event that you cannot pass it within the form or to the URL where the results of the attribute request or a pseudonym may be found.

wpseudo is an optional parameter used to specify a pseudonym request as either a SOAP envelope or a pseudonym response. The response is likely to come in a wpseudoptr or a pointer.

Where browser-based clients are anticipated, there is no mechanism to reliably discover the home realm of the client, unlike with a SOAP client. To this end, WS-Federation provides the possibility of a Home Realm Discovery Service. This is often performed by a silent redirect to the discovery service, which will return the realm in the whr parameter if successful as well as redirect the session to the desired destination.

The WebBinding assertion is to be used when the application architect needs to allow the browser client to make requests of token services. You can think of this as the back-end translator of HTTP GET and POST requests for a SecurityTokenService. This is accomplished through the /fed:WebBinding element with the following attributes and elements:

/fed:WebBinding/wsp:Policy: This identifies a nested wsp:Policy element that defines the behavior of the WebBinding assertion.

/fed:WebBinding/wsp:Policy/sp:TransportToken: This specifies that a transport token is required.

/fed:WebBinding/wsp:Policy/fed:Authentication: This indicates the required token type for authentication to the service.

/fed:WebBinding/wsp:Policy/fed:AuthenticationToken/ wsp:Policy: This is used to indicate a nested policy used to specify a choice of formats for the authentication token.

/fed:WebBinding/wsp:Policy/RequireSignedTokens: The security architect in me urges that every application architect use this particular element. The presence of this control remediates all injection and substitution attacks if the signature is validated. Signed tokens can also prevent successful man-in-the-middle attacks, which are the hardest attacks to defend against and virtually impossible to detect. Unfortunately, the default value is false, but if this element is specified, then it sets the value to be true.

/fed:WebBinding/wsp:Policy/RequireBearerTokens: This element, if present, indicates that Bearer Tokens are required. The default is that they are not required.

/fed:WebBinding/wsp:Policy/RequireSharedCookies: Cookie Monster need not tremble; this is merely to facilitate home realm discovery. If present, it sets the property to be true; otherwise the default value is false.

/fed:WebBinding/wsp:Policy/Base64Url: Where present, this sets the requirement for XML parameters to be base64 encoded. The default value is false. There is no security value in encoding these values; base64 is readily recognized, and most tools used for web and SOA hacking have the ability to decode base64.

Where WS-Federation is used with WS-Policy, the policy needs to assert three elements to provide support for authorization. While none of them is mandatory, I recommend that the architect consider the role they may play in not only securing the application but also enhancing the security operation to ensure interoperability and transparency. They are:

/fed:RequiresGenericClaimDialect: This does just what the name implies.

/fed:IssuesSpecificPolicyFault: This lets the requester know that the service will issue the fed:SpecificPolicy Fault if the security requirements for a specific request are beyond those of the base policy.

/Fed:AdditionalContextProcessed: This value in the policy ensures that if the fed:AdditonalContext parameter is specified in the request for a security token, it will be processed.

Where WS-Federation provides Fault strings to the consumer of the service, the following Fault codes are provided. For the most part, their meaning is self-evident:

- fed:NoPseudonymInScope
- fed:AlreadySignedIn
- fed:NotSignedIn
- fed:BadRequest
- fed:NoMatchInScope
- fed:NeedFresherCredentials
- fed:SpecificPolicy
- fed:UnsupportedClaimsDialect
- fed:RstParameterNotAccepted
- fed:IssuerNameNotSupported
- fed:UnsupportedEncoding

*3.4.6 Authorization without WS-Federation*

WS-Federation has a lot of build in controls designed to be used for authorization modeling, and SAML attributes are frequently used for attribute-based authentication; however, not all SOAs are designed with the need for federated identity services. All SOAs, however, need to process authorization checks. While we already discussed authorization models in the abstract, this would be a good moment to review the mechanics of the implementation of those authorization models.

While all authorization models should look to enforce the principle of least privilege and separation of duties, if not also the principle of least authority, there is a variety of mechanisms that can be used to evaluate if access should be granted. WS-Federation and SAML both provide mechanisms for attribute-based authorization but are not necessary to facilitate this flexible means to authorize an individual. Another mechanism for authorization is resource-based authorization.

Attribute-based authorization can be either designed into the application formally or can be evaluated at run time based upon an algorithm. Which approach to take largely depends upon the business needs; however, I would recommend that in considering those business needs, consider the needs for security audit in the design. Where authorization is algorithm based, an audit of the individuals authorized for access means the manual processing of the algorithm in the review of the application. Many third-party auditors are not going to be satisfied with script outputs that automate the application of the authorization algorithm to list authorized members. It largely depends upon how technical they are and how well they understand the script used to enumerate the account population. Such scripts should be well documented with the intent of being evaluated by a third party as part of an audit.

What attribute-based authorization provides to you is the flexibility to grant access on a dynamic basis. If, for example, the individual has attribute y & z as well as comes from company a, then authorize, but if they had attribute p & q instead, do not. Those attributes could be queried over LDAP from a directory server, they might be metadata-stored within the SOAP message, or they might be queried from references provided in the token. This allows for very granular levels of authorization where many different factors can be considered for authorization, allowing different access levels to the same team depending upon other factors than a common reporting structure.

As an alternative approach to granting access based upon the presence of some set of attributes, you can assign mathematical values to the data found within the attributes evaluated for access and functionality.

This policy is adaptive, so that the service provider can strengthen or loosen the constraints upon access without impacting the rest of the application in response to changing business requirements, in response to a security incident, or as a result of a contract negotiation.

Access is authorized when the mathematical processing of the aggregate result of the algorithm equals or exceeds a defined threshold for access. This permits an authorization model where attributes are not evaluated equally based upon presence or absence but rather some attributes are allowed to be considered as more indicative of a reason to authorize access to either data or functionality. Where the attributes required are insufficient for access, either it can be denied or the service provider can query for additional attributes. Once queried, these additional attributes allow for a re-examination of the algorithm and may adjust the decision to authorize use or decline the request.

Resource-based authorization, on the other hand, tends to be managed by predetermined criteria such as all members of group x are authorized for access to y. This requires the groups to be maintained by some identity provider and for access control matrixes or lists to be created around the matrix. Auditing this is simple as one simply checks the membership of the group authorized for function x to determine who has access to that function. This allows easy administration of authorization based upon a common reporting structure and is often how most system administration authorization controls are implemented. However, this kind of authorization is not very granular unless many groups are maintained.

Where authorization checks are data oriented rather than application function oriented, for each data element one must grant access to create, read, update, or delete. Either resource-based or attribute-based authorization models work and allow scale and effective checking for each object in the data set. Usually, this is done through data groupings or classifications, such as access to sensitive data, access to classified data, access to public data, access to top-secret data, and so on. This allows for ease of management and auditing while scaling to large and complex data sets, though if the authorization is attribute based rather than resource based, careful logging is essential. This authorization model provides the most granular and specific control of access, carefully and deliberately ensuring that the principle of least privilege and the principle of least authority are both enforced.

The problem with data-based authorization models is that you need to evaluate access for each field. Functionality-based authorization models group data based upon those elements needed to perform a specific task. This makes them more efficient than data-oriented authorizations, specifically because data elements may be accessible through multiple application features, each of which need to be authorized either on a functional or data-specific basis. Evaluating on an element-by-element basis will require performing more authorization checks.

Authorization models are not mutually exclusive, and one can readily combine techniques. Thus, individuals who are members of group x with attributes p & q are permitted read access to sensitive data, but not to top-secret data, which requires attribute r as well as p & q. Write access to classified data only is permitted, and so on. A common approach is to use functional testing except where data is specifically sensitive and then to use attribute-based checks within the functional test.

Having a preset and common identity store can be helpful, but for many service-oriented applications, there is no native centralized identity store, which is where WS-Federation and SAML come in handy. They provide a virtual centralized identity store by unifying access across multiple-account stores. Because of the rigors involved in trying to define resource authorization models across a distributed account store, most application and security architects resort to attribute-based authorization models.

For those service-oriented application architectures, which can leverage a common identity store, LDAP lends itself well as a data query language which returns many and diverse attributes for a user account without a need to pull from the many related tables of a relational database. For those who have skipped to this chapter and not read the chapter on identity architectures, LDAP allows both relational and object-oriented queries of data from a distributed data store in a simple read-oriented syntax. You can readily use it as the basis to define a resource-based authorization model leveraging LDAP groups or the hierarchical tree structure of the directory itself. LDAP may also be readily leveraged for attribute-based authorization by leveraging the manifold attributes stored within the directory.

By now you may be wondering why I have not referenced a standard or delineated a catalog of that standard's attributes and objects. There is no WS-Authorization standard, nor is there one planned. WS-Federation provides a mechanism through which authorization can be standardized across corporate boundaries, as does SAML; however, the logic of attribute processing for feature or data or feature-on-data authorization checking is and remains a business logic function.

The information needed to process authorization decisions may pre-exist in an identity store, or that identity store may need to be created for the application. The nature of that information may be best represented as the variable properties of an object or through the commonly shared properties of many items in relationship with many individuals. The architect's options are bound mostly by history. If there is an existing identity store that must be used for the application as it contains information on the relevant accounts mapping to the individuals who will be using the application, then this identity store will be used along with its properties.

If that identity store is a relational database, then group memberships and resource-based modeling is likely for an authorization model so as to best leverage the ability of a relational database to relate a member to a group or a group to its members as well as matrixes of authorizations for each data element and the four basic data manipulation functions. Relational databases do not perform well when repeated queries are made against divergent relationships against the same data set if insufficient attributes are provided for authorization and the authorization model is to query for missing attributes before denying access.

If, however, the pre-existing identity store is a distributed or local directory where the information about the individual account is stored as an attribute or object of that account, then attribute-based access modeling is more likely.

One authorization model I have not discussed is the so-called role-based authorization model. This is because roles can be defined in terms of attributes or in terms of resources or some combination of the two. Role-based authorization models are often an attempt to apply rigor to attribute-based authentication models, wherein roles are defined as attribute groupings, which map back to business roles within the organization. While this methodology of authorization management is quite popular with various security analysts, as with other attribute-based models, this can be problematic to audit and manage.

If the organization decides to build an attribute-based authorization model, the organization should also build and document an auditing framework. If the identity store is not queryable, which it often is not when auditing service-oriented applications, then the audit framework needs to test the controls by querying the logs. To this end, it is imperative that authorization decisions are carefully logged with all the data elements used to evaluate the decision regarding access captured for each authorization test.

Regardless, it is important to understand that with the exception of SAML and custom tokens issued under WS-Federation or proprietary tokens issued by a token service provider, credentials will not have attributes that can be used for attribute-based authorization. X509v3 certificates may be incredibly secure, but they have few attributes that can be used. Passwords have no attributes. The initial SAML assertion may carry attributes but may not be the ones required; unless you are using WS-Policy to enforce your requirements, it is not likely that an SAML assertion will contain what is needed. Thus, policy-less attribute authentication models will require queries for any missing attributes. Any time a security system needs to query the source system, this creates a performance impact. Thus, while attribute authorization models provide better and more scalable mechanisms to control the use of your application and its data, they may adversely impact application performance, which is to be avoided at all costs. The reality that all security architects must face: A secure and slow application will never be used where faster and less secure options are available.

### 3.4.7 WS-Addressing

WS-Addressing defines two constructs used to convey information usually provided by transport protocols and messaging systems: endpoint references and message information headers. The endpoint references may be used to provide the information needed to access a web service endpoint or to direct a message to that endpoint. It uses the XML information set and conveys the endpoint locations using XMLNamespaces. The information can be exposed in a WSDL or a WS-Policy.

There are three basis usage scenarios:

Dynamic generation of the service endpoint descriptions
Identification and description of specific service instances
Flexible and dynamic exchange of endpoint locations

To do this, the WSDL description model is extended to include endpoint references instead of WSDL service elements. These references contain the following properties:

Address: A mandatory URI identifying the end point.
Reference properties: xs:any (0-unbounded), providing the number of individual properties required to identify an endpoint.
Reference parameters: xs:any (0-unbounded), providing the number of individual parameters associated with the endpoint to facilitate a particular interaction.
Selected port type: QName (0..1), the QName of the primary portType of the endpoint.
Service-port: QName, NCName (0..1))(0..1), the QName identifying the WSDL service element which contains the description of the service endpoint.
Policy: wsp:policy (0..unbounded), a variable number of XML policy elements describing the behavior, requirements, and capabilities of the endpoint.

These properties can be expressed with the following attributes and elements:

/wsa:EndPointReference: This is used to an endpoint reference with the following properties:
/wsa:EndPointReference/wsa:Address/: This is a required element of type xs:any URI specifying the address of the endpoint reference.
/wsa:EndPointReference/wsa:ReferenceProperties/: An optional element containing the elements conveying the reference properties.
/wsa:EndPointReference/wsa:ReferenceProperties/{any}: Those properties.

/wsa:EndPointReference/wsa:ReferenceParameters/:     An optional element containing the elements conveying the reference parameters.

/wsa:EndPointReference/wsa:ReferenceParameters/{any}: Those parameters.

/wsa:EndPointReference/wsa:PortType: This optional element provides the value of the selected port type as an xs:Qname

/wsa:EndPointReference/wsa:ServiceName: This optional element specifies the `<wsdl:service>` definition that contains the WSDL description of the endpoint as an xs:QName.

/wsa:EndPointReference/wsa:ServiceName/@PortName: This optional attribute specifies the name of the `<wsdl:port>` corresponding to the endpoint being referenced as an xs:NCName.

/wsa:EndPointReference/wsa:Policy: This optional element specifies a relevant policy.

/wsa:EndPointReference/{any}: Allows additional elements to be specified.

/wsa:EndPointReference/@{any}: Allows additional attributes to be specified.

When a message needs to be sent to the endpoint, the information in the endpoint reference is mapped to the message. While the specification defines a binding for this purpose using SOAP, other bindings may be used for other protocols. To use the SOAP binding, you must copy the address property in the endpoint reference to the destination header in the SOAP message. Each reference property and associated parameter becomes a header block in the SOAP message.

Because multiple copies of an endpoint reference are likely to be received, the specification defines rules for keeping track and clarifying the behavior regarding message transmission. Strict conformance to these rules in one's implementation will provide a more reliable application, but if the application architect needs to guarantee message delivery, the architect will wish to explore WS-ReliableMessaging. The rules are simple: if the endpoints have the same address and the same reference properties, then the two endpoints are considered the same. Embedded policies are not considered authoritative and may be stale or incoherent with the policies now associated with the endpoint.

This is important for the security architect to understand. With the assumption that polices may change and may change frequently, these polices are not a place to enforce security controls unless with each policy change, the endpoint reference is also changed. Such dynamic and frequent change may be required for a number of reasons as the service may connect a message to different endpoints or different variations on the endpoints based upon choices made during the session. As an example, if the service provider is providing a travel application, choice of airline will provide different endpoints chosen at run time, and if the traveler is someone who is a frequent traveler, the policy for that airline will be different, sometimes markedly so, than the policy for an individual who has never flown that airline before.

The WS-Addressing message information headers augment the message with abstract properties that enable the identification and location of the desired endpoints. One of the properties which is very helpful is the ability to request a reply from the endpoint. The reply can be an application message, fault, or any other message, but must contain the message id to which it is replying. The properties available are:

Destination: A mandatory URI containing the address of the intended recipient.

Source endpoint: A reference to the origination endpoint.

Reply endpoint: If a reply is expected or needed, then the message must contain the reply endpoint property with the contents necessary to formulate a meaningful reply.

Fault endpoint: This is a reference for where faults are to be directed. Like with the reply endpoint property, when this is present, there must be a message ID that matches the source.

Action: This mandatory property provides a URI that uniquely identifies the steps to be taken as a result of receiving the message. It is recommended that the URL identify a corresponding property, input, output, or message within a WSDL port type.

Message ID: This is a mandatory property containing a URI that uniquely identifies the message. This must be globally meaningful but because of Network Address Translation (NAT), firewalls, Dynamic Host Configuration Protocol (DHCP), and so on, that may be impossible; so where that is the case, an anonymous URI may be provided, but an out-of-band method must be provided to process replies and faults.

Relationship: This is a property expressing, by pairing a QName with a URI, a relationship regarding how this message relates to another message. Reply messages must contain this property, referencing the message ID property of the message with the QName of wsa:Reply.

The message information header blocks function as a unit to express the end-to-end characteristics of a message. As such, this information is designed to be static and immutable. To express these characteristics, the message header block may contain the following attributes and elements:

/wsa:MessageID, an optional element which is used to convey the message id as an xs:anyURI. Should the wsaReplyTo or wsa:FaultTo be used, this element becomes mandatory.

/wsa:RelatesTo, an optional repeating element which provides a relationship between a message id and its message through a URI, QName pair.

/wsa:RelatesTo/@RelationshipType, an optional attribute used to convey the relationship type in the form of a QName. The default value is wsa:Reply.

/wsa:ReplyTo, this optional element is used to provide the value for the reply endpoint.

/wsa:From, an optional element used to provide the value of the source endpoint.

/wsa:FaultTo, an optional element used to convey the destination for fault processing.

/wsa:To, a required element used to convey the value of the destination using xs:anyUIR.

/wsa:Action, a required element used to convey the action property using xs:AnyURI.

There are two mechanisms in the standard for associating an action in a WS-Addressing message with a WSDL port type. The first is through explicit association using the wsa:Action attribute. The second is to leverage the default action plan which has the format of [target namespace]/[port type name]/[input|output name], where "/" is a literal character, not an indication of division or proportion.

To remain compliant with the WS-Addressing standard, endpoints must include the required message headers on all fault messages. These may be sent to the source endpoint or the reply endpoint if present. Messages use the following properties to communicate faults:

Code: the fault code

Subcode: the fault subcode

Reason: The English reason for the fault

Detail: The details of the fault are not required. If using SOAP 1.1, only code and subcode are needed; SOAP 1.2 provides the ability to express both reason and detail.

To properly secure WS-Addressing messages, the body and all relevant headers need to be signed by the initial sender, though some elements may also be signed by various relay points. Addresses specified in wsa:Form, wsa:ReplyTo, and wsa:FaultTo most certainly should be signed to prevent redirection to an invalid endpoint. If confidentiality is a requirement, then the message information header blocks may be encrypted except those fields required for delivery. The application should ensure that the wsa:MessageID is used and that its uniqueness is verified. This value should be signed to ensure its integrity and authenticity.

### 3.4.8 WS-ReliableMessaging

One of the main problems with building a distributed application which depends upon services often rendered by other companies in other locations is resiliency. The WS-ReliableMessaging specification is an OASIS standard with the goal of providing resiliency to service-oriented applications, which leverage the WS-Security standards suite. WS-ReliableMessaging addresses issues of availability, control, and integrity but not confidentiality, authenticity, or utility.

The specification defines a protocol that enables a reliable messaging (RM) source to determine the disposition of any message it transmits so as to resolve any doubts about the delivery or the order of delivery for any messages it transmits. It can determine if it has received any particular message already, filter out duplicates, and place messages back in the intended order. It can also guarantee the delivery of these messages. This makes the WS-ReliableMessaging a key standard to conform to if the organization's service-oriented application needs to be resilient to changes in network status.

Messages are sent between RM sources and RM destinations in sequences. For the protocol to work as desired, the architect must ensure the following:

> For all messages created within each sequence, the source must have an endpoint reference that uniquely identifies the destination.
>
> The source must have the ability to create a sequence with the destination.
>
> The source must be capable of formulating messages that conform to the destination's policies as stated in their WS-Policy.
>
> If the destination's policies mandate a secure exchange of messages, then the source and destination must have a security context.
>
> Each message must be assigned a message number within the sequence. These are whole numbers starting at 1, assigned in numerical order to the messages in the order of intended delivery.
>
> The RM destination must send acknowledgement messages, containing in one or more AcknowledgementRange child elements the message number of the message received.
>
> When a sequence is not terminated properly, the RM source should retransmit all unacknowledged messages.

The WS-Policy of the destination needs to specify the delivery assurance policy that the source must comply with. The available options are:

> AtLeastOnce: Messages may be sent more than once, as the source retries each message until an acknowledgment is received.
>
> AtMostOnce: Messages may only be delivered once; the destination will filter out all duplications. The source is not required to retransmit messages that were not delivered.
>
> ExactlyOnce: If the source receives an error, it must retransmit the failed message until it is acknowledged as successfully

delivered. However, it is not to retransmit messages that were acknowledged as received.

InOrder: Obviously, the InOrder policy may be specified with any of the others. When specified, no subsequent messages may be sent until an acknowledgment is received that the prior message is received. Only then the next message in the numerical sequence may be sent.

Because sending single messages in sequence is remarkably inefficient, many application architects will look to piggyback RM protocol header blocks onto messages already targeted to the same endpoint. This is doable. It can even be automated so that the reliable messaging sender can make the determination if it will piggyback its messages into other messages. However, this means that the destination must be prepared to handle messages with RM protocol header blocks in any message received. This can place an untoward burden on the RM infrastructure.

Considering the role of WS-Addressing in identifying endpoints and specifying replies, it makes sense to leverage WS-Addressing within WS-ReliableMessaging. When the application architect wishes to use WS-Addressing in combination with WS-ReliableMessaging, the architect must ensure that the proper constraints on the wsa:Action header are put in place. These constraints are:

- The wsa:Action association must be between the WS-RM namespace URL and the local name of the child element of the SOAP body.
- A sequence request must use the wsa:Action (IRI) of http://docs.oasis-open.org/ws-rx/warm/200702/CreateSequence. If the acknowledgement message has no element content in the SOAP body to associate with, the IRI must be http://docs.oasis-open.org/ws-rx/warm/200702/SequenceAcknowledgement.
- If the acknowledgement request has no element content in the SOAP body to associate with, the IRI must be http://docs.oasis-open.org/ws-rx/warm/200702/SequenceAckRequested.
- If a fault is to be generated, it must use an IRI of http://docs.oasis-open.org/ws-rx/warm/200702/fault using codes of S11:Client for the sender and S:11 for the receiver in SOAP 1.1, and S:Sender with S:Receiver for SOAP 1.2.

To create a sequence, the RM sends a CreateSequence element in the body of a message to the RM destination that will reply with either a CraeteSequenceResponse or a CreateSequenceRefused fault. The CreateSequence element has the following elements and attributes:

/wsrm:CreateSequence: The element requests the creation of a new sequence, which must be responded to with either a CreateSequenceResponse or a CreateSequenceRefused. This element must not be sent as a header block.

/wsrm:CreateSequence/wsrm:AcksTo: This is a mandatory element in any CreateSequence request, sending the wsa:EndPointReferenceType specifying the endpoint reference to which SequenceAcknowledgement header blocks are to be sent.

/wsrm:CreateSequence/wsrm:Expires: This optional element expresses as an xs:duration the duration of the sequence. If the value is PTOS, the sequence never expires. This value creates a potential security issue and should be carefully considered before implementation.

/wsrm:CreateSequence/wsrm:Expires/@{any} allows the addition of new attributes.

/wsrm:CreateSequence/wsrm:Offer: This optional element allows the RM source to specify a sequence for the destination to use.

/wsrm:CreateSequence/wsrm:Offer/wsrm:Identifier: This optional element is used to provide an absolute URI that uniquely identifies a sequence offered to the destination.

/wsrm:CreateSequence/wsrm:Offer:/wsrm:Identifier/@{any} allows the addition of new attributes.

/wsrm:CreateSequence/wsrm:Offer/wsrm:Endpoint: This mandatory element is used to provide the endpoint reference to which sequence life cycle messages, acknowledgment requests, and fault messages are to be sent.

/wsrm:CreateSequence/wsrm:Offer/wsrm:Expires: This optional element expresses as an xs:duration the duration of the sequence. If the value is PTOS, the sequence never expires. This value creates a potential security issue and should be carefully considered before implementation.

/wsrm:CreateSequence/wsrm:Offer/wsrm:Expires/@{any} allows the addition of new attributes.

/wsrm:CreateSequence/wsrm:Offer/wsrm:IncompleteSequence Behavior: This optional element should always be present. It predefines how the destination should behave in the event of an incomplete sequence. Possible values are:

DiscardEntireSequence

DiscardFollowingFirstGap

NoDiscard

Obviously that which is specified needs to meet business requirements. Here the application and security architects should strongly consider issues of data integrity, data utility, as well as, of course, data availability.

/wsrm:CreateSequence/wsrm:Offer/{any} allows the addition of new elements to convey new information.

/wsrm:CreateSequence/wsrm:Offer/@{any} allows the addition of new attributes.

/wsrm:CreateSequence/{any} allows the addition of new elements.

/wsrm:CreateSequence/@{any} allows the addition of new attributes.

For every /wsrm:CreateSequence, you will get a /wsrm:CreateSequenceResponse. These will carry the Identifier of the /wsrm:-CreateSequence. The /wsrm:CreateSequenceResponse has the following elements and attributes available to it:

/wsrm:CreateSequenceResponse: Like with /wsrm:CreateSequence, this must not be sent as a header block.

/wsrm:CreateSequenceResponse/wsrm:Identifier, a mandatory element with the value of the absolute URI which uniquely identifies the sequence.

/wsrm:CreateSequenceResponse/wsrm:Identifier/@{any} allows the addition of new attributes.

/wsrm:CreateSequenceResponse/wsrm:Expires/@{any} allows the addition of new attributes.

/wsrm:CreateSequenceResponse/
   wsrm:IncompleteSequenceBehavior provides the behavior
   that the destination will exhibit upon closure of the sequence.
   It has the same options and security implications as the element in the request.
/wsrm:CreateSequenceResponse/wsrm:Accept: This element is
   used to accept the offer of the corresponding sequence offered
   in the wsrm:Offer element by the requester.
/wsrm:CreateSequenceResponse/wsrm:Accept/wsrm:ActsTo:
   This mandatory element specifies the endpoint reference to
   which the sequenceAcknowledgment header blocks and
   faults related to the created sequence are to be sent.
/wsrm:CreateSequenceResponse/wsrm:Accept/{any} allows the
   addition of new elements.
/wsrm:CreateSequenceResponse/wsrm:Accept/@{any}    allows
   the addition of new attributes.
/wsrm:CreateSequenceResponse/{any} allows the addition of
   new elements.
/wsrm:CreateSequenceResponse/@{any} allows the addition of
   new attributes.

Either the source or the destination may close a sequence. These
should never be just terminated, as that would trigger the actions
specified in the wsrm:IncompleteSequenceBehavior, which may not
be the desired effect. If the source wishes to terminate a sequence,
it sends a CloseSequence element in the body of a message to the
destination. Any messages received after this should not be processed by the recipient. The response to this should include the
SequenceAcknowledgement to all messages up to and including
this message, but to no subsequent ones. The source should include a
LastMsgNumber element in the CloseSequence element to allow the
destination to properly validate that it has received all the messages in
the sequence or through a fault.

If the recipient wishes to close a sequence, then it should send a
CloseSequence in a body of a message to the AcksTo endpoint of
the sequence. It must include a final SequenceAcknowledgement and
must include the Final element. The /wsrm:CloseSequence element
has the following elements and attributes available to it:

/wsrm:CloseSequence/wsrm:Identifier, a mandatory element specifying the absolute URI of the closing sequence.

/wsrm:CloseSequence/wsrm:LastMsgNumber, a highly recommended optional element specifying the highest message number of the sequence traffic messages. It is not as if not having this value accomplishes anything; all it does is increase the reliability of a protocol designed to be reliable. There is no need to worry about saving bits here; using this value is a good thing.

/wsrm:CloseSequence/wsrm:Identifier/@{any}

/wsrm:CloseSequence/{any}

/wsrm:CloseSequence/@{any}

The response, /wsrm:CloseSequenceResponse, predictably has a /wsrm:CloseSequenceResponse/wsrm:Identifier element as well as the ability to be extended through /wsrm:CloseSequenceResponse/wsrm:Identifier/@{any}, /wsrm:CloseSequenceResponse/{any}, and /wsrm:CloseSequenceResponse/@{any}.

A sequence that has been closed can still be used. However, there are times when it is desirous to prevent the reuse of a sequence. When a source has completed its use of a sequence and there are valid reasons to prevent its reuse, it should issue a TerminateSequence instead of a CloseSequence. The destination may now safely reclaim any resources dedicated to that sequence in closing it. The TerminateSequence, like the CloseSequence, makes use of the wsrm:Identifier and wsrm-LastMsgNumber, with the Identifier a required element and the LastMsgNumber a highly recommended value that enhances the reliability of a protocol whose goal is reliability. The response is a TerminateSequenceResponse, with wsrm:Identifier as a mandatory element. Both the TerminateSequence and TerminateSequenceResponse can be extended with Identifier/@{any}, and attributes and elements may be added to each of TerminateSequence and TerminateSequenceResponse through the use of /{any} and /@{any} to add new elements and attributes, respectively.

Sequences are re-established using the /wsrm:Sequence element. This protocol element associates a message with a previously closed but not terminated sequence. The request must assign a mustUnderstand attribute with a value of 1/true, and the response must understand the

Sequence header block. This element has the following elements and attributes:

/wsrm:Sequence/wsrm:Identifier, an absolute URI which must
be present which uniquely identifies the sequence.
/wsrm:Sequence/wsrm:Identifier/@{any}
/wsrm:Sequence/wsrm:MessageNumber, a mandatory element
indicating the position within the sequence, often the number
after the number used to previously close the sequence.
/wsrm:Sequence/{any}
/wsrm:Sequence/@{any}

Much like parents wishing to know that their teen has heard what they have said, WS-ReliableMessaging uses the AckRequested header block to ask for an acknowledgement from the destination that the source has been heard and understood. This may be done any time, every time (with every message), or at no time, depending upon the requirements of the business. Destinations in receipt of these requests must respond with a Sequence acknowledgment header block to the AcksTo endpoint reference or generate an UnknownSequence fault. The AckRequested header block uses a /wsrm:Identifier to identify the absolute URI representing the sequence to which the request applies, and the SequenceAcknowledgment reply uses the same element with the same value in its response. The element contains as possibilities:

/wsrm:SequenceAcknowledgment/wsrm:Identifier, the absolute
and unique URI which is being acknowledged.
/wsrm:SequenceAcknowledgment/
wsrm:AcknowledgmentRange/@Upper
/wsrm:SequenceAcknowledgment/
wsrm:AcknowledgmentRange/@Lower
/wsrm:SequenceAcknowledgment/
wsrm:AcknowledgmentRange/@{any}
/wsrm:SequenceAcknowledgment/wsrm:None: Specifically, this
means the destination is not receiving any messages in the
specified sequence.
/wsrm:SequenceAcknowledgment/wsrm:Final: This element
must be included when a sequence is closed and the destination receives an SequenceAcknowledgment request.

/wsrm:SequenceAcknowledgment/wsrm:Nack: This is used to indicate the message number of an unreceived message in the sequence. If this is received, the source should retransmit this message or issue a fault.

/wsrm:SequenceAcknowledgment/{any}

/wsrm:SequenceAcknowledgment/@{any}

### 3.4.9 WS-Coordination

WS-Coordination provides a defined set of instructions to coordinate the behavior of various web services within the SOA. It is used to maintain process integrity and functionality. WS-Coordination can manage any of the protocols typically used to call services and provide them with the required information. This is most applicable when those services are distributed among many entities but can be equally useful when the application is internally distributed across data centers. The protocol lacks the message-tracking features of WS-ReliableMessaging, but those could be added through the ability to extend the protocol.

These transactions may be short-lived, best executed through WS-AtomicTransaction, or they may be long, extended, and complex and leverage WS-BusinessActivity. This volume will not look at those protocols, but it is worth looking at WS-Coordination as a more flexible and scalable alternative to WS-ReliableMessaging, providing both integrity and authenticity assurances across many systems.

The protocol defines three basic roles: that of an activation service, that of a registration service, and that of a coordinator. The activation service is used to create the context for an activity. This will contain the necessary information needed to allow the service to register itself, using either the registration service provided by the activation service or another provided by a trusted coordinator.

The coordination service has the following elements and attributes available to it:

/CreateCoordinationContext/CoordinationType, a mandatory element, which provides a unique identifier as a URI for the activity.

/CreateCoordinationContext/Expires, an optional element, which provides the expiration for the CoordinationContext as an unsigned integer. Including this element improves the security of establishing a coordination context as it binds the context in time, which helps prevent unauthorized use.

/CreateCoordinationContext/CurrentContext: This element is ironically optional, as if it is absent then the activation service will create a new context, but if present, it provides the information needed to participate in the context.

/CreateCoordinationContext/{any} allows the addition of additional elements.

/CreateCoordinationContext/@{any} allows the addition of new attributes.

The element CreateCoordinationContextResponse is used in the response. This carries an Identifier, a coordination type, and the address of the RegistrationService using a wsa:Address. There may be duplicate Registrars, and the protocol has no means to detect the presence of duplicates. The problem is, of course, that this functionality can be maliciously used by an attacker to spin up a pseudo-duplicate that is malicious in nature.

The registration with the context uses the /Register element with the following subelements and attributes:

/Register/ProtocolIdentifier, an element providing the URI of the coordination protocol.

/Register/ParticipantProtocolService, an element used to provide location of the endpoint reference.

/Register/{any} allows the addition of additional elements.

/Register/@{any} allows the addition of new attributes.

When a service registers with a coordination service, the coordination service will send back a /RegisterResponse/CoordinatorProtocolService, which will contain the endpoint reference. The /RegisterResponse element has no other subelements, unless it is extended.

In the event of a fault, WS-Coordination must include an action property of http://docs.oasis-open.org/ws-tx/wscoor/2006/06/ fault. Much like faults in WS-ReliableMessaging, the faults must have a Code, SubCode, Reason, and Detail, where the Code property is either Sender or Receiver.

To secure WS-Coordination coordinators and messages, WS-Coordination relies upon WS-Trust, WS-Policy, and WS-Security.

When the coordination context is created, the message is secured using WS-Security, which is validated on the recipient by WS-Policy. This is done through the establishment of claims bound to the identity of the coordination center's creator. The context creator requests them from the coordination center, which can then demand proof of identity from the requester. The coordinator should also provide a shared secret used to indicate authorization to register with the coordination context. This secret is communicated using a security token and a wst:Req uestSecurityTokenResponse element inside a wst:IssuedTokens header. This is mapped to the context using a wscoor:Identifier element in a wsp:AppliesTo element with the wst:RequestSecurityTokenResponse.

This shared secret may be delegated to other messages using a wst:IssuedTokens header. This should be both encrypted and signed but not by the shared secret. A key derived from the shared secret may be used to secure a message using WS-SecureConversation. The body and all relevant headers should be signed, with the wscoor:CoordinationContext header signed with the body by the same key.

Again, what this protocol is missing is a method to ensure the delivery and processing of messages, but this can be added through extending the elements and attributes. Extending, however, can cause interoperability issues and so should be considered carefully for an externally facing SOA.

### 3.4.10 WS-Transaction

A defined set of instructions to handle atomic (individual) transactions and business transactions for long-term operations, WS-AtomicTransaction is an alternative to Business Process Execution Language (BPEL), and is designed to be used with WS-Coordination for the processing of short-duration transactions. Long and complex transactions should be handled by WS-BusinessActivity or by BPEL.

As with any of the web services' suite, it is assumed the source is aware of the destination policies and must be capable of meeting those requirements to engage with the destination. WS-AutomicTransaction has two basic protocols: Completion and Two-Phase Commit. The Completion protocol is used to instruct the coordinator which transactions to commit or abort. The coordinator will accept instructions to commit and rollback and will respond with Committed or Aborted.

There should be no surprise that there are two phases of Two-Phase commit: Volatile Two-Phase commit and durable Two-Phase commit. They are both used to allow multiple participants to participate in the commit protocol, wherein each must respond before the commit is acted upon. Once the volatile-phase commit is complete, the application may then act on the durable phase, again seeking responses from those participants involved in the durable phase of the transaction. Here, the protocol permits the following values: prepare, rollback, and commit. The responses are Prepared, ReadOnly, Aborted, and Committed. The definition of these terms match those expected from commonsense use of English; so I will not waste space in enumerating the terms.

WS-AtomicTransaction is essentially a policy assertion leveraging WS-Policy and WS-Policy Attachment as a framework and grammar for expressing its capabilities and requirements. The policy assertion uses the /wsat:ATAssertion element, which specifies that an atomic transaction coordination context must be flowed in the requester's message. It has one predefined attribute: /wsat:ATAssertion/@ wsp:Optional = "true", which is a compact notation for two policy options: one with and one without the assertion.

Where present, the assertion has the subject WSPOLICYATTACH, using wsdl:binding/wsdl:operation. You cannot use a wsdl:portType as a WS-AtomicTransaction specifies concrete behavior, and the port type is an abstract construct.

AtomicTransaction faults must include http://docs.oasis-open. org/ws-tx/wsat/2006/06/fault as the fault action URI. As with WS-ReliableMessaging, faults must have a code and subcode but may or may not have a reason or use detail, with the code set to either Sender or Receiver.

Because WS-AutomicTransaction leverages WS-Coordination for its communications, it also leverages the same security controls and has the same concerns. As it is a single transaction, there is no need to use WS-ReliableMessaging like controls on its messages.

Ws-BusinessActivity (http://docs.oasis-open.org/ws-tx/wstx-wsba-1.2-spec-os.pdf) is basically an extension of WS-AtomicTransaction, essentially allowing the stringing together of multiple transactions in a workflow, allowing for a MixedOutcome and a response to this. Also, the BusinessActivity may not be the automated response of an application or service but may involve human action and there may be significant time involved between the initiation of a transaction and its completion. This allows use in manufacturing and other assembly activities.

WS-BusinessActivity models business functions into a hierarchical model with parent tasks and subordinate tasks. Subordinate task results may or may not be rolled up into the results of the parent tasks, and faults that occur in child processes may or may not impact the processing of other subordinate tasks or the parent task. Subordinate tasks may terminate without necessarily impacting other subordinate tasks or parent processes. Tasks may provide outcome without waiting to be queried, and tasks may be tentative in nature, so that preliminary outcomes may be made available which may be changed as the task is completed properly. This is rather important when tasks are dependent upon other tasks that are long-running.

Applications using this protocol have the flexibility to have processes in various states and even have processes dependent upon other incomplete processes advance using incomplete results. Valid coordinator states include Completed, Fail, Compensated, Closed, Canceled, Exist, and CanNotComplete. The participant will accept or transmit these states: Close, Cancel, Compenstate, Failed, Exited, and NotCompleted. The coordinator and the participant may use either GetStatus or Status to query each other.

There is a modification to this protocol that offloads onto the coordinator the responsibility of tracking tasks and their I/O so that the participants all query the coordinator, not each other. This protocol is called the BusinessAgreementWithCoorinatorCompletion protocol, and participants that register for this protocol must use http://docs. oasis-open.org/ws-tx/wsba/2006/06/CoordinatorCompletion

The specification recommends using the mechanisms described in WS-Security to secure the messages between participants and the coordinator in a context defined by WS-Trust and WS-SecureConversation. Specifically, messages should be signed, and signing keys should be protected.

## 3.5 SAML

Much like WS-Federation, SAML is where application, identity, and security architectures collide. SAML provides a mechanism for seamless authentication and authorization between divergent applications, organizations, and identity communities. Unlike WS-Federation, SAML is self-contained; there are no external objects upon which it depends for success. Also, unlike WS-Federation, the use of SAML guarantees the use of a secure token, where WS-Federation itself must rely upon policy set in WS-Policy and WS-Trust to define the tokens that are allowed and the required settings.

SAML provides the authentication service for web services-based SOA. It is not mandatory and not supported by all platforms and vendors. There are major compatibility issues between the different versions of SAML, where products that support SAML 2.0 will not likely also support SAML 1.1. SAML is commonly used to extend trust boundaries, allowing for federated identity. SAML assertions will contain information necessary to provide both authentication and authorization.

SAML, originally designed for SSO between applications, permits identity federation, wherein multiple companies are engaged in the management of a credential, its authorization, and authentication to services.

It was developed due to limitations in other tokens such as cookies to carry sufficient information securely to establish trust between two organizations. The basic use case is that an identity provider presents to the service provider that the identity provider knows and trusts the credentials that were passed to it by the authenticator and will ensure that the credential holder has the right to use the service provider.

A good example of this use case would be a travel reservation system that provides to the airline the frequent flyer information it collected, to the rental car company the membership and license information it collected, and to the hotel, the credit card information needed to reserve a room. In this example, the individual may not have even authenticated to the travel reservation system but only collected that information as part of its handling of a specific reservation by a guest user of the application. Because all of the above information represented to the service providers by the travel reservation system acting as the identity provider will be later validated upon check-in to each specific identity consumer, the risk of trusting this unauthenticated security assertion is minimal.

Now, I have used some technical terms in my example that I need to more precisely define and then illustrate how they work. Specifically, "assertions," "identity provider," and "service provider" are specific terms of the SAML specification with particular meanings that do not always map to expectations. Before I get into that, let us take a look at the SAML document itself. As with WS-Security, I am going to dive into the particulars of the schema so that a security architect who is inexperienced with SOAs may become exposed to these details in the context of a discourse on architecture instead of implementation.

### 3.5.1 Assertions

SAML is primarily a specialized XML document that contains assertions. An assertion is a package of data that supplies one or more statements made regarding a credential by the system, which authenticated it, called an SAML authority or asserting party. The SAML specification defines three different types of assertion statements:

> Authentication: The subject of the assertion was authenticated by a specific means at a particular time. An authentication is performed by an identity provider, which is in charge of authenticating credentials and keeping track of other information about them. Older versions of the SAML standard may use the term "authentication authority" instead of "identity provider," which was introduced in version 2.0. The identity provider may do other things besides authentication; so it is more precise to discuss this as an identity service provider; however, identity provider is the technical name for the authenticator in the SAML specification, with service provider the specific and technical name of the authorization agent. As these are often components of the same application, it is not incorrect to discuss them as identity service providers.
>
> Attribute: The subject of the SAML assertion is associated with attributes most often provided by the identity provider. These may or may not be associated with subsequent authorizations.
>
> Authorization decision: The assertion may contain at least one and perhaps more records of authorizations or rejections of authorization requests by the identity provider. These are sent by the identity provider to be used by downstream services that trust the SAML authority to properly authenticate for the distributed application.

Like with much XML, the basic structure of an assertion is generic, governed by the schema. The specifics within an assertion provide the information needed for the applications that depend upon the assertions and will vary somewhat between organizations. All assertions are usually made regarding a subject, represented by the <Subject> element, but this is optional, and other elements may be used.

The basic structure of an assertion for SAML 2.0 is:

```
<saml:sssertion xmime:saml = "urnoasis:names:tc:SAML:2.0
:assertion"
  Version = "2.0"
  IssueInstant = "2013-01-18T18:00:00Z">
<saml:Issuer>
  www.somecompany.com
  <saml:Issuer>
  <saml:Subject>>
    <saml:NameID Format = "urn:oasis:namestc:SAML:1.1:nam
    eid-format:emailAddress">
    J.doe@somecompany.com
  </saml:NameID>
  </saml:Subject?
<saml:AuthnStatement
  AuthnInstant = "2013-01-18T18:00:00Z" SessionIndex =
  "4733749595874"">
  <saml:AuthnContext>
    <saml:AuthnContextClassRef>
      urn:oasis:names:tc:SAML:2.0:ac:classes:PasswordPr
      otectedTransport
    </saml:AuthnContextClassRef>
  </Saml:AuthnStatement>
</saml:Assertion>
```

This assertion shows that the person holding the email address of j.doe@somecompany.com was authenticated at 2013-01-18T18:00:00Z by a service provider using a password-protected mechanism.

The SAML schema provides the standard syntax for many basic elements, which like most XML standards, may be used but are not mandated. The first is the Name Identifier. Name Identifiers allow many different organizations to refer to the same credential holders with different elements. As two or more organizations may actually use the same Name Identifier to refer to entirely different credentials, SAML provides the concept of name qualifiers to allow the same identifier to be used differently by different organizations.

Name Identifiers consist of the following element types:

BaseID: A BaseID is an extension which allows applications to add new kinds of identifiers. It has a complex type, called a BaseIDAbtractType, which as the name suggests is abstract and therefore usable only as the base of a derived type. It includes the attributes NameQualifier, which is an optional attribute, which provides a mechanism to federate identifiers from various different credential stores without collisions and SPNameQualifier, which is an optional attribute which further qualifies an identifier with the name of a service provider or its affiliate.

NameIDType: This complex type is used when an element serves to represent an entity by a string-valued name. This type underlies both the NameID and the issuer elements and is more restricted than the BaseID element. It provides a number of optional attributes. NameQualifier is an optional attribute used to federate names from different credential stores without collision. SPNameQualifier is an optional attribute used to federate names on the basis of their relying party or parties. Format is an optional URI reference used to represent the classification of string-based identifiers. If no Format attribute is provided, unlike other attributes, there is a default Format value of:
Urn:oasis:names:tc:SAML:1.0;nameid-format:unspecified

SSProvidedID is an optional attribute that provides the name used by the service provider or affiliation for the entity in question. This allows the integration of SAML with existing naming structures.

NameID: The NameID element is of type NameIDType, and is used in `<Subject>` and `<SubjectConfirmation>` elements. It is often used as one of the components of the credential.

EncryptedID: The EncryptedID element is of the EncryptedElementType type and holds the content of an unencrypted identifier element, encrypted as per the XML Encryption specification. This element contains the following elements:

<Xenc:EncryptedData> is a required element containing the encrypted content and associated encryption details as mandated by XMLEnc. The Type attribute should be present, and if present must be http://www.w3.org/2001/04/xmlenc#Element. The content must contain an element that has the type of NameIDType or AssertionType or a type that is derived from BaseIDAbstractType, NameIDType, or AssertionType.

<Xenc:EncryptedKey> contains the wrapped decryption key as defined by XMLEnc. Where present, each wrapped key should include a Recipient attribute that specifies the entity, which is authorized to decrypt the content. This should be the URI of the recipient. The ciphertext must be unique. Where the entire assertion is encrypted, the <Subject> element supplies the identifier of the subject of the assertion.

The following extract from the schema shows the <EncryptedID element and the EncryptedElementType complex type:

```
<complexType name = "EncryptedElementType">
<sequence>
<element ref = "xenc:EncryptedData"/>
<element ref = "xenc:EncryptedKey" minOccurs = "0"
maxOccurs = "unbounded"/>
</sequence>
</complexType>
<element name = "EncryptedID" type =
"saml:EncryptedElementType"/>
```

Issuer: The <Issuer> element, along with the complex type NameIDType, provides information about the issuer of the SAML assertion. This element uses a string to convey the issuer's name and permits descriptive data. Unlike most elements of this type, if no format is provided with the element, then the value of urn:oasis:names:tc:SAML:2.0:nameid-format:entity is in effect. The following extract from the schema shows the definition of the element:

```
<element name = "Issuer" type = "saml:NameIDType"/>
```

There are also elements which are specific to assertions either that they make or as references to assertions already made.

The `<AssertionIDRef>` element makes such a reference using a unique identifier. The identity of the authority is not identified as part of the reference. The schema extract which shows how it is defined is:

```
<element name = "AssertionIDRef" type = "NCName"/>
```

More useful, especially in Web 2.0 applications is the `<AssertionURIRef>` element that refers to the assertion using a URI as its reference. Unlike the `<AssertionIDRef>` element, the `<AssertionURIRef>` can actually be used to retrieve the corresponding assertion if not present. The following schema extract shows how it is defined:

```
<element name = "AssertionURIRef" type = "anyURI"/>
```

The last two elements associated with assertions are the `<Assertion>` and `<EncryptedAssertion>` elements. The `<Assertion>` element is a complex AssertionType type, which specifies the basic information common to all assertions. It includes the following elements and attributes:

Version is a required attribute. Most modern SAML assertions will have the value of "2.0", but may be "1.1" or "1.0".

ID is of type xs:ID and must follow the requirements specified for identifier uniqueness. This is a required attribute.

IssueInstant is a required attribute, which shows the time of issue in UTC. Because this is in UTC, it is a good practice where SAML assertions are used in SOA to have all the logs written with UTC timestamps.

Assertions must have the `<Issuer>` element, which is the specific SAML authority making the statements in the assertion. This should be unambiguous but does not need to be the signer of the assertion.

The `<ds:Signature>` element is an optional element used to protect the integrity and authenticate the identity of the issuer of the assertion.

While the `<Subject>` element is optional, it is most often present as it provides the subject of the statements of the assertion.

Where the `<Conditions>` element is present, it defines conditions necessary to assure the validity of the assertion or of its use.

Where the `<Advice>` element is present, it may be used in processing the assertion under certain conditions but may be ignored.

As an alternative to the `<Subject>` element, any one of the following statement elements may be used: `<Statement>`, `<AuthnStatement>`, `<AuthzDecisionStatement>`, or `<AttributeStatement>`.

The `<EncryptedAssertion>` element represents the assertion but the contents are encrypted. It contains the following elements: `<xenc:EncryptedData>`, which is required and contains the encrypted content and details as well as the `<xenc:EncryptedKey>` element, which is optional. Where present, it will contain the Recipient attribute, which should be the URI of the authorized recipient.

Much of the security of the SAML assertion depends on the elements and attributes in the subject. The `<Subject>`, as an element, should have an identifier `<BaseID>` with either `<NameID>` or `<EncryptedID>` and possibly a `<SubjectConfirmation>` element which contains information which permits the confirmation of the subject. Where present, this will contain a Method attribute containing a protocol or other mechanism for validation. It is common to have a URI as the reference or the use of `<ds:KeyInfo>`.

The element `<SubjectConfirmationData>` has the SubjectConfirmationDataType as a complex type with the following optional attributes: NotBefore, NotOnOrAfter, Recipient, InResponseTo, Address, or Arbitrary attributes or elements.

The KeyInforConfirmationDataType, which is a complex type, constrains the `<SubjectConfirmationData>` to contain just one or more `<ds:KeyInfo>` elements. Different keys may be used to confirm the subject with different parties.

Conditions elements may be used to place additional restrictions on the use or validity of SAML assertions. `<Conditions>` may contain elements and attributes such as NotBefore, NotOnOrAfter, `<Condition>`, `<AudienceRestriction>`, `<OneTimeUse>`, and/or `<ProxyRestriction>`. If present, they are considered using the following rules of order:

> If no subelements or attributes are supplied by a `<Conditions>` element, then the assertion is considered valid with respect to any conditions.
>
> If any element or attribute of a `<Conditions>` element is found to be invalid, the entire assertion is invalid.
>
> If any element of the attribute of a `<Conditions>` element cannot be evaluated for any reason, then the assertion cannot be validated and is considered to be indeterminate.

The `<Conditions>` element may serve as an extension point for new conditions. The ConditionAbstractType is a complex type but can be used only as the basis of a derived type.

As SAML assertions may be viewed by many service-based applications as part of the distributed architecture, there may be information within the assertion that should be restricted to a particular application or company. The `<AudienceRestriction>` and `<Audience>` elements may be used to indicate this, but these are voluntary and cannot be enforced. The use of encryption and multiple keys guarantees that only the desired destination can inspect the sensitive parts of an assertion.

The `<OneTimeUse>` element is particular to each use of the assertion. When an assertion is received with this element, the application should check with the SAML authority to verify if the assertion has already been used, and if so, either request a fresh assertion or deny access depending upon business requirements.

The `<AuthnContext>` element allows an organization to provide to consumer organizations details of the context of the authentication that can then be used to evaluate the risk of trusting the authentication for their service and the data therein.

While the <Authncontext> element would be found within the assertions part of the SAML document, it is complex enough; so I will discuss it in a subsequent section. It tends to be used only by organizations with a high concern for security.

The <Attribute> element and the <AttributeStatement> element are both optional elements that can be used to provide unspecified application-specific information. Where confidentiality is required, the <EncryptedAttribute> element can be used instead. The actual value of the attribute would be conveyed in the <AttributeValue> element, which is of xs:anyType type, which allows any well-formed XML to be the content.

The <AuthzDecisionStatement> is an orphaned element that will not see further development as the rest of the standard grows. This is used to capture the results of decisions made by requests for access by the assertion. The specific resource for which access is requested is captured as a URI by the relying party.

Related is the DecisionType, which defines the possible values to be reported as the status of an authorization decision statement. The values of Permit, Deny, and Indeterminate are returned as required.

The <Action> element is restricted to providing the name of an action on the specific resource for which permission is sought. It uses the Namespace attribute to refer to the resource.

The final element found in SAML assertions is the <Evidence> element. It has the EvidenceType complex type and is used to convey one or more assertions or references used in issuing authorization decisions. This is a critical element for logging, forensics, and various troubleshooting needs. It can contain one or more of these elements: <AssertionIDRef>, <AssertionURIRef>, <Assertion>, and/or <Encrypted Assertion>.

The schema, as provided by www.w3.org, as with all other XML documents, is downloaded as part of the processing of the authentication, enforcing version compliance. You will note that there are elements within this assertion that are compliant with both versions 1.1 and 2.0 of SAML.

Backward compatibility against all versions of the SAML standard was not a goal of version 2.0, and you will need to verify which version(s) of SAML are supported by your identity provider. I will take up the differences in a subsequent section, but I highly recommend using SAML 2.0 wherever there is a choice.

### 3.5.2 Protocol

SAML protocol messages can be exchanged using a variety of transport protocols. SAML is encoded in XML as a set of request–response pairs. These are defined as follows:

These request and response messages are derived from common XML types. The requester sends an element derived from the RequestAbstractType to an SAML responder, which responds with an element conforming to the StatusResponseType. Under certain circumstances, an SAML response may be generated and sent without the responder having received a request. Common protocol actions are:

- Returning a requested assertion
- Performing authentication
- Registering a name
- Terminating a name registration
- Retrieving a protocol message that has been requested
- Performing a near-simultaneous logout
- Providing a Name Identifier mapping

Elements and types in the SAML protocol space are written with the samlp: prefix, with those used in assertions written with the saml: prefix.

The RequestAbstractType is a complex type, which has many attributes and elements as possible values.

ID is a required attribute, of type xs:ID and must be unique. This value must be in both the request and the response and must match.

Version is another required attribute. Mostly modern applications support SAML 2.0.

IssueInstant is a required attribute that records the time of the request in UTC.

Destination is an optional attribute containing a URI indicating the address to which the request has been sent. It is thought to be a useful means to prevent malicious forwarding. If present, the recipient must validate that this matches the destination. In practice, if an SAML assertion is intercepted by a man-in-the-middle attack, it is a trivial matter to change this as there is no signing of the value within the document; so the use of this presumes that a man-in-the-middle attack cannot happen, which is no longer a viable assumption.

Consent is an optional attribute indicating under what conditions consent has been obtained in the sending of the request. If no value is provided, this is assumed to be "unspecified" by default. Unfortunately, where Consent has been populated with data, <ds:Signature> is optional. In practice, it should be mandatory.

<saml:Issuer> is an optional element indicating the element that generated the request method.

<ds:Signature> is regrettably an optional element. It authenticates the requester and provides message integrity against a man-in-the-middle attack. No modern implementation of SAML can be truly secure unless this is present and properly validated by the recipient.

<Extensions> is an optional element containing extensions mutually agreed upon by the sending and recipient parties.

The StatusReponseType is a complex type with mandatory and optional elements and attributes.

ID is a required attribute, in the type of xs:ID and must not only be unique but also match the value provided in the request.

InResponseTo is an optional attribute that is a reference to the identifier of the request. It must be present when the document is sent in response to an SAML request, and it must match the ID of the request. This is a means to identify when an SAML protocol is sent as a response to a request or under other circumstances.

Version, IssueInstant, Destination, Consent, <saml:Issuer>, <ds:Signature>, and <Extensions> have much the same properties in the response as they do in the request.

<Status> is a required element containing the status of the corresponding request. The <Status> element contains the following elements:

<StatusCode>, a required code representing the status of the activity carried out. It has the attribute Value, which is a required value containing a URI reference of:
urn:oasis:names:tc:SAML:2.0:status:Success
The meaning of this response is self-evident
urn:oasis:names:tc:SAML:2.0:status:Requester

There was an error on the part of the requester
urn:oasis:names:tc:SAML:2.0:status:Responder

There was an error on the part of the responder
urn:oasis:names:tc:SAML:2.0:status:VersionMismatch

The version of the request message is not supported

The `<StatusCode>` may have a secondary `<StatusCode>` element embedded within it, with more specific details. The available options are (for the most part, the message is self-explanatory):

urn:oasis:names:tc:SAML:2.0:status:VersionMismatch
urn:oasis:names:tc:SAML:2.0:status:AuthnFailed
urn:oasis:names:tc:SAML:2.0:status:InvalidAttrNameOrValue
urn:oasis:names:tc:SAML:2.0:status:InvalidNameIDPolicy
urn:oasis:names:tc:SAML:2.0:status:NoAuthnContext
urn:oasis:names:tc:SAML:2.0:status:NoAvailableIDP
urn:oasis:names:tc:SAML:2.0:status:NoPassive
urn:oasis:names:tc:SAML:2.0:status:NoSupportedIDP
urn:oasis:names:tc:SAML:2.0:status:PartialLogout
urn:oasis:names:tc:SAML:2.0:status:ProxyCountExceeded
urn:oasis:names:tc:SAML:2.0:status:RequestDenied
urn:oasis:names:tc:SAML:2.0:status:RequestUnsupported
urn:oasis:names:tc:SAML:2.0:status:RequestVersionDeprecated
urn:oasis:names:tc:SAML:2.0:status:RequestVersion
TooHigh
urn:oasis:names:tc:SAML:2.0:status:RequestVersionTooLow
urn:oasis:names:tc:SAML:2.0:status:ResourceNotRecognized
urn:oasis:names:tc:SAML:2.0:status:TooManyResponses
urn:oasis:names:tc:SAML:2.0:status:UnknownAttrProfile
urn:oasis:names:tc:SAML:2.0:status:UnknownPrincipal
urn:oasis:names:tc:SAML:2.0:status:UnsupportedBinding

`<StatusMessage>`, an optional message returned to the requester.

`<StatusDetail>`, an optional attribute containing implementation specific details.

*3.5.2.1 Assertion Query and Request Protocol*   A set of queries by which existing SAML assertions may be obtained, these may be on the basis of a reference, subject, or statement type.

The `<SubjectQuery>` element is an extension point, which allows new SAML queries to be defined that specify a particular SAML subject. The associated type, SubjectQueryAbstractType, is an abstract type and therefore suitable only as the basis of a derived type. It does, however, add the `<saml:Subject>` element to the related RequestAbstractType.

The Assertion Query and Request Protocol allows the application to request additional assertions by subject and statement type or reference. The most useful element of this protocol is the `<AssertionIDRequest element>` which uses the `<saml:AssertionIDRef>` element to request a specific assertion by its defined identifier, as this is a very precise way to get exactly the assertion the application requires.

The `<SubjectQuery>` element can be used to query by subject where the precise ID is not known. Its SubjectQueryAbstractType is a complex and abstract type that permits new SAML queries to be constructed.

The `<AuthnQuery>` can be used to inquire as to what assertions regarding authentication have been made regarding the specified subject. It must not be used to request a new authentication. The element's type is AuthnQueryType which is an extension of SubjectQueryAbsractType and provides the following elements and attributes:

SessionIndex is an optional attribute that specifies a filter for possible responses. If this is present in the query, then one `<AuthnStatement>` element in the returned assertions must contain a SessionIndex attribute that matches that in the query.

`<RequestedAuthnContext>` is an optional element, which allows you to specify the authentication context you are seeking additional assertions on. If this is in the query, then at least one `<AuthnStatement>` in the returned response must contain an `<AuthnContext>` element that satisfies the element in the query. The RequestedAuthnContextType is a complex type that defines the following elements and attributes:

```
<saml:AutnnContextClassRef>
<saml:AutnnContextDeclRef>
```

Comparison:    `<saml:AuthnContextClassRef>`    and `<saml:AuthnContextDeclRef>`    are    both    optional elements in the query and specify one or more URI references either regarding the successful or declined authentication. Comparison is an optional attribute that specifies the comparison method used to evaluate the context and may be "exact", "minimum", "maximum", or "better" with a default value of "exact".

The `<AttributeQuery>` element is used to query for specified attributes regarding the subject of the assertion. It is of type AttributeQueryType, which extends SubjectQueryAbstractType with the element `<saml:Attribute>`.

The `<AuthzDecisionQuery>` is used to get the answer for the query, should the requested actions be permitted for the subject of this assertion considering the evidence presented in the query. This is an orphaned feature of SAML 2.0, with no further development planned.

The final element in the Assertion Query and Request Protocol is the `<Response>` element. This has the complex type ResponseType that extends StatusResponseType, adding the elements:

```
<saml:Assertion>
<saml:EncryptedAssertion>
```

*3.5.2.2 Authentication Request Protocol* This protocol defines the `<AuthnRequest>` message that causes a `<Response>` to be returned containing one or more assertions relevant to the credential. This is usually entered by a service provider with the identity provider returning the `<Response>`.

This permits a principle to obtain assertions containing authentication statements to establish a security context. An SAML authority that accepts this protocol is also termed an identity provider.

The contents of the returned assertions depend upon the context of the query and the exact means by which the credential holder authenticates to the identity provider. In other words, you will not find information on password acceptance in an assertion when the credential used was an x509v3 certificate.

The authentication request protocol may reference any of the these potential credential holders, many of which might be the same acting principle:

- Requester
- Requested subject
- Attesting entity
- Relying party
- Identity provider

The `<AuthnRequst>` element is used to request from the identity provider an assertion containing an authentication statement. A key thing to consider is that there is no need for the requester of the assertion to be the same as the presenter of the request. The requester may be a relying party, especially in a complex distributed service-oriented application.

It is very important that the `<AuthnRequest>` be signed or otherwise authenticated. Signing this is the best means to prevent common attacks against authentication, but it is only truly effective if the recipient application actually verifies the signature.

`<AuthnRequest>` has the complex type AuthnRequestType, which is an extension of RequestAbstractType. While the elements and attributes it adds may be in principle optional, they may be required by a specific implementation. These are:

```
<saml:Subject>
<NameIDPolicy>
<saml:Conditions>
<RequestedAuthnContext>
<Scoping>
ForceAuthn
IsPassive
AssertionConsumerServiceIndex
AssertionConsumerServiceURI
ProtocolBinding
AttributeConsumingServiceIndex
ProviderName
```

The `<NameID>` policy element contains the processed Name Identifier from the subject of assertions coming from an `<AuthnRequst>`.

Its NameIDPolicyType is a complex type that defines the following optional attributes:

Format, which specifies the URI reference to the Name Identifier format and references the specification of the format.

SPNameQualifier specifies that the assertions subject's identifier is to be provided in the namespace of a service provider other than the requester.

AllowCreate is a boolean value used to indicate if the identity provider is permitted to create a new identifier to represent the credential holder. By default, this is false. When this is used, if the content is not understood by the identity provider, the response must contain an error `<Status>`. It is a good practice to also have it include at least one second-level `<StatusCode>`. As with all security and authentication objects, the more details provided for logging and debugging, the better.

The `<Scoping>` element specifies those identity providers trusted by the requester to authenticate the credential as presented in the request. This is often presented with specific context to permit better validation. Its type is a complex type called ScopingType and has just two elements and an attribute.

`<RequesterID>` identifies (where present) the group of requesting entities upon whose behalf the requester is acting.

`<IDPList>` is a list of identity providers with associated information that the requester deems acceptable to respond to the request. It has a type of IDPListType, which is a complex type defining the elements of `<IDPEntry>` which is information about a single identity provider, and `<GetComplete>` which is a URI reference that can be used to retrieve the complete list of providers if the items listed in `<IDPList>` are not complete. `<IDPEntry>` has three attributes, ProviderID, Name, and Loc that contain the unique identifier of the provider (required), a human readable name of the identity provider, and a URI reference of the location of a profile-specific endpoint of the authentication request protocol.

ProxyCount specifies the number of proxies permitted between the requestor and the provider and may be set to 0 to indicate that no proxying is permitted.

*3.5.2.3 Artifact Resolution Protocol*   This provides the means to obtain assertions through a reference called an artifact. This is often used when, for whatever reason, there is a size limit on the data that can be transported. Instead of sending an SAML message, a reference is sent as an artifact using the binding. This artifact must provide a mechanism that can be used to determine who sent it and must be used only once. The underlying message may need additional protections such as mutual authentication, and so on, from the protocol binding used to resolve the artifact.

The `<ArtifactResolve>` element is used to request that the SAML protocol message be returned as an artifact. The original transmission is governed by the specific protocol binding that is being used. We will explore SAML bindings at length later. The `<ArtifactResolve>` element should be signed, which will protect the integrity of the artifact.

The `<ArtifactResolve>` element is used in a message to request the `<ArtifactResponse>` element. `<ArtifactResolve>` has the complex type ArtifactResolveType that extends the RequestAbstractType and adds the required element, `<Artifact>`

The `<Artifact>` element will be discussed more in the section on SAMLBind.

Like the `<ArtifactResolve>` element, the `<ArtifactResponse>` should be signed. `<ArtifactResponse>` has the complex type ArtifactResponseType that extends the StatusResponseType and adds the optional wildcard element that must match the SAML protocol message being returned.

*3.5.2.4 Name Identifier Management Protocol*   This provides the means to change the value or format of the name of the credential holder. This can be sent by either the service provider or identity provider. This can also be used to terminate the association between the credential and either the identity provider or service provider. All of this is done with a properly formatted `<ManageNameIDRequest>`. This protocol is generally not used for temporary credentials but for those credentials which need to be managed on a long-term basis.

The `<ManageNameIDRequest>` element has the complex type ManageNameIDRequestType that extends the RequestAbstractType adding the following elements:

```
<saml:NameID>
<saml:EncryptedID>
<NewID>
<NewEncryptedID>
<Terminate>
```

The message must have either the `<saml:NameID>` or `<saml:EncryptedID>` element and use either "New" or `<Terminate>` to call the required action on the part of the identity provider.

The `<ManageNameIDResponse>` element must match the `<ManageNameIDRequest>`. It is of StatusReponseType, adding no additional elements or attributes to the type. Both the Request and the Response should be signed to protect their integrity.

*3.5.2.5 Single-Logout Protocol*   This protocol performs a mostly synchronous logout of all sessions associated with the credential. This can be initiated by the credential holder (the principle), by session timeout, or application logic. This can also be initiated by any of the service providers that the credential holder is connected to. In either event, the provider or the principle issues a `<LogoutRequest>` message. The `<LogoutRequest>` element has the complex type of LogoutRequestType, which extends RequestAbstractType.

This type provides the `<saml:NameID>` or `<saml:EncryptedNameID>` or `<saml:BaseID>` element as well as optional `<NotOnOrAfter>` with a date timestamp as a value and `<Reason>` as another optional (but highly recommended) element. Whichever ID element is used, it must match that of the principle as understood by the service provider. It may also contain the `<SessionIndex>` element that must match the index value of the current ongoing session.

When a message containing a single logout request is received by a service provider, it must be answered by a `<LogoutResponse>` message.

This will be of <StatusReponseType> with no additional content specified. The service provider must also authenticate the request, to prevent a denial-of-service attack from succeeding. It is for this reason that it is best if both the request and response are signed. All sessions open with the service provider must be invalidated, and any messages that arrive after the <LogoutRequest> message must also be invalidated, unless they arrive after the <NotOnOrAfter> date/timestamp which expires the logout. Failure to send such a value could result in an inability to reauthenticate the principle for a defined period of time. If the service provider is unable to invalidate the session with all known sessions, then this must be indicated in the <LogoutResponse> status.

*3.5.2.6 Name Identifier Mapping Protocol*   This protocol provides a mechanism to enable linking between credentials, mostly used in identity federation. It allows service providers who do not share credentials to use the same assertions to provide authentication and authorization to resources. The mapped identifier in the MNameIDMappingRequest> should be encrypted using the <saml:EncryptedID> element, but both <saml:BaseID> and <saml:NameID> are supported for those organizations that care less about security of their authentication framework than the convenience offered by an SSO into multiple applications.

Not only is one of <saml:EncryptedID> or <saml:BaseID> or <saml:NameID> required in the use of this protocol, but the <NameIDPolicy> element is also required. The <NameIDMappingRequest> element is of complex type NameIDMappingRequestType, and the associated <NameIDMappingResponse> element is of NameIDMappingResponseType, which is also a complex type. This latter response type extends the StatusResponseType, adding the element choice of either <saml:NameID> or <saml:EncryptedID>. Both messages should be signed.

### 3.5.3 *Authentication Context*

Context is an important consideration in the authentication of a token. Considerations for items external to the security token being presented may prevent the unauthorized use of a compromised credential. What context is considered by each company and service provider is a matter of some weight and must be carefully evaluated for the continued trade-off between the value it provides to the authentication decision and the time and effort involved in making that decision, along with any associated delay.

In essence, this allows the authenticating entity to make a risk-based decision regarding the authentication request. Considering that the SAML assertion is being trusted by third parties who often have no role in that authentication, the more information that can be conveyed about the process through which authentication happened, the better the analysis can be. This can also allow organizations using SAML to make many of the same decisions that users of WS-Federation can regarding the authorization of use, where the same token in one context allows access to x, but in a different context, allows access to both x and y.

To enable the capture and representation of this context, SAML provides a predefined schema that categorizes the information regarding context into:

Identification: The process and mechanism by which the association between the subject and identity is made.

Technical Protection: How the credential is kept secure.

Operational Protection: Procedures to ensure the identity is valid (audits, records review, etc).

Authentication Method: How the credential was authenticated, such as a password being provided or a certificate being validated.

Governing Agreements: The legal or contractual framework under which the authentication happened.

There are theoretically infinite combinations of these data elements to create context. However, the actual use cases are somewhat less infinite, and services in the same industry will most often have the same or similar requirements for trust. The standard allows for the development and use of Authentication Context Classes that are commonly in use. This allows for a greater degree of interoperability, simplifies implementation decisions, and allows a greater use of relying parties.

The following classes are predefined by the standard. Of course, this is readily extensible.

Internet Protocol: This is used when a provided IP address is part of the means to authenticate an individual or organization.

Internet Protocol Password: This is used when in addition to an IP address, a user name and password are required for authentication.

Kerberos: This is used when a Kerberos ticket is used to authenticate. As Kerberos is like SAML, and does not map directly back to a particular user, Kerberos presumes prior authentication, but there is no indication what that might have been.

MobileOneFactorUnregistered: This is used to indicate that a particular mobile device was authenticated. There is no implication that any particular user of that device was ever authenticated.

MobileTwoFactorUnregistered: This reflects the authentication of the device, and a secondary authentication, such as a PIN or password.

MobileOneFactorContract: This reflects a mobile device bound by a contract but with no secondary authentication of the user of that device.

MobileTwoFactorContract: This reflects a mobile device under contract that leveraged a second factor such as a PIN or biometric.

Password: This reflects the use of a password over an unprotected HTTP session. This particular context should be used only where security is not a business requirement.

PasswordProtectedTransport: This reflects the use of a password where the HTTP was protected by SSL, TLS, IP security (IPSec), or some other tunneling mechanism.

PreviousSession: This is used to indicate that the principle has used the service in the past but provides no information on how that prior session was authenticated.

Public Key–X.509: The principle was authenticated through a validation of an x.509v3 certificate as part of an x.509 PKI.

Public Key–PGP: The principle was authenticated through a PGP PKI.

Public Key–simple PKI (SPKI): The principle was authenticated by means of a digital signature as part of an SPKI infrastructure.

Public Key–XML digital signature: The principle was authenticated through the rules specifying the use of XML digital signatures. This is often used for application-to-application authentication decisions.

Smartcard: The principle presented a smartcard that was validated by the authentication authority.

SmartcardPKI: The principle presented a smartcard containing an x.509v3 certificate to the authentication authority. The certificate was unlocked with a PIN.

SoftwarePKI: The principle used an x.509v3 certificate stored within software. This is often used for application-to-application authentication.

Telephony: The principle used a fixed-line telephone number via a telephony protocol such as ADSL or ISDN.

Telephony ("nomadic"): The principle authenticated using a line number with a user suffix and a password. Often this is used to indicate the use of a phone card.

Telephony (personalized): The principle used a fixed-line telephone number with a user suffix transported over a telephony protocol such as ADSL or ISDN.

Telephony (authenticated): The principle used a line number, a user suffix, and a password.

Secure Remote Password: The principle used a Secure Remote Password as defined in RFC 2945.

SSL/TLS certificate-based client authentication: The principle authenticated by means of a client certificate over an SSL/TLS encrypted tunnel created by mutual authentication of the client and the server.

TimeSyncToken: This is used for principles that use one-time pads, such as RSA's SecureID, which are time-synchronized tokens.

Unspecified: This means "we authenticated the principle, but we're not going to tell you." This could only be used in environments where security is not a concern.

Obviously, the above elements only make up a portion of the Authentication method context. As the schema may be extended, other authentication tokens can be suggested, such as geolocation, shared secret, special cookie, and so on. There are means to authenticate a computer system for reuse for a secondary authentication and there are also means to authenticate through biometrics such as by using the computer's camera to do facial recognition. The possibilities are really endless.

### 3.5.4 Bindings

Mappings of SAML request or response messages to other communications protocols are called SAML protocol bindings. The binding should allow the transmission of any SAML message derived from samlp:RequestAbstractType or samlp:StatusResponseType. As with other parts of the SAML specification, the OASIS Security Services Technical Committee has recognized that the protocols that were available when SAML was developed are not the only protocols that SAML will need to work with; so they laid out guidelines for expansion. These are actually useful to survey before we begin to look at how SAML protocol bindings work as they form the basis of the existing protocol bindings.

Each binding must specify three pieces of identifying information, a URI that uniquely identifies the binding, contact information for the author, and references to prior work, which the new binding updates or replaces.

The binding must describe the interactions between the parties involved in the binding. Any restrictions on applications or use must be defined. The binding must identify the parties using it for each interaction, specifying any intermediaries, and the method of authentication that was used by each. The means to ensure message integrity must be specified as well as the means to ensure message confidentiality if required. Error states must be identified, especially regarding the handling of SAML. Security considerations must be documented, with a consideration of how threats to message integrity and confidentiality should be managed in the implementation of the binding. Lastly, but rather importantly, the binding must have documented support for protocol metadata. This metadata may be used to perform authorization decisions or other application processing regarding the SAML assertion or protocol.

By default, SAML requires that SSL or TLS be used and that the server authenticate itself to the client based upon the contents of the certificate. This provides some protection against man-in-the-middle attacks if the application checks not only the subject DN and subjectAltName, which are checked by default but also the signer's subject DN and subjectAltName, effectively walking the certificate chain. This should be compared to the known signer, which can be validated through other mechanisms, pre-establishing the authority, which was authorized by the business entity to sign its communications. As SAML assertions are often sent over many relays, SAML provides internal mechanisms for parties to authenticate with each other; however, this is optional. I would highly recommend that these are used, however, as an authentication token, which is not in and of itself reliable and is not a good foundation for ensuring that application use is limited to authorized individuals.

The most common SAML binding is to SOAP. As we have reviewed, SOAP has nothing in it natively to secure its messages or transports, so using it to send SAML is problematic, as to ensure that SAML is usable for its intended purpose, the binding must ensure reliability, integrity, and confidentiality, elements for which SOAP was not designed.

SAML must be enclosed with the SOAP body. As SAML does not use the SOAP encoding system, SAML messages can be sent without re-encoding. SAML is sent using a simple request–response model. A service requestor sends a SOAP message containing an SAML request to the SAML responder. There can only be one SAML request or response per message. The response must contain an SAML element or a SOAP Fault. The Fault must not be generated for items within the scope of SAML, such as the request not being authorized.

While the SAML assertion will be in the SOAP body, the requester or responder may add arbitrary headers to the SOAP message. While these may not be used to process the SAML assertion, they may be used for proper routing. As SAML processes that accept SAML over SOAP must also accept SAML over SOAP over HTTP, there may also be arbitrary HTTP headers defined by the service provider. SAML may also be sent over HTTP directly, and we will look at that later. One example of a typical HTTP header value when sending SAML over SOAP over HTTP is to set the Cache-Control header field to "no-cache, no-store" or set the Pragma header field to no-cache. This prevents proxies and other HTTP relays from storing a local copy of the assertion.

Where the SAML assertion is refused, the SAML responder should simply return a "403 Forbidden" response, and when access is granted, a simple "200 OK" message should be sent along with an `<samlp:Status>` element in the SAML response within the SOAP body.

Where the application architect wishes to use the reverse HTTP binding for SOAP (PAOS) to send SAML assertions, there is a pre-defined SAML binding to PAOS. This can allow a service provider to advertise the ability to act as a SOAP intermediary or responder to SAML requests. The PAOS binding has two message exchange patterns.

An HTTP requester sends an HTTP request to an SAML requester that responds with an HTTP response containing a SOAP envelope with an SAML request. Then the HTTP requester sends a request to the original SAML requester containing a SOAP envelope containing an SAML response. To facilitate this, the HTTP Accept Header field must indicate the ability to accept the application /vnd. paos+xml content type and the HTTP PAOS Header field must be present, specifying at least the version "urn:liberty:paos:2003-08." Much like with traditional SOAP bindings, SOAP messages containing SAML responses in their body must only contain the SAML message or assertion in the body. HTTP headers should also prevent the caching of SAML by using the Cache-Control and Pragma header fields.

Where it is necessary to bind SAML to HTTP redirects, the HTTP Redirect Binding provides a mechanism to transmit SAML within a URL parameter. To limit the size of the parameters, the architect should plan on encoding this information, especially if larger or more complex content is desired.

Due to the nature of the communication afforded by HTTP, RelayState data may be included with the SAML protocol message transmitted with this binding. However, the value must not exceed 80 bytes in length. As this can be tampered with, some sort of integrity protection should be implemented, but due to space constraints, signing the data is not a viable alternative. I would recommend, however, that in the absence of at least a checksum to be used to verify the information integrity the responder reject the message with a Fault. Where an SAML request is sent with RelayState data, the response must be with a protocol binding that supports a relay state mechanism, placing the same RelayState parameter in the response.

Where SAML is sent over HTTP, URL encoding techniques are used, as sent using the HTTP GET method. As there are many URL encodings, I recommend specifying the encoding mechanism in metadata. There is a predefined parameter of SAMLEncoding that should be used for this purpose. The entirety of the SAML message must be in the query string.

Where no query string encoding is specified, the DEFLATE encoding mechanism is understood to be used. Where used, the following procedure should be followed.

Any signature on the SAML protocol message must be removed. This does not include signatures with the SAML message itself, such as a signed assertion. The rest of the message is then compressed, base64-encoded with both line feeds and white space removed. This is then URL-encoded and added as a query string called SAMLRequest or SAMLResponse. Any RelayState data must also be URL-encoded and placed in a query string parameter called RelayState. If the original data was signed using an XML signature, a new signature must be attached.

As already noted, XML signatures cannot be URL-encoded. To use XML signature, there is a way around: Using the SigAlg query string parameter, identify the value of the algorithm as a URI. The signature is constructed from a concatenation of the RelayState (if using), SigAlg, and SAMLRequest or SAMLResponse depending upon if you are signing a request or a response. This can be constructed as SAML(Request/Response) = value&RelayState = value&Sig = value where the result is an octet string fed into the algorithm identified by the URI. The result must be encoded using base64 and provided as the query string parameter Signature.

To exchange SAML assertions using the HTTP binding, the client sends an HTTP request, using a GET. The SAML request is returned encoded into the response's Location header, with an HTTP status of either 303 or 302. The response may be immediate or may be delayed. The responder may choose to render a form to collect metadata. When the SAML response is returned, it should place it into the Location header, encoded with either a 302 or 303 code.

If the application or security architect wishes to use a POST instead of a GET, SAML supports an HTTP POST binding. This binding may be composed of an HTTP Redirect and the HTTP Artifact bindings to use two existing bindings instead of a new one, but the HTTP POST binding allows the SAML protocol message to be transmitted in the base64-encoded content of an HTML form. This is desirable when the business requirements specify that such requests must be authenticated. Considering that SAML is designed to authenticate an individual client to many target service providers, I highly recommend that the identity provider authenticate the client with other credentials and leverage this particular binding.

When using this binding, you may use a RelayState, but it must be placed in a hidden form control named RelayState within the same form as the rest of the SAML message. The SAML XML is form-encoded using the base64-encoding rules, with the results placed into a hidden field called either SAMLRequest or SAMLResponse depending upon the nature of the state. The action attribute of the form must be the recipient HTTP endpoint, with the method attribute being POST. Unlike HTTP Relay Binding, with this binding, the SAML message is delivered to the message recipient in an HTTP request and sent to the user agent in an HTTP response. In other words, the user agent sends the request to an SAML requester for the SAML request and the response is sent back to the user agent, who then submits the form to the SAML responder. The SAML responder may or may not request additional information, but once sufficient metadata has been collected, it sends the form back to the user agent targeted at the SAML requester. The SAML requester now responds back to the user agent with the SAML assertion.

As with the other bindings, you should use the Cache-Control and Pragma header fields to turn off caching. It is important to remember that SAML assertions are tokens used for authentication and authorization, but there is nothing in the binding process that authenticates the user agent. Consider the use of an x509v3 certificate, a one-time pad, or if nothing else a password to request the SAML assertion. Sign the message, placing the Destination XML attribute into the root of the protocol message. This attribute must contain the URL to which the sender has instructed the user agent to deliver the message. The recipient must verify that this matches. If nothing else, the transport for the request, issuance, and use of the SAML assertion should be over SSL/TLS encrypted tunnels.

SAML can also use the HTTP Artifact Binding to send the request and response by reference in an artifact. A separate binding such as the SAML SOAP binding (the usual case) or SAML HTTP Relay binding is used to exchange the artifact for the actual protocol. To resolve the artifact, a direct communication patch must exist between the SAML message sender and recipient in the reverse direction. If using SOAP, the receiver of the message and artifact must be able to send an `<samlp:ArtifactResolve>` request back to the artifact issuer, and state must be maintained while this request is pending. This has implications for environments using load balancers.

There are two ways to encode the artifact for the binding: place into a URL parameter called SAMLart or into an HTML form control into a hidden attribute called SAMLart, using GET or POST, respectively. The security professional may have a bias for the HTML form as this can be signed, providing protection for message integrity.

RelayState data may be included with an SAML artifact transmitted with this binding, but the value may not exceed 80 bytes and should be integrity-protected using any of the techniques mentioned for the HTTP Relay binding. The RelayState must be placed into a query string parameter called RelayState, or if using a form, into a hidden form control called RelayState.

If using a form, the action attribute of the form must be the recipient's HTTP endpoint for the protocol, with the method attribute set to POST.

The artifact itself is a short opaque string, with a mandatory two-byte artifact-type code and a two-byte index value specifying the endpoint for the artifact resolution service of the issuer. The SAML_ artifact itself is a base64-encoded transformation of the TypeCode, EndpointIndex, and RemainingArtifact. SAML artifacts should have a unique identifying URI. The SourceID component of the artifact can be constructed by taking a SHA-1 hash of the Identifying URI. Do not convert this to hexadecimal. The MessageHandle value is constructed from a cryptographically strong random number of at least 16 bytes in size, padded to a total length of 20 bytes.

The TypeCode for the SAML architect is 0x004. It is assumed that the destination site would maintain a matrix of SourceID values to indexed URL endpoints for the corresponding SAML responder. Those SourceID values must be unique, and there should be no way to derive MessageHandle if you do know the SourceID. When the SAML artifact is received, the receiver determines if the SourceID belongs to a known issuer, and the location of the SAML responder is obtained using the EndpointIndex before sending the SAML `<samlp:ArtifactResolve>` message.

When this binding is used, the request for and transmission of the artifact over the request/response of HTTP simply has the artifact reference as the message content. When the artifact is received, the recipient opens a direct exchange with the artifact issuer using the Artifact Resolution Protocol, usually over SOAP. HTTP is not an option for this step. Once the artifact has been retrieved, it is discarded and the SAML protocol message is resumed or completed. This binding can be used for either half or the entire SAML protocol exchange. If only used for half, then SAML HTTP Redirect or the SAML POST binding may be used for the other half.

The basic workflow is:

The user agent accesses a resource at the SAML requester and initiates a need for an SAML protocol exchange.

The SAML artifact is returned in an HTTP redirect or XHTML form control targeted at the SAML responder. If the application architect determines it is best to use an HTTP redirect, the artifact is returned encoded in the HTTP response's Location header, with a status of either 302 or 303.

The User agent goes to the SAML responder, using either the redirect or the form.

The SAML responder sends the `<ArtifactResolve>` to the SAML requester.

The SAML requester then responds with an `<ArtifactResponse>` containing the original SAML message.

The SAML responder then interacts with the user agent if it requires more information to complete the request.

The SAML artifact is returned to the user agent, targeted through either a redirect or a form directed at the SAML requester.

The SAML requester takes this and initiates an `<ArtifactResolve>` message to the SAML responder.

The SAML responder sends the `<ArtifactResponse>` to the SAML requester.

The SAML requester takes the `<ArtifactResponse>` and sends an HTTP response to the user agent, completing the SAML exchange.

As with other SAML bindings, the HTTP header should have both a Cache-Control and Pragma fields set properly not to cache the contents. All of the transmissions should be over SSL/TLS, as otherwise there is no protection of either message confidentiality or of integrity. While the artifact itself is sent over a direct communication, the rest is all indirect and subject to both interception and redirection attacks. The artifact issuer must authenticate the sender of any `<samlp:ArtifactResolve>` messages before returning the message or risk delivery of the artifact and the actual token to the wrong party. It need not be said that if nothing else, this authentication should be over an encrypted tunnel. Artifacts that do not resolve properly should be placed into a matrix of unallowed artifacts. These may be recycled at some point, depending upon the risk tolerance of the organization.

SAML URI Binding provides a protocol-independent means to request and respond to SAML requests. Unlike the other bindings discussed thus far, this binding is not a request/response flow, but rather supports the encapsulation of an `<samlp:AssertionIDRequest>` with a single `<saml:AssertionIDRef>` as the resolution of the URI. The result is an SAML assertion, though not a complete SAML protocol response.

These URLs must map to a specific SAML assertion; so the URI must be unique per assertion. If reused, then the same assertion will be retrieved or an error indicating the assertion is no longer available. This binding should only be used where the assertion provides no real security or where there are sufficient other controls in place to guarantee that the requester is trusted AND the contents cannot be modified in transit. In my recommendation, the only conditions that would enable such trust is a strong authentication of TLS using client-side certificates. The URI syntax is completely flexible, as long as within it there is a query string with a parameter named ID, which maps to the SAML assertion ID. The assertion may be returned as a MIME type of application/samlassertion+xml. This should be signed by the sender and should also be encrypted. Upon receipt, the signature should be validated.

As with the other protocol bindings, this protocol binding must be set to not be cached using the Cache-Control and Pragma header variables.

### 3.5.5 Profiles

Profiles define and restrict the use of SAML within an application or message. As examples, one kind of profile defines how SAML may be added to SOAP messages, designating how SAML errors should be reflected as SOAP Faults. Another kind of profile restricts the implementation of SAML, which is a rather flexible standard regarding the use of attribute naming. By restricting this use, a better assurance of interoperability may be achieved.

While the W3 OASIS consortium predefines a set of profiles, others may be submitted, allowing the standard to be extended so that the enhancements become a shared resource for the security community. Regardless of whether a profile is predefined or custom-defined, it needs to follow the guidelines given below:

- It must have a URI that uniquely identifies the profile, provide contact information regarding author, and reference any previous profile that this profile updates or references.
- It must describe the interactions and restrictions on interactions involved in the profile.
- It must identify the parties involved in each interaction.
- It must specify the method of authentication involved, if any, and the acceptable authentication type.
- It must specify the level of support for message integrity and the mechanism used to enforce it.

- It must identify any error states that can be anticipated, especially those regarding SAML assertions and messages.
- It must identify security considerations, threats, and countermeasures.
- It must identify SAML confirmation methods.
- It must identify SAML metadata used by the profile.

The confirmation method is actually one of the more important security features of SAML. It is used to convey that the request or message came from a system that is associated with the subject of the assertion within the context of a profile. There are three methods commonly used: holder of key, sender vouches, and bearer. Holder of key is considered to be the subject of the assertion by the asserting party. Bearer is considered to be the subject of the assertion but this may be subject to optional constraints such as date/time filters. With sender vouches, no information is available about the context of the assertion, and other means should be used to determine if the application should process the assertion further.

SAML is often used to provide SSO into multiple applications with a single set of credentials. There are a number of profiles that have been created to support this. The Web Browser SSO Profile allows for a web user who has been authenticated to one application to be trusted by other components of the distributed application as long as the user maintains the session with the browser that initiated that session.

The workflow involved is:

- An HTTP request is made to the service provider.
- The service provider determines identity provider.
- A request for authentication `<AuthnRequest>` is issued by the service provider to the identity provider.
- The identity provider either identifies or fails to identify the principle.
- The identity provider issues `<Response>` to the service provider.
- The service provider grants or denies access to the principle.

Another commonly used profile is the enhanced client or proxy client (ECP) profile. This is a profile wherein the system entity knows how to contact an appropriate identity provider and supports the SAMLbind or reverse SOAP binding.

The workflow involved is:

- The ECP issues HTTP request to the service provider.
- The service provider issues the `<AuthnRequest>` to the ECP.
- The ECP conveys the `<AuthnRequest>` to the identity provider.
- The identity provider identifies/fails to identify the principle.
- The identity provider issues `<Response>` to the ECP, targeted at the service provider.
- The ECP conveys the `<Response>` to the service provider.

Based upon the response, the service provider grants or denies access.

Of course, this is only truly reliable if the `<AuthnRequest>` is signed by a trusted signer. SOAP Headers should be integrity-protected, using either SOAP Message Security or by leveraging an SSL/TLS tunnel.

Discovering an appropriate identity provider can be a challenge. This is why the Identity Provider Discovery Profile was developed. This relies upon a cookie, which is written in a domain common between identity and service providers. This cookie is called the common domain cookie. The name of this cookie must be "_saml_ip", and must be formatted as one or more Base64-encoded URI values delimited by a space. The cookie must be set with a path prefix of "?", and the domain set to ".[common-domain']"; the cookie must be marked as secure.

As the end of the session for a distributed application is a key security control, the Single Logout Profile has been established to log out an account in all components of the distributed application. The workflow for this is as follows:

`<LogoutRequest>` issued by session participant to an identity provider.

Identity provider determines session participants.

`<LogoutRequest>` issued by identity provider to session participant/authority.

Session participant/authority issues `<LogoutResponse>` to identity provider.

Identity provider issues <LogoutResponse> to session participant.

As the logout request may use either a synchronous or asynchronous binding, there is a workflow for both use cases. In the case that the session participant uses an asynchronous binding, such as HTTP redirect or artifact binding using SAMLBind, the identity provider may use either an asynchronous or synchronous method to communicate the logout message, but an asynchronous method is preferred because it provides the best chance of successfully communicating the logout to other session participants.

If a synchronous binding such as the SOAP binding using SAMLBind is used, then the identity provider should propagate the logout messages using a synchronous binding. The requesters must authenticate themselves.

### 3.5.6 Metadata

SAML 2.0 added support for metadata, with the idea that it would be used to provide data regarding the role of the service provider and its profile. This allows the dynamic exchange of metadata between organizations in a standardized way. Each role is described by an element of the base type of RoleDescriptor, which is in turn collected into the <EntityDescriptor> container element. Where a service provider wishes to document its relationship with other organizations, it can use the <AffiliationDescriptor> element. All metadata uses the urn:oasis:names:tc:SAML:2.0:metadata namespace, using the common namespace prefix of md:.

The metadata specification also defines a number of simple and complex types it uses to define metadata elements and attributes. The first of these types is the entityITType, which is used to represent an entity ID, but restricts the URI to 1024 characters. As with all ID, this value must be unique across all entities which interact, and specifically refer to an entity.

The EndpointType allows the provider to convey the Binding, Location, and, if desired, ResponseLocation for the entity. Binding and Location are mandatory, though the format of Location depends upon which Binding is supported. Each binding is assigned a URI to identify it. ResponseLocation is used to specify other endpoints to be used in the protocol exchange. This does not provide a mechanism for making an environment highly available or fault tolerant, and cannot be used to balance load. Rather it specifies where to find the SAML responder or other endpoints in the protocol exchange. However, if the organization provides multiple ResponseLocation URI, it can be used as a means to balance load or identify locations to use in the event of a failure. There is nothing, however, to prevent these other locations from being used, so they will need to be active, and there is no algorithm used to distribute load; so there will be no assurance that load is evenly distributed. I would discourage organizations from using this feature to provide load balancing specifically.

The IndexedEndPoint extends the EndPoint type with two elements, index that is required and isDefault. Each endpoint is assigned a unique integer that can be referenced in a protocol message. This only needs to be unique among child elements of the same parent. isDefault identifies the default instance to be used. It is assumed to have a value of false if not present.

The localizedNameType extends a string value name type with the standard XML language attribute. The localizedURIType does the same for the URI type.

Metadata may be used to describe either a single entity or multiple entities. Where used for a single entity, the <EntityDescriptor> is used as a root element; otherwise, it is the <EntitiesDescriptor> element that must be used. The <EntityDescriptor> element can be used to identify both predefined roles or additional roles as the organization can extend the type. It should be noted that all extensions must be agreed upon by all involved in the exchange, issuance, and acceptance of the SAML assertions.

The predefined roles are:

- SSO identity provider
- SSO service provider
- Authentication authority
- Attribute authority
- Policy decision point
- Affiliation

The EntityDescriptorType is a complex type with the following elements and attributes:

entityID: This is a required attribute specifying the unique identifier of the SAML entity.

ID: This is an optional attribute providing a document unique identifier for the element. This is often referenced when signing.

validUntil: This is an optional attribute used to indicate the expiration time of the metadata contained in the element and any container elements.

cacheDuration: This is an optional attribute used to indicate how long a consumer should cache the metadata.

<ds:Signature>: This is an optional XML signature authenticating the element and contents.

<Extensions>: This provides, optionally, the means to extend the EntityDescriptorType.

<Organization>: This is an optional element used to identify the organization responsible for the SAML entity described by the element.

<ContactPerson>: This is an optional element providing a person to contact at the organization. Multiple <ContactPerson> elements may be specified.

<AdditionalMetaDataLocation>: This is an optional sequence of one or more alternative locations to query additional metadata regarding the SAML entity. This allows the provision of metadata that does not conform to the SAML specification but which can be used to make authorization decisions.

One or more of the following:

```
<RoleDescriptor>
<IDPSSODescriptor>
<SPSSODescriptor>
<AuthnAuthorityDescriptor>
<AttributeAuthorityDescriptor>
<PDPDescriptor>
<AffiliationDescriptor>
```

When this is used as a root element of a metadata instance, the element must contain a validUntil or cacheDuration attribute, and I would recommend that these values always be present.

The EntitiesDescriptor element has the following elements:

ID, an optional attribute providing a document unique identifier for the element. This is often referenced when signing.

validUntil, an optional attribute used to indicate the expiration time of the metadata contained in the element and any container elements.

cacheDuration, an optional attribute used to indicate how long a consumer should cache the metadata.

Name, an optional string that identifies a group of SAML entities in the context of some deployment.

`<ds:Signature>`, an optional XML signature authenticating the element and contents.

`<Extensions>` provides, optionally, the means to extend the EntityDescriptorType.

`<EntitiesDescriptor>` or `<EntityDescriptor>`, which is a list of one or more SAML entities' metadata or a nested group of additional metadata.

Much like the EntityDescriptor element, when this is used as a root element of a metadata instance, the element must contain a validUntil or cacheDuration attribute, and I would recommend that these values always be present.

The `<Organization>` element allows basic information about the organization responsible for the SAML entity or role to be conveyed. It is an optional element used for information dissemination. It can have:

`<OrganizationName>`: One or more names, not formatted for human use.

`<OrganizationDisplayName>`: One or more names, formatted for human use.

`<OrganizationURL>`: One or more URLs where more information about the organization may be obtained.

`<Extensions>`: This provides, optionally, the means to extend the `<Organization>` element.

The `<ContactPerson>` element provides basic information about the person responsible for the SAML entity or role. This has the following elements and attributes:

contactType, a required attribute with the possible values of technical, support, administrative, billing, and others. Obviously, there may be some overlap as to how organizations leverage these values, but do not assume that a technical contact is a support contact unless specified.

`<Company>`, an optional string providing a human readable company name for the contact.

`<GivenName>`, optional.

`<SurName>`, optional.

`<EmailAddress>`, zero or more in the mailto: URI format.

`<TelephoneNumber>`, zero or more telephone numbers. These should include the country code and all subsequent codes.`<Extensions>`:

Most of SAML metadata exists to describe roles that can be used programmatically by the application in the processing of the SAML assertion and in the use of the SAML protocol.

The `<RoleDescriptor>` element is an abstract element that can be used to convey common descriptive information intended to assist in the uniform processing of roles. New roles may be defined by extending this type, which contains the following elements and attributes:

ID, an optional attribute provides a document unique identifier for the element. This is often used when signing.

validUntil, an optional attribute used to indicate the expiration time of the metadata contained in the element and any container elements.

cacheDuration, an optional attribute used to indicate how long a consumer should cache the metadata.

protocolSupportEnumeration, a required white space delimitated set of URIs that identifies the set of protocol specifications supported by the role element. This set must include the SAML protocol namespace URI.

ErrorURL, an optional attribute that can be used to provide a location to direct a user for problem resolution.

<ds:Signature>, an optional element used for an XML signature which is used to authenticate the containing element and its contents. I would encourage that the application architect always sign SAML metadata.

<Extensions>, optional element for metadata extensions.

<KeyDescriptor>, an optional element used to provide information about the cryptographic keys the entity uses when acting in the role described by the SAML metadata.

<Organization>, an optional element used to specify the organization associated with the role.

<ContactPerson>, an optional element used to specify contacts associated with the role. This is identical to the<ContactPerson>within the <EntityDescriptor> element.

The <KeyDescriptor> element, as I just mentioned, is used to provide information about the cryptographic keys that an entity uses to sign data or to receive encrypted keys. This element consists of the following elements and attributes:

use, an optional attribute, specifying the purpose of the key being described. Values are KeyTypes and consist of either encryption or signing or both.

<ds:KeyInfo>, a required element which identifies the key. This element conforms to XMLSig.

<EncryptionMethod>, an optional element specifying the algorithm and algorithm-specific settings where encryption is supported. This element conforms to the xenc:EncryptionMethodType complex type.

The SSODescriptorType is an abstract type, which provides the base for both the SPSSODescriptorType and IPSPSSODescriptorType. This type extends the RoleDescriptorType. This type contains the following elements:

<ArtifiactResoltuionService>, which will contain zero or more elements that describe indexed endpoints which support the Artifact Resolution Protocol.

<SingleLogoutService>, which will contain zero or more elements used to support the Single Logout profile.

<ManageNameIDService>, which will contain zero or more elements that describe endpoints that support the Name Identifier Management profile.

<NameIDFormat>, which will contain zero or more elements that enumerate the name identifier format supported by the system entity acting in the defined role.

The <IDPSSODescriptor> element extends the SSODescriptorType, adding the following additional elements and attributes:

WantAuthnRequestsSigned, an optional element requiring the use of signatures for any <samlp:AuthnRequest> messages received. I highly recommend its use wherever practical. Where absent, the value is considered false.

<SingleSignOnService>, which will be used to convey one or more elements of the EndPointType describing endpoints that support the Authentication Request profile.

<NameIDMappingService>, which will contain zero or more elements that support the Name Identifier Mapping profile.

<AssertionIDRequestService>, which will contain zero or more elements used to describe endpoints that support the profile of the Assertion Request protocol.

<AttributeProfile>, which will contain zero or more elements used to enumerate the attribute profiles supported by the identity provider.

<saml:Attribute>, which will contain zero or more elements that identify SAML attributes supported by the identity provider.

The <SPSSODescriptor> element extends the SSODescriptorType with content specific to service providers. This element contains the following elements and attributes:

AuthnRequestSigned, is an optional attribute that indicates if the <samlp:AuthnRequest> messages sent by this service provider will be signed. If omitted, this is assumed to be false. I highly recommend that these requests are always signed unless there is absolutely no requirement for security, and SAML is just being used to provide convenience.

<AssertionConsumerService>, which will contain one or more elements describing indexed endpoints that support the profiles of the Authentication Request protocol.

<AttributeConsumingService>, which will contain zero or more applications or services that require or desire the use of SAML attributes. In essence, it defines a particular service in terms of the attributes the service provider requires or desires. It will contain the following elements and attributes: index, a required attribute specifying a unique integer value isDefault, an optional attribute used to identify the default service provided by the service provider. Where not indicated, this value is assumed to be false.

<ServiceName>, one or more language-qualified names for the service.

<ServiceDescription>, zero or more strings that describe the service.

<RequestedAttribute>, one or more elements specifying attributes required or desired by the service provider. This will have the attribute of isRequired when the <RequestedAttribute> is not optional.

The <AuthnAuthorityDescriptor> extends the RoleDescriptorType for the authentication role, or more specifically, for service providers which respond to <samlp:AuthnQuery> requests. This contains the following additional elements:

<AuthnQueryServices>, which is a list of one or more EndPointTypes.

<AssertionIDRequestService>, which is a list of zero or more endpoints that support the Assertion Request protocol or the URI binding for assertion requests.

<NameIDFormat>, which is a list of zero or more URIs which provide the identifier formats supported by the service authority.

The <PDPDescriptor> is an extension of the RoleDescriptorType to provide content specific to policy decision points or SAML authorities that respond to `<samlp:AuthzDecisionQuery>` messages. It contains the following elements:

- `<AuthzService>`, which is a list of one or more endpoints which support the profile of the Authorization Decision Query protocol.
- `<AssertionIDRequestService>`, which is a list of zero or more endpoints that support the profile of the Assertion Request protocol or the URI binding for assertion requests.
- `<NameIDFormat>`, which is a list of zero or more URIs that enumerate the Name Identifier formats supported by this authority.

`<AttributeAuthorityDescriptor>` extends the RoleDescriptorType to describe attribute authorities. These authorities support the information needed to customize the application for the specific identity presented in the SAML assertion and perhaps influence authorization decisions regarding access to application functionality and data. Such authorities will respond to `<samlp:AttributeQuery>` messages and may be described with the following elements:

- `<AttributeService>`, which is a listing of one or more endpoints that support the Attribute Query protocol.
- `<AssertionIDRequestService>`, which is a list of zero or more endpoints that support the AssertionRequest protocol or the URI binding for assertion requests.
- `<NameIDFormat>`, which is a list of zero or more URIs which contain the Name Identifier formats supported by the authority.
- `<AttributeProfile>`, which is a list of zero or more URIs which enumerate the attribute profiles supported by the authority.
- `<saml:Attribute>`, which is a list of zero or more elements identifying the SAML attributes supported by the authority.

The `<AffiliationDescriptor>` element provides an alternative to the sequence of role descriptors provided by `<EntitiesDescriptor>`. The `<AffiliationDescriptor>` element provides a summary of the individual entities that make up the affiliation along with information about the affiliation. This is communicated using the following elements and attributes:

- affiliationOwnerID, a required attribute that specifies the unique identifier of the entity responsible for the affiliation. This may not be a member of the affiliation, but if it is, then this ID must be listed in the `<AffiliateMember>` element.

ID, an optional attribute that provides a document unique identifier, usually used as a reference when signing.

validUntil is an optional attribute that indicates the expiration time of the metadata contained in the element. While this may be optional, I highly recommend that a meaningful value be set for this attribute.

cacheDuration is an optional attribute indicating the maximum amount of time that a consumer should cache the metadata. While this may be optional, I highly recommend a meaningful value be set for this value.

`<ds:Signature>`, an optional element containing the signature which authenticates the contents of the message. I highly recommend that all SAML messages are signed unless SAML is not being used for security. Simply put, unsigned SAML messages cannot be trusted.

`<AffiliateMember>` is a list of one or more elements enumerating the members of the affiliation by their unique identifier.

`<KeyDescriptor>` is a list of zero or more elements providing information about the cryptographic keys that are used by the affiliation as a whole.

`<Extensions>`: I have called repeatedly for the use of signatures to guarantee the integrity and authenticate the information presented in SAML assertions and metadata. SAML metadata can be signed using a `<ds:Signature>` element. There are other mechanisms that can be used to protect the metadata, such as if it is provided by the publisher through a secure channel directly. However, organizations should not entirely trust their "secure" channels, and signing the metadata can protect its integrity in the event that the secure channel is compromised in any way, including ways that are undetectable to the receiving party.

When signing metadata, it is not necessary to sign the entire message. Simply signing the identifier attribute value of the metadata is sufficient. This can be done by listing the URI to the identifiers in the `<ds:Reference>` of the signature.

There are two ways to publish metadata documents for SAML. You can use a well-known location by dereferencing the entity's unique identifier, or by publishing the location in DNS. Where a consumer supports both, it must use DNS before it looks in a well-known location. Where the document requires retrieval, this should be protected by TLS/SSL. As a consumer, I would hesitate to trust unsigned metadata.

If publishing through a well-known location, you must use a URL pointing to the location of the document, though a redirect can be used. The mime type must be application/samlmetadata+xml. This document must provide the metadata only for the document with the matching entityID. The root element of the document must therefore have a `<EntityDescriptor>` (not `<EntitiesDescriptor>`) with the matching entityID of the URL.

If you are going to use DNS to publish this information, you should use the Name Authority Pointer (NAPTR) Resource Record. If you do this, strongly consider using the Domain Name System Security Extensions (DNSSEC) to sign your zone file to prevent tampering or hijacking. Quality DNS providers support this functionality free as part of their service.

When you need to retrieve this information, parse the unique identifier and extract the fully qualified domain name. Look in the order field for the order in which to process each NAPTR resource record returned. The preference field indicates the preferred order of use to the resolving application. This may be ignored. The flag field will either contain the U flag, indicating the output will be a URI, or it will be null.

The service field is specific to SAML processing and declares the modes by which instance documents are to be made available. This is a multivariate field, consisting of a service field prefix with two possible variables: PID2U or NID2U representing either an entity's unique identifier to the metadata URL or the resolution of a principle's NameID into a metadata URL. This prefix is followed by a protocol, either HTTPS or UDDI (which will be an https URL to a WSDL), then to a class, service type, and si. You do not always need class, service type, and si. Class identifies if the referenced metadata document is for a single entity or many. If many, then the entity defined by the unique identifier must be a member of a group of entities within the document described by either `<AffiliationDescriptor>` or `<EntitiesDescriptor>`. Service type allows the entity to publish metadata specific to a service role or service as a distinct document. The si variable allows the publisher to either directly publish the metadata for a service instance or articulate a SOAP endpoint.

As an example, PID2U+https:entity represents the entire metadata document that is available over HTTPS.

Each Service Record will have Regex and Replacement fields, which allows when processed that all input strings will result in valid https URL or UDDI WSDL document addresses. Once the identifier is parsed, the application would perform a DNS query for the domain's NAPTR resource records, getting back one or more responses. These should be resolved according to the order field, or if desired, the preference field. These are opened iteratively until a terminal NAPTR resource record is read. This will provide the application with a well-formed URL to retrieve the metadata document.

The DNS domain will define a TTL. Any location caching should not exceed the life of that TTL; otherwise, the application may be working with obsolete information. This can present a problem, as many organizations like to set a short TTL to facilitate expedient deployment of DNS changes, sometimes as short as 15 minutes. This would mean the application would have to query DNS every 15 minutes for a fresh NAPTR record.

### 3.5.7 Versions

Unlike most Internet protocols, SAML was not designed with backward compatibility with earlier versions as a goal. Backward compatibility has been the Achilles' heel of many applications, operating systems, and protocols, with legacy vulnerabilities and flaws carried forward so as not to break older implementations. Later versions of SAML are not guaranteed to work with earlier versions; so it is imperative that all producers and consumers are using the same version.

SAML also uses versioning internally to define different versions of an assertion. These two uses of versioning are independent of each other and recorded differently within the assertion. However, they are both used to validate that consumers and producers are working with the same assumptions.

The SAML schema versioning, reflected in the version attribute of the `<xs:schema>` element, will be in the form of Major.Minor, and will reflect the version of the schema used. It is important in application design to include verification logic of the schema version used so that the desired functionality can be ensured.

Assertions, however, have their own versioning, to indicate changes to the assertions by identity providers, service providers, relays, and so on. These use the <Assertion> element's Version attribute. This is also in the form of Major.Minor, and governs the processing of the assertions.

SAML also has support for protocol versioning, which defines the schema support, syntax, semantics, and processing rules. In general, a requester should issue requests with the highest SAML version it supports. When what is supported is unknown, application logic must support version based rejections and a fail would open to a down-level version with less desirable functionality. It is best to verify versions supported during the application-design phase to prevent attacks that reduce the version to a more readily compromised version of the protocol.

### 3.5.8 Security and Privacy Considerations

SAML assertions often include statements regarding the attributes and authorizations of an individual. This information should be kept private between the individual and the organization, especially if the service provided is financial or health related. To this end, the organization's privacy policy must publish how they handle the information within the assertions. Confidentiality of that information can be assured if it always transverses public networks over encrypted tunnels, where both the cryptographic keys of the tunnel endpoints are properly validated and the DNS-provided values are validated. This last step is made much easier if the DNS domain has been signed using DNSSEC.

For some services, anonymity is desired. While WS-Federation has a preset mechanism for defining how anonymity is maintained, SAML does not. In fact, because of the use of authorities, at best partial anonymity is possible. An authority makes an assertion about someone, after all. They must be a member of a set of authorized individuals. Privacy can be protected through anonymity where the subject of the SAML assertion is not mapped to the individual about whom it is made. This does not mean by any means that anonymity is assured. Even where no logs are kept of the authentication, usage patterns can always be used to identify one individual against another.

SAML may be a security protocol used for authentication and authorization, but it must be remembered that SAML assertions themselves are not confidential, and there are other attacks against integrity that must be considered. It is essential to get this right, as the assertions are designed to be used across corporation boundaries and transcend both services and applications. This comes from a complete information security architecture.

Let us look at the realistic threats to SAML assertions and then consider the techniques required to protect them:

- Collusion between a principal and service provider
- Collusion between a principal and identity provider
- Collusion between the identity provider and service provider
- Collusion between two or more principals
- Collusion between two or more service providers
- Collusion between two or more identity providers
- Denial-of-service attacks
- Man-in-the-middle attacks
- Replay attacks
- Session hijacking

Attacks against the authentication engine must be considered as they may result in unauthorized use of an authorization and SAML assertions issued to the wrong party. In essence, the entire ability to trust the SAML authorities' assertion that individuals are who they claim to be and are properly authenticated depends upon the strength and resilience of that authentication process.

Therefore, the following additional threats must be considered:

- Brute force attacks
- Key compromise
- Redirection attacks
- Credential theft

No technology is immune to attack. While I have gone on at great length about the strengths of public key cryptography as an authentication token, these keys can be granted to the wrong individual through impersonation, and there are mechanisms to attack the key store. As an example, a cross-site scripting attack that tricks the browser to prompt for the key pair might gain access to the private as well as the public key if the underlying private key is not protected by the browser's key store. Of course, such protections are easily circumvented if the cross-site scripting attack convinces the user to unlock their private key with a fallacious prompt. Even if the private key is stored on a smart card locked by a 30-character passphrase, if the user enters that long passphrase because they have been tricked, the game is over and trust is destroyed.

As there is no patch for stupidity, the entire security infrastructure depends upon trusting that the user's authentication is authentic. All communications with that user and all communications between service and identity providers must be over an IPSec, IPv6, or SSL/TLS encrypted tunnel. This provides confidentiality and integrity during transit, as long as keys are validated. The messages can be encrypted. XML encryption can be used; however, you must remember that this provides encryption of only selective components of the message and that this encryption is no protection unless XMLSig was used to sign those components of the message. Otherwise, if the message is intercepted, the encrypted components are readily replaced with other encrypted components, and even the encryption key can be substituted if the data is not signed.

Strongly authenticated IPSec, IPv6, or SSL/TL protect well against the following threats:

- Man-in-the-middle attacks
- Replay attacks
- Session hijacking
- Redirection attacks

There are also in protocol ways to prevent against some of these attacks. While most application traffic will be sent over secured protocols, you can add additional protection against replay attacks by signing the message and using a message timestamp. Upon receipt, the recipient will check the signature and timestamp to validate that the message is authentic and has not been tampered with. It will then check the replay cache for the value of that signature. If that signature value is already in the cache, something or someone is executing a replay attack, and the attack fails. Otherwise, the signature and timestamp are added to the cache.

Man-in-the-middle attacks can be overcome without encrypted tunnels by encrypting and signing the messages before they are sent. What needs to be remembered if this is to be relied upon as a strategy to mitigate this risk is that any element within the SAML message that is not signed can be replaced or modified without notice, even if it is encrypted, and any element within the SAML message that is not encrypted is visible to any attacker or for that matter the network administrators of any switch, router, or firewall through which the messages transverse.

To protect against other attacks, you must use techniques that fall far outside what SAML is capable of. The collusion attacks can only be prevented by sound business practices. No technology can prevent them. Denial of service, brute force, key compromise, or credential theft are all very hard to prevent. There is nothing in SAML or in web services that can prevent these attacks from succeeding. The application architect must rely on the security architect putting in place other layers of protection.

Unfortunately, and unlike WS-Security, SAML by itself is incapable of enforcing controls such as messages must always transverse public networks via encrypted tunnels. This is where WS-Policy and WS-Trust add value, along with overheads and complexity. All security is a trade-off between protection and performance. With modern computers, that trade-off is less than ever. If, however, the application architect can design their distributed service-oriented application in such a way that all traffic transverses public networks via encrypted channels, then SAML provides everything needed to distribute authentication, authorization, and identity management across multiple organizations securely.

## 3.6 Kerberos

Kerberos ticketing systems are a legacy authentication and authorization service that must be considered. Although designed before service-oriented applications were conceived, Kerberos was designed for the kind of distributed authentication and authorization that distributed and service-oriented applications need. Kerberos has seen wide implementation for operating system authentication, both on the Unix/Linux and Windows platforms because it facilitates the ability to sign onto manifold systems with the same trusted and trustable credentials.

Much like with an STS, Kerberos tickets are issued by a central issuing service called the Kerberos Distribution Center (KDC). This system functions as an authentication broker, where the client authenticates to the KDC, which issues a ticket. This ticket is then used to authenticate the client to any and all systems and applications to which the client needs access. This is accomplished by the client requesting access, the system asking the KDC if the client has authenticated and can be granted access, and the KDC sending the system or application a service ticket, which provides the proof of authentication and the required information needed for authorization.

While this sounds very much like the tokens issued by an STS, there are some critical differences. When tokens expire, there is no notice provided, and active sessions may continue uninterrupted. The Kerberos ticket is encrypted by the client, not by the KDC, and if the client does not protect the key properly, the token can be compromised. Depending upon implementation, Kerberos tickets can be replayed, especially in implementations where they have a long lifetime. Sending the Kerberos tickets over secure network tunnels such as over TLS/SSL encrypted networks can reduce this risk but not eliminate it, because unless the tunnel is client-authenticated with an x509v3 client certificate, it is vulnerable to a man-in-the-middle attack. As there is no mechanism in Kerberos to check the certificate of the server, Kerberos cannot detect a successful man-in-the-middle attack.

Because of the vulnerability to man-in-the-middle attacks and replay attacks, Kerberos is only deployed internally. However, in no small part due to the integration with Microsoft products, Kerberos sees wide usage, even as a token used for authentication into service-oriented applications.

Like x509v3 certificates, Kerberos tokens do not convey much information beyond the successful authentication into the KDC of the specific client. Thus authorization decisions must either be resource based or depend heavily upon postauthentication authorization queries into an attribute repository. For service-oriented application in an internal Windows-based ecosystem, Active Directory is readily query-able over the LDAP protocol, providing a rich hierarchical object-oriented identity store with attributes.

## 3.7 x509v3 Certificates

Client-side authentication using x509v3 certificates are the only way to ensure that SSL/TLS tunnels are secure from both man-in-the-middle attacks and redirection attacks. Man-in-the-middle attacks involve putting a false certificate between the client and the server. While a certificate error may be generated, most individuals and applications will ignore this error, and the error will only be generated if the false certificate was not issued from a legitimate but different CA than the one that certified the legitimate link. Redirection attacks involve spinning up a system in parallel to the legitimate system, with a false certificate, and using either DNS hijacking or forced rerouting (through a BGP attack) to direct the client to the wrong system which may proxy the actual service. Those attacks are devastating, but were considered theoretical until about 2008 when they started becoming common. What makes them so devastating is that there is no way for the service provider to know that their customer was a victim of the attack; the ability to detect and defend against these attacks depends entirely on the client.

The use of client-side certificates prevents either attack, as both sides of the network connection authenticate each other. Normally in an SSL/TLS handshake, the client authenticates the server. With a client-side certificate, the server will also authenticate the client. As the redirection or man-in-the-middle attacks will not have the private key of the client, the server's authentication of the client will fail, and the attack will fail. While this will also result in a failed authentication, it protects the client from credential and service theft in a way that no other credential can do.

X509V3 certificates can be used to do more than just create a truly secure network tunnel. They can also be used to authenticate to the service provider. There are two limitations, however, to the technology. The first is also its strength. The client certificates cannot be forwarded. While this prevents injection, man-in-the-middle, replay, redirection, and hijacking attacks for which other tokens are vulnerable, it also limits the use of strongly authenticated TLS/SSL to point-to-point solutions. The second limit is that the certificate cannot carry metadata, limiting its use to just strong authentication.

## 3.8 OpenID

The needs for identity federation extends far beyond service-oriented applications, and as such OpenID was created to meet those needs. Application owners that leverage OpenID can allow their customers to use those credentials to authenticate into any application that leverages OpenID. Each authentication must be explicitly authorized in the specific session, allowing a user to authenticate into GoodReads, as an example, using their Facebook ID, as a secondary example. This provides an authentication, which functions as a substitution for a locally managed user account and password, while not having the support issues associated with a client certificate.

While OpenID looks to simplify registration so that an individual need only register for one of the OpenID-compliant systems and then leverage this to use all the others, it provides more convenience than security. OpenID requires the use of TLS, and is vulnerable to man-in-the-middle attacks, replay attacks and injection attacks unless a client certificate is actually used. Because OpenID was designed for RESTful systems by humans, it provides access to various applications but is not designed to facilitate application-to-application authentication. It is widely used among various social applications such as Facebook, LiveJournal, LinkedIn, Google, and many others. However, it requires the use of cross-origin resource sharing of JavaScript, and as such faulty implementations will expose the user to a variety of attacks including cross-site scripting and cross-site request forgery. Because of this, and the availability of SAML which does not have these vulnerabilities, I would recommend that any service-oriented application using web services use SAML instead of OpenID unless the application is socially oriented and places the risk of lost registrations higher than account compromise.

- Clients cannot determine if they are connected directly to the terminal service provider or to an intermediary service provider, allowing scalability and load balancing.
- Clients can have their code extended on a temporary basis by servers. Examples include JavaScript run within a browser or Java applets.
- Clients and servers have a uniform interface consisting of identification of resources usually through URIs, manipulations of these resources, self-descriptive messages, most often through MIME types, and the use of hypermedia as the engine of application state.

## 4.3 WebSockets

Modern web applications are increasingly being written using HTML5 WebSockets. This allows tremendous reduction in the number and volume of calls, as an application no longer has to use URL sequences to derive all the data from another location but may access it directly by HTML WebSockets. This eliminates the polling and streaming, which were solutions to resolve limitations in earlier versions of HTML. These sockets allow for bidirectional communications that prior to HTML5 could only be accomplished using heavier protocols such as SOAP.

WebSocket constructors take up to two arguments: a mandatory URL and an optional protocol as a string or an array of strings. If not present, it is considered equivalent to an empty array. When invoked, the user agent must:

- Parse the URL's components to obtain host, port, resource name, and if secure. If this fails, throw a SyntaxError (equivalent to a SOAP fault).
- If not flagged as secure, but the entry script uses a secure protocol such as TLS, then throw a SecurityError.
- If the client attempts to connect to a port which is forbidden the user agent, then throw a SecurityError.
- If protocols are absent, let protocols be an empty array.
- If any of the values in protocols is present, and a string, let protocols be an array of just that string.

- If any of the values in protocols are duplicates or in other ways compromise the Sec-WebSocket-Protocol header fields, then throw a SyntaxError.
- Set the Origin value of the ASCII serialization of the origin of the entry script as ASCII lowercase.
- Return a new WebSocket object.
- Establish a WebSocket connection.

The WebSocket has three major variables, readyState, networking, and messaging, along with a few minor ones. The readyState attribute represents the state of the connection as a numeric value of 0–3, where:

0 = CONNECTING
1 = OPEN
2 = CLOSING
3 = CLOSED

The bufferedAmount attribute returns the number of bytes of data that have been queued using the send() command but not yet sent. This does not reset to zero once the connection closes. This value is used to throttle data transfer, so that the application traffic does not overflow the network throughput. Attackers could easily change this value to cause a denial of service if they are able to execute a man-in-the-middle attack on the socket.

When a WebSocket object is created, the binaryType IDL attribute is set to "blob" (binary large object), and the send (data) method transmits the data. If the data are actually a string, they are sent as a sequence of Unicode characters. If in either case the blob or string exceeds the size of the buffer, then the application must either increase the size of the ArrayBuffer through increasing the bufferedAmount attribute or close the WebSocket.

The security flag just mandates that the WebSocket must be sent over Transport Layer Security (TLS). There is nothing within HTML5's WebSockets to enforce any other security control. This makes WebSockets an excellent application interface for applications that do not need to be exposed to the Internet but means that service-oriented applications will need to depend upon fatter but more robust protocols such as SOAP if there is a need to ensure the delivery of data with its integrity intact and its authenticity ensured.

# 5

# OTHER SOA PLATFORMS

## 5.1 DCOM

Distributed Component Object Model (DCOM) is a set of remote procedural call libraries designed for the Microsoft Windows operating system. DCOM is often used within an enterprise-specific service-oriented architecture (SOA) and is an alternative to SOAP or Representational State Transfer (REST). It is a legacy technology that has been largely replaced by Microsoft by their Windows Communication Framework but is still maintained by the company that published the specifications as an open standard.

DCOM extends the Component Object Model over a network by providing facilities for creating and activating objects, providing a means to manage object references and provide object interface queries. Remote procedure call (RPC) is relied upon for authentication, authorization, and message integrity.

## 5.2 CORBA

Common Object Request Broker Architecture (CORBA) is a platform-agnostic method of RPCs with predefined mappings into many common languages designed to allow different applications written in different languages to interchange instructions and data. CORBA is often used within an enterprise-specific SOA and is an alternative to SOAP or REST.

CORBA is an object-oriented framework. This means that CORBA applications are composed of objects, which are individual instances of software and data that represent something as a unified whole. Objects inherit from common parents, so a shopping cart for user x would be a shopping cart object of type x with all the properties of the common shopping cart but just the data from user x.

To create an interface for CORBA applications, you define an interface using Interactive Data Language (IDL). This is independent of language and serves much the same function as a user layer interface in the framework. The client is unaware of the transactions of the back-end system, which manipulates, processes, stores, and communicates with this front-end system. IDL needs to be defined specifically and strictly.

CORBA has built-in specifications for load balancing, resource control, and fault tolerance, allowing it to be used for large scalable applications. Because CORBA is a framework, it has many different components that can be leveraged, some of which provide the means to bring the power of CORBA to a web services application.

Probably the most useful thing about CORBA to readers of this book is the ability to integrate with web services through a Web Services Description Language (WSDL), essentially using the WSDL as a means to map to an IDL. While IDL files can be generated from a WSDL, the generated files tend to lack the information needed to create an interaction translation gateway. This generated file should be supplemented with an Identifier Information File and a SOAP Information File. I need to note that while WSDL can handle HTTP and Multipurpose Internet Mail Extensions (MIME), CORBA can only map to SOAP, which rather restricts the ability to front-end CORBA applications with a web service.

## 5.3 DDS

Data Distribution Service (DDS) was developed to provide a mechanism to distribute data in a publish/subscribe model. It is an alternative to SOAP or REST but is rarely used in modern implementations. However, as legacy application may leverage this standard, it is worth a few words.

DDS was developed to allow real-time applications to model some of their communications as pure data-centric exchange, where they stream (or publish) their data to applications that are interested. The key goal of the specification is the predictable distribution of data with minimal overhead. There are hooks into quality of service (QoS) to allow alignment and control of network resources.

DDS can scale to deliver data to thousands of subscribers in real time, using a model called Data-centric publish–subscribe using a "global data space." Applications that wish to contribute to this space become publishers, and applications that wish to leverage this information become subscribers. The Data Local Reconstruction Layer is used by subscribers to access the data as if it was local.

## 5.4 WCF

Windows Communication Foundation (WCF) is a Microsoft-specific technology designed for building web services using Microsoft products. It is a replacement for DCOM and is an alternative to SOAP and REST. Unlike DCOM, WCF was designed to work with web services and to support an SOA. This framework is still actively supported by Microsoft and is well worth understanding. I am not going to dive into this to the same depth as I have dived into other web services components for the simple reason that unlike Web Services Business Process Execution Language (WS-BPEL) among others, the WCF framework is platform specific. It is worth noting, however, that WCF does support many of the WS standards. The following is a list of WS standards supported by WCF:

- WSDL
- WS-Policy
- WS-PolicyAttachment
- WS-MetadataExchange
- WS-Addressing
- WS-SecureConversation
- WS-Trust
- WS-ReliableMessaging
- WS-AtomicTransaction
- WS-Coordination
- SOAP
- WSS SOAP Message Security

WCF has the following features and capabilities:

- The ability to automate workflow services (a WS-BPEL competitor)

- Data transfer and serialization
- Session instancing and concurrency (instead of WS-Concurrency)
- Control of the transport layer
- Controls of queues, reliable sessions, and transactions
- Metadata
- Exposure to non-SOAP interfaces
- Support for Asynchronous JavaScript and XML (AJAX) and JavaScript Object Notation (JSON)

I would encourage anyone using WCF to use them in a standards-compliant manner, especially with regard to anything at the presentation layer. The closer a WCF application is to strict compliance with the WS standards, the more transparent the ability to integrate other applications with an application developed using WCF will be.

The one area where I do want to spend a little bit of time is with WCF workflow. Workflows are an excellent way to control the coordination of the asynchronous work within a distributed application. WFC workflow is built on service contracts that describe the service and the data received. These data are represented as either data contracts or message contracts depending upon the nature and use of the data. As with WS-BPEL, the service exposes metadata about the workflow in WSDL.

There are three basic activities: the Receive activity, the SendReply activity, and the TransactedReceiveScope activity. Unlike in WS-BPEL that can handle the entirety of the business logic internally, WCF uses message queues. The two bindings that are predefined are NetMsmqBind and MsmqIntegrationBinding. Both have a ValidityDuration property that specifies for how long the message queue may be considered valid. It is very important that these durations be set based upon any transaction dependencies.

### 5.5 .Net Passport, Windows Live ID

.Net Passport is a Microsoft propriety alternative to Security Assertion Markup Language (SAML), which was not supported in Microsoft products until recently. In many ways, Passport was ahead of its time and its function is more analogous to the emerging OpenID. Passport is still supported in both Microsoft products and service providers that leverage the technology, but it has been rebranded as Windows Live ID.

Windows Live ID can be used for a platform-independent authentication service and can also be used to provide delegated authentication. The platform-independent authentication service, called Web Authentication, is used for sites and services completely unaffiliated with the Microsoft cloud services. Microsoft recently announced that they are discontinuing support of this as they migrate people to their Live Connect service.

To accept and process a Live ID from Live Connect, you need to validate their authentication token, which is encoded as a JSON web token. These tokens are signed, and the verification process includes checking the signature of the token. The verification routine can be called using a simple URL for RESTful SOA; for other systems, there are various application programming interfaces (APIs) that can be called built into the Android, iOS, Windows Phone, and Windows store.

## 5.6 WS-BPEL

To permit workflows to transcend the boundaries and controls of a single corporation, BPEL was developed. It is based upon Business Process Markup Language (BPML), an extension of XML as a formal metalanguage for modeling business processes, which provides an abstract execution model for describing collaborations and transactions. WS-BPEL is one of the more complicated of the web services standards, so I highly recommend reading the standard and supporting literature. As with all other discussions on the various web services standards, I am going to cover the salient points that an application architect or a security architect would need to grasp in the design of their application. WS-BPEL allows the capability to:

- Describe the logic of business processes through composition of services
- Compose larger processes from smaller processes
- Handle synchronous and asynchronous operations
- Invoke services in series or parallel

- Selectively compensate completed activities in case of failure
- Maintain interruptible long-term transactional systems
- Resume interrupted or failed activities or both
- Route incoming messages to the appropriate service
- Correlate requests within and across business processes
- Schedule activities based upon predefined times
- Define order of execution
- Handle both message- and time-related events

With BPEL, business processes can be described in three distinct ways:

a. As executable business processes wherein the exact details of the process are defined and follow the orchestration paradigm.
b. As abstract business processes or public message exchange. These are not executable and follow the choreography paradigm.
c. In the orchestration paradigm, a central process (which can be another service) takes control and coordinates the execution of different operations in the services involved in the operation.

The choreography paradigm does not rely upon a central process but is a peer-based system where each service knows when to execute its operations and with what other services to interact.

WS-BPEL was created to provide business with a means to build automated business processes that are stateful, are long running, and involve two or more parties without revealing the complexities of internal decision-making using BPEL. WS-BPEL is a competitive standard to the WS-Cooperation suite and has many of the same design goals: a repeatable process for multiparty business transactions.

There are three basic concepts that are fundamental to successfully deploying WS-BPEL:

Business processes include data-dependent behavior, where transactions cannot complete without key information that may be processed by another service. It is important to specify exceptional conditions where things do not go well as well as those conditions where all the data are provided as expected.

Long-running transactions are often multiple nested processes each with their own data requirements. A business process's success across a distributed system will often depend upon the coordination of the delivery of the outcome of those processes.

WS-BPEL is structured so that there are two basic kinds of processes, Abstract and Executable. Executable processes are fully defined and can be executed, while abstract processes are not fully defined in the XML and cannot be executed. The full executable construct is made available to abstract processes, giving both equal expressive power, but abstract processes have two mechanisms for hiding internal business logic: the omission I have already mentioned, which prevent them from being executable, and the use of opaque tokens. This separation between abstract and executable content is similar to WSDL, and as much as possible, WS-BPEL is compatible with WSDL, but there are three areas where they are not compatible:

Fault naming

Overloaded operations' names of WSDL port types are not supported by WS-BPEL.

WSDL port types that contain solicit-response or notification operations.

WS-BPEL activities perform the process logic. There are two kinds of activities, basic and structured. Basic activities describe the steps of the process behavior. Structured activities encode logic flow and can contain other basic or structure recursively.

All activities have standard attributes and elements. The name attribute is used to provide machine-processable names for activities. Only those names in scopes are processed. The suppressJoinFailure attribute is used for parallel and control dependencies' processing.

Each activity can leverage optional containers, `<sources>` and `<targets>`, which contain the standard elements of source and target. These can be readily extended using namespace elements. They are used to establish and keep track of synchronization relationships.

WS-BPEL business processes each have one main activity of one of the following types:

`<invoke>`: When clients need to make a call into an existing WS-BPEL session, they use the `<invoke>` activity, which is usually used to call a basic activity, but the call can include other activities such as a compensation and fault handler. These invokes can be one-way or bidirectional. Invoke activities may use the optional inputVariable and outputVariable variables. When used, they must be messageType variables with a QName which matches the QName of the input and output message type used in the operation. A variable can be used instead, creating a temporary anonymous WSDL message variable, where the copying of the element data between this anonymous WSDL message and the element variable acts as a single virtual `<assign>` with a copy element where the keepSrcElementName attribute is set to "yes." Otherwise, this functions as a normal `<assign>`.

The one-way invocation needs only the inputVariable, while two-way invocations require the outputVariable as well. The `<toPart>` element may be substituted for the inputVariable, and the `<fromPart>` element may be substituted for the outputVariable. When a fault is returned, it may result in a WSDL fault message, in which case the fault will only be known by its QName. To allow for identification of the specific fault, the QNames must be structured to be the target namespace of the corresponding port type and the fault name.

When `<invoke>` activities are associated with compensation activities, a `<compensationHandler>` can be invoked either explicitly or by default for the enclosing scope. An implicit `<scope>` activity will assume the name of the `<invoke>`, and will include the supressJoinFailure, if any, and any `<sources>` and `<targets>`.

I have made a number of references to WSDL and the uses for which WS-BPEL depends on and uses WSDL. While multipart WSDL messages may be created from WS-BPEL variables using inputVariables or outputVariables, the elements `<toParts>` or `<fromParts>` allow the creation of anonymous and temporary WSDL variables. The `<toPart>` elements act as a virtual `<assign>`, wherein each `<toParts>` acts as a `<copy>`, copying data from the fromVariable to the anonymous temporary variable referenced in the part attribute of the `<toPart>` element. If copying from an element variable to an element part, then the keepSrcElementName will be set to "yes". There must be a one-to-one mapping of parts to `<toParts>`. Parts not represented by <toParts> will be discarded. <FromParts> elements may also be mapped to explicit WSDL ports or an anonymous temporary WSDL can be created following the same processes, with the data copied from the <fromPart> to the part based upon the value of the toVariable.

<Receive> and <reply>: Business processes are build on the pairings of <receive> and <reply> activities, which may be modified through <pick> and <onEvent> activities. The <receive> activity specifies the partnerLink which contains the myRole used to receive messages and the portType and operation it expects the partner to invoke. Receive specifies the variable used to receive the message data. This may be specified using the variable attribute or through the use of the <fromPart> element; they are mutually exclusive. Both the <receive> activity and <pick> activity with the createInstance attribute set to "yes" will instantiate a business process in WS-BPEL, as will an <extensionActivity> child element if it receives inbound activity. All of these are considered start activities.

With the exception of <scope>, <flow>, <sequence>, and <extensionActivity> activities, all activities must be started by a start activity. The <extensionActivity> can only be called without a start activity if it functions by itself as a start activity for another activity, and it must not be a repeatable activity. A business process may have multiple start activities, but the initial start activity must complete before any other start activities are allowed to execute.

Any inbound message may initiate the start activity. If a process has multiple start activities with a correlation set, then all of its start activities must have at least one correlation set in common, and these must have the initiate attribute set to "join". Once an inbound message matching the single process instance initiates the business process, the remaining messages are delivered to the <receive> activity of the already created instance.

The variable referenced by the variable attribute in a <receive> (or a reply for that matter) must be a messageType variable with a QName which matches the QName of the input (for the <receive> action) or output (for the <reply>). A <receive> will not complete until it receives a matching message from the process, but the process cannot enable two or more activities from two messages with the same partnerLink, portType, operation, and correlationSet. If two or more such messages are received, then the process will throw a bpel:conflictingReceive fault. If the correlationSets differ, but the other variables are identical, then a bpel:ambigousReceive standard fault is thrown. If all messages received have the same correlation, this may cause a race condition if the `<receive>` activity is not already started. If it is started, then there should be no issue.

`<assign>`: The `<assign>` activity is used to update variables with new data.

`<throw>`: The `<throw>` activity is used to generate faults. Faults in WS-BPEL are defined by their name and optional fault data. Thus, for faults that result from messaging activity, there is no need to keep track of the port type or operation that was underway. Because of this, if any faults have a common name, there is no means to distinguish between them, making them useless for diagnostic purposes.

`<exit>` is an activity which terminates a business process.

`<wait>` is used to delay a process until a certain point in time has been reached. This can be expressed as either a deadline-expr (deadline expression) or a duration-expr (duration expression) as a uniform resource identifier (URI).

`<empty>`: This activity indicates nothing is happening or a "no-op". This allows synchronization of concurrent activities.

`<sequence>`: This activity is used to define a group of activities to be performed in alphabetical order.

`<if>` is an activity which is used to select activities from a set of choices with `<elseIf>` and `<else>` conditionals marking the choices which will be in the format of "anyURI".

`<while>` is an activity which is used to define a child process which operates as long as the defined process remains true. This process is defined using the attribute "condition" defined by an "anyURI" value.

`<RepeatUntil>` is an activity which is used to define a child process which operates until a defined process becomes true. This process is defined using the attribute "condition" defined by an "anyURI" value.

`<ForEach>` is an activity which executes its child activity exactly N+1 times. N is the value of the `<finalCounterValue>`—`<startCounterValue>` and is an integer. If the "parallel" variable is set to "yes", then each of the iterations happens simultaneously. A `<completionCondition>` may be used to allow the completion of the calling `<forEach>` activity without all called activities in the `<scope>` complete.

`<pick>` is an activity, which like `<receive>` or `<reply>`, can initiate another action.

`<OnMessage>` is another activity, like `<pick>`, `<receive>`, or `<reply>`, which can initiate another action.

`<flow>` is an activity which allows the application architect to specify one or more activities to happen concurrently. `<links>` can be used within the `<flow>` to define control dependencies.

`<scope>` is an activity used to define nested activities with their own `<partnerLinks>`, `<messageExchanges>`, `<variables>`, `<correlationSets>`, `<faultHandlers>`, `<compensationHandlers>`, `<terminationHandlers>`, and `<eventHanders>`.

`<compensate>` is an activity used to start compensation on all scopes within a superordinate activity, which have completed successfully in the proper order. It is used within a fault handler, another compensation handler, or termination handler.

`<compensateScope>` is an activity, like the `<compensation>`, which is used to start a compensation on a specified inner scope, which has already completed. It is used within a fault handler, another compensation handler, or termination handler.

`<rethrow>` is an activity to resend a fault.

`<validate>`: This activity is used to ensure that the values of the variables match their XML and WSDL definitions.

`<extensionActivity>` is an activity used to extend WS-BPEL. Any such extension must use a name = "NCName" and must include a suppressJoinFailure value.

`<ExtensionAssignOperation>` is another activity used to extend WS-BPEL; however, in this case, if the "mustUnderstand" variable is not set to "yes" and if the activity is not understood by WS-BPEL, it will not be executed.

When the business process needs to depend upon external XML schema or WSDL definitions, the `<import>` element can be used. This element uses a mandatory attribute of "importType" to identify the type of document being imported through an absolute URI which identifies the encoding language used in the document. Other variables include location and namespace. The location attribute contains a URI defining the location of the document. This location is neither mandatory nor be used when present. The namespasce attribute also specifies a URI, but in the case of a namespace attribute, it must be an absolute URI. This is used when the external names referenced in an import are not namespace qualified.

Throughout this volume, I have discussed service clients and service providers. One important innovation in WS-BPEL is the notion of partnership. WS-BPEL defines <partnerLinks> as bidirectional peer-to-peer conversational relationships. Instead of using endpoint references, it uses <sref:service-ref> to represent the data needed to describe the various partner relationships. The <partnerLinkType> describes the relationship between two services by defining the roles placed by each of the services. It specifies the portType provided by each service to receive messages. Each <role> specifies exactly one WSDL portType. As this type is not native to WSDL, it is usually defined as a child element of the <wsdl:definitions> element.

More than one <partnerLink> can be described by the same partnerLinkType. Each <partnerLink> is named, and the name is used for all service interactions with that service. Within a <partnerLink> definition, the attribute myRole is used to indicate the role of the business process, and the role of the partner is communicated with the partnerRole attribute.

As you no doubt remember from our review of WSDL, WSDL makes an important distinction between port types and ports, wherein port types are abstract functionality used by abstract messages where ports provide the means to understand how to access information. Ports communicate service endpoints and other public deployment-related information including public keys. Bindings are used to tie together a specific port to a specific port type. These may be static or dynamic and may be discovered dynamically.

Within WS-BPEL, endpoint references are used as a means to dynamically discover port-specific data. An endpoint reference allows WS-BPEL to dynamically select a provider for a particular service and remotely invoke their operations. Those endpoint references associated with the partnerRole and myRole within a partnerLink are described as service reference containers (sref:service-ref). This has an optional attribute called a reference-scheme used to provide the URI of the reference interpretation scheme. The URI of the reference-scheme is not necessarily the same as the URI of the `<sref:service-ref>`. The URI in the reference-scheme should be used when the URI in the `<sref:service-ref>` is ambiguous.

Within a message, there is generally application data and protocol information. When working with WS-BPEL, there is a third kind of data, business process data, which can be thought of as business protocol data. It is treated as protocol data within the design and referencing of the XML, though it does not describe the message context such as how it is transmitted, secured, and so on. WS-BPEL processes need to be able to access and manipulate both kinds of protocols.

To allow the expression of these business protocols, WS-BPEL has defined variable properties. Properties allow the isolation of initialization logic from information manipulation logic. These are defined through `<vprop:property>`. The names given should be indicative of function and as it is likely that these properties will be mapped to many messages, the names should clearly delineate that function globally.

Property names may also be used as aliases to variable values or specific message parts. However, when this is done, the `<vprop:propertyAlias>` element is used with either a messageType and part or type or element. When it is defined with a messageType and part, then the messageType, expressed as a QName, will be globally available to the business process as the name of the alias. However, if the `<vprop:propertyAlias>` element is defined using a type or an element attribute, then the propertyName is the name by which the alias is known.

As with all programming languages, variables provide a means to hold information about the state of the processes. With WS-BPEL, these may be made globally available to partners or may be only available internally. WS-BPEL supports three means to declare variables: WSDL message types, XML schema types, and XML schema elements. No matter what the means used are, the name of the `<variable>` must be unique for the variables within the defined scope. While it is possible to have the same variable name used in multiple scopes to store different data, this is not a very good idea, and a naming convention for variable names, which convey scope and data to be stored is a good technique to allow reuse without confusion or name collision. Unfortunately the "." character cannot be used in a name as it is a delimiter. I would encourage the use of multiple words strung together with capitalization used for readability, much like the various names used within WS-BPEL itself. Variables resolve to the nearest closing scope regardless of the type of the variable; thus, if a variable is defined locally, it will be used instead of a remotely defined variable.

The variable type can be specified using the messageType, type, or element attribute, and one of those three must be used to specify the type where messageType indicates a WSDL type, type an XML schema type, and element an XML schema element. When a process starts, global variables are uninitialized and local variables are uninitialized within their scope. They are initialized when assigned values or when some parts in the message type are assigned values. If the business process attempts to read or process a variable which has yet to be initiated, a bpel:uninitializedVariable fault must be thrown.

Variables can be changed during the execution of a process, and sometimes they are changed in ways that break type. The `<validate>` activity validates all variables listed in the variables attribute against their XML definitions. The `<validate>` activity can be passed the names of the variables to validate using the BPELVariableName with the variables listed with a white space delimiter. When a deviation is found, a bpel:invalidVariables fault is thrown.

While it is possible to turn off variable validation, this creates not only the potential for application logic errors not being caught but also the possibility that an attacker could manipulate the application data and data types to destroy the authenticity of data, its integrity, and utility.

In support of application and process logic, WS-BPEL supports a number of logical expressions. These include boolean, deadline, duration, unsigned integer, and general expressions. The `<assign>` activity is used to copy data from one variable to another as well as to initialize a variable with data.

In the delivery of messages to the right WSDL port of the service, they not only need to be delivered to the right port but also the correct instance of the process that provides the port. As an SOA is not an object-oriented structure where stateful interactions are mediated by object references, which allow the discovery of the correct object with the appropriate state and history for the interaction, business data and protocol headers are leveraged.

These exchanges may nest and overlap and are not global, spanning the entire interaction between process and partner but relate just to aspects of the interaction. The same data sets may be correlated with different actions. WS-BPEL provides correlationSets as a mechanism to keep track, using a pairing of the name as an NCName and the properties as a QName-list. The name must be unique among the names of all the correlationSets within the immediate scope.

The properties in a correlationSet are defined using XML schema simple types, and any message which interacts with or participates in the set simply needs to carry information that matches or initiates a correlationSet to participate in that set. However, the information must match exactly to be included in an existing correlationSet. However, messages may be sent with a particular initiate value that must be observed. If initiate is set to "yet", the activity must attempt to initialize the correlation set, and throw a fault if the set is already created. If the initiate attribute is set to join, the message must create a set if not already created, and if it is already in existence, join that set unless the data is not consistent with the data already in the set. If initiate is set to "no", the message cannot initiate a correlationSet, and a fault is thrown if a set does not already exist. Messages can carry the tokens of more than one correlation set, with business logic defining how this is handled.

Business logic can be defined using structured activities where the order in which a collection of activities is defined. This may be done through sequence control such as `<sequence>`, `<if>`, `<while>`, `<repeatUntil>`, and `<forEach>`, with a deferred choice specified by `<pick>`. Because the applications are distributed and dependent upon external factors not in the control of a particular process's execution, there are situations where the dependent link fails, and the suppressJoinFailure is set to "yes" leading to a situation where the false condition must not be initiated and the fault bpel:joinFailure must not be generated. The outgoing links must be assigned a status of "false", and this must be propagated across the entire path formed by successive links until a join condition is reached which evaluates to "true". This ensures that a valid activity can always be executed.

While `<scope>`s provide context, they do not do so in isolation. Scopes can be nested hierarchically, with a `<process>` construct acting as root. They both share the same syntax and constructs and the following distinctions:

The `<process>` is not an activity.

Neither the compensation nor termination handlers can be attached to a `<process>`.

The `<process>` cannot be isolated using an isolate construct.

Each scope has a primary activity, though this may be as simple or as complex as needed. If complex, a scope can have an arbitrary depth to it, limited by the complexity of the process. All variables, messages, and correlationSets are accessible to the parent of the scope, but the scope can only declare variables, messages, and correlationSets within itself.

When the activities within a scope complete, all service interactions dependent on the partner links and message exchanges declared in the scope need to be completed. When an inbound message activity is left in such a state, it is considered orphaned. In the event that a partner link or message exchange cannot be completed within a child scope, a bpel:missingReply must be thrown. When the fault is thrown, no matter how many orphaned IMA there are, they are all covered by the single fault.

WS-BPEL has a robust error handling precisely because business processes can be of long duration and their successful completion depends upon proper handling of the errors. Where possible, the application architect should leverage the ability of WS-BPEL to handle errors with application-specific activities, which attempt to reverse the actions of the work, which is being abandoned because of the error. This is called compensation. This can be predefined in the scope alongside the logic of the business process, using the `<compensationHandler>` element. Because these may need to run opposite ongoing processes because of the failure of a subordinate scope, they should be defined within their own scopes. The process keeps track of all iterations of a scope, no matter how many executions in a "for" loop or "while" loop, and the compensationHandler will have full access to the state with full transaction set.

Depending on how the `<compensateScope>` is called allows the alteration of what is rolled back. If `<compensateScope>` is called with regard to a specified target of a specified child scope, then only the activity within that child scope is reversed. However, the default activity of calling a `<compensate>` is that all child scopes are rolled back. If such an activity happens in a "for" loop or a "while" loop, all transactions are reversed in the opposite order of the initial execution. If an uncaught fault occurs while executing a compensation handler or if compensation activities are terminated, then all running instances must be terminated.

Each scope may have a set of event handlers that run in parallel with the scope and are invoked when a corresponding event happens. There are two kinds of events, inbound messages that correspond to WSDL operations and alarms which trigger after a time-set trigger. Event handlers must contain at least one `<onEvent>` or `<onAlarm>` element, which defines the actions that are executed upon the event condition. `<OnEvent>` events function pretty much like a `<receive>` activity, with similar variables and constraints as well as compensations. Event handlers are enabled when the parent scope starts.

The `<onAlarm>` event is a time-driven event, with at least one `<for>`, `<until>`, or `<repeatEvery>` expression, though `<for>` and `<until>` are mutually exclusive. If the specified duration ever equals zero, then a bpel:invalidExpressionValue is thrown. The clock is started when the parent scope starts, with the alarm triggered when the specified time conditions are met.

When a scope's primary activity is completed, the event handlers are disabled; however, the existing running event handlers must be permitted to complete, and the completion of the scope is delayed until they finish.

If a scope has the isolated attribute set to "yes" when initialized, then that scope is considered isolated. Isolated scopes may not contain other isolated scopes but may contain normal scopes. In the event that a normal scope is executed from the inside of an isolated scope, it must access all external variables through the constraint of the isolated scope. It is useful to isolate a scope to control concurrent access to shared resources, partner links, and control dependency links. The results of the isolated scope remain the same no matter what other scopes do to the shared values, so that if two isolated scopes access the same external variables, the results of each scope are unaltered no matter which scope executes first or what ever is the order of processing of the variables. Compensation handlers of isolated scopes are not started until the isolated scope completes, unlike with a normal scope where the compensation handler operates in parallel with the scope's processing.

So far we have looked at executable processes within WS-BPEL. Abstract processes have their own uses and are a powerful feature of the standard. Abstract processes are defined using a common base with profiles to refine for separate use cases. This common base does not have well-defined semantics. The common base must have an abstractProcessProfile, with a value referring to an existing profile definition. All constructs of executable processes are permitted, though certain constructs may be hidden through the inclusion of opaque language extensions or through omission. Four types of opaque tokens are enabled: activities, expressions, attributes, and from-specs. While abstract processes must comply with the need to validate the syntax, it may omit the createInstance activity.

An opaque activity is an explicit placeholder for an executable WS-BPEL activity and any activities nested therein. This executable activity uses all the nonopaque attributes defined by the opaque activity it replaces, as well as any elements or expressions. Opaque activities can be used to create a process template that marks the points of extension in a process; another is hiding an activity, which is a join point for several links when creating an Abstract process from a known executable process. Opaque expressions allow the ability to present outcomes and alternatives without exposing how the outcome was derived.

Not only are attributes hidden, but their values may also be opaque. Those opaque attributes actually hide where the data is stored once the corresponding message is received.

Another technique to hide processing is omission, which can be used when the location can be detected deterministically. Omission is restricted to those attributes, activities, expressions, and from-specs that are syntactically required by WS-BPEL and have no default value.

It is important to note that WS-BPEL has no native security controls, though it is binding-neutral. Because messages may be modified or forged, the use of WS-Security or at least signing the messages is encouraged. Signatures should include the semantically significant headers and the message body. To prevent replay attacks, messages should include a message timestamp within the signature, allowing the detection of duplicate transmissions.

# 6

# AUDITING SERVICE-
# ORIENTED ARCHITECTURES

The auditing of a service-oriented architecture (SOA) will involve inspecting the Web Services Description Language (WSDL) and WS-Policy for each service to make certain that only those functions desired for the workflow can be called, that all services that provide sensitive functionality or operate on data, which remains confidential require authentication, that data are encrypted, and that encrypted data are signed. The auditor must also verify that authentication and authorization are logged by the service, and that logs can record who did what, when, and with what authority. A key thing to look for, but is not a requirement, is that the clock setting on all the audit logs is the same. While it is a fundamental requirement that all systems that log get their time from a centralized time service such as Network Time Protocol (NTP), there are benefits and problems from placing what are often globally deployed systems into the same time zone. If you so place them, then cross-system log correlation for both audits and troubleshooting becomes trivial. However, any user-focused troubleshooting becomes problematic, as the time zone the user is located in may not (and probably will not) match the time zone the systems are set to. Also, if the time zones are set centrally, then auditing conformance to time-based authorization checks becomes hard, as discrepancies must be accounted for. This is one of those many areas where there are no right answers, just trade-offs and corporate styles. The auditor should check, however, that the corporate standard for time zone setting is followed for all systems in scope.

Because the SOA is a complex multiplatform cross enterprise unity of capabilities in the service of business objectives, properly auditing any SOA for compliance with internal or external standards will take time and diligence. However, no shortcuts should be taken as a flaw caught in an audit may prevent the business from compromise by a criminal who found a service without authentication or sensitive data that remained unencrypted.

## 6.1 Penetration Testing

First, I must clarify that penetration testing is not hacking but rather an extension of the quality assurance (QA) process and of the audit process. QA testing is testing of application functionality and performance to verify that it is bug-free and responsive. Looking for security vulnerabilities is simply looking for a certain class of bugs; however, instead of testing the normal use of an application or platform, you perform abusive tests designed to force the application to do things for which it is capable but not designed to do. In essence, you are exposing hidden functionality that is not part of the specifications and therefore should be eliminated.

It is an extension of the audit function insofar as it is a validation that the controls you have implemented are effective as designed, where findings are control gaps or areas where the penetration tester was able to compromise a control.

Despite very impressive security controls to guarantee the integrity of data, the utility of process, and the confidentiality and availability of information, there are numerous ways to attack successfully even the best-protected web service.

Many web services are not authenticated properly; often authorization is not checked after authentication. Most importantly, the service logic itself may be used in ways that the developers never intended.

In the absence of proper account lockout policies, web services accounts can be brute forced using a SOAP message that contains account after account. Proper logging can record this but may not alert you to the attack unless the log is monitored.

Web services messages can have their sessions hijacked when the session is maintained with either cookies or information in the SOAP header.

### 6.1.1 Reconnaissance

More than almost any other technology, SOAs may expose their features to passive reconnaissance techniques. Universal Description, Discovery and Integration (UDDI), where used, provides a wealth of information on where the service and its components are located. It is for this reason more than any other that UDDIs are not commonly used.

WSDLs, as discussed earlier, also provide a wealth of information on the service. More than a UDDI, the WSDL is a gold mine for an attacker and provides the penetration tester with a road map to how to approach the application.

WSDLs are often found through simply appending "?wsdl" to the end of a URL. You look in the WSDL for open methods and resources that are unprotected. Service tags, easily found with a `<service.*?>` regex pattern, define the name of the service and how to engage it.

**Exhibit 6.1**

While any web browser can read and parse the syntax of a WSDL file, using a browser to read the syntax manually is an inefficient way to look for vulnerabilities. There are a variety of free tools, which can be leveraged to parse and test web services. One of the more useful tools is WSDigger by McAfee Foundstone. You simply load the URL for the WSDL into the tool. URLs for WSDLs are usually easily found by appending a ?wsdl to the end of a URL, but obviously they will most often be found when the file extension is a .asmx or .jws indicating a J2EE or .Net-based web service.

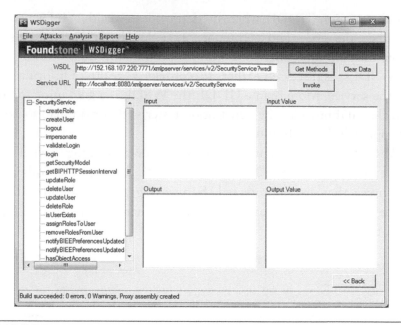

**Exhibit 6.2**

Simply selecting the service you wish to exploit will provide details on the data expected and allow for manual testing of the service's response to data.

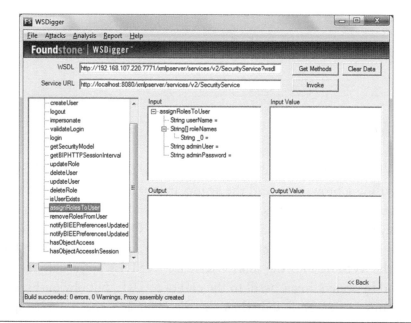

**Exhibit 6.3**

WSDigger provides the vulnerability analyst or penetration tester with not only the ability to parse out any control but also to feed the tool with input data for testing.

WSKnight is another WSDL enumeration tool that can make finding vulnerabilities easy. The circle in Exhibit 6.4 shows a service call in a WSDL that does not require authentication. This particular WSDL is for a commonly used enterprise-class business analytics tool published by Oracle.

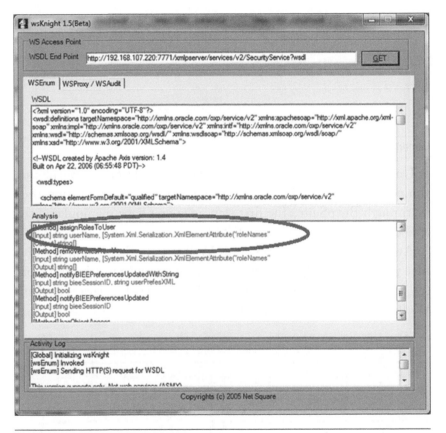

**Exhibit 6.4**

Buby is a free BurpSuite plugin written by Ken Johnson which can not only enumerate a WSDL and manually test it for input handling but also scan the file for common vulnerabilities. Buby is a ruby extension, which relies on jRuby, rubyGems, Savon, and Nokogiri.

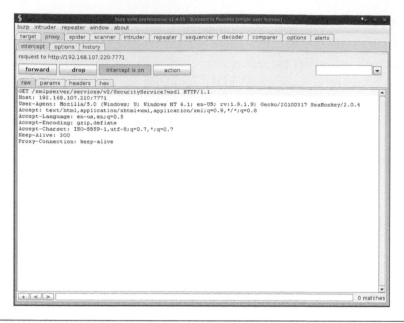

**Exhibit 6.5**

Unlike with other web services testing tools, to test using BurpSuite, you configure BurpSuite as a proxy and direct the application traffic through BurpSuite. The first step once you have manipulated the application is to enumerate the WSDL.

Another plugin for BurpSuite is WSDLER. This plugin requires that you are running burpsuite 1.5.1 or later, and must be run from the command line, started with the following syntax: java -classpath Wsdler.jar;burp.jar burp.StartBurp.

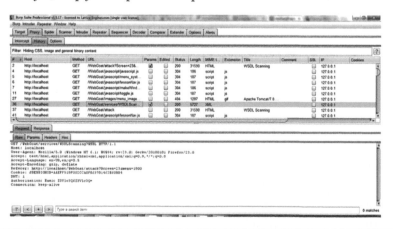

**Exhibit 6.6**

As with other tools, WSDLER will parse WSDL to make the parameters easily identifiable. These parameters can be sent to other aspects of the BurpSuite to allow attacks to be planned and executed. This allows BurpSuite to bridge the gap between reconnaissance and attacking the service provider.

Another tool that allows you to not merely evaluate and parse WSDL is WS-Attacker. Named as if it were a web services standard, WS-Attacker is a web services application testing tool, which enumerates a WSDL file, identifies vulnerabilities, and allows for attack execution. Unlike BurpSuite, WS-Attacker is not an attack proxy, so you do not access the application through the tool as if you are using it normally while the tool examines the application for areas of weakness. Instead, you load the WSDL into the tool, which then becomes a client of the service, which exposes areas of attack.

You should use both attack proxies and web services clients and SOAP-based clients in testing your service-based application to provide a completeness of review.

### 6.1.2 Injection Attacks

Before we get into how to inject malicious data successfully into Extensible Markup Language (XML), I want to take a moment to explain two different kinds of XML parsing. Simple API for XML (SAX) parsers parse the XML one line at a time, and Document Object Model (DOM) parsers parse an entire document in memory. Both have advantages, and both have vulnerabilities.

Injecting data into XML will impact each parser differently. When the XML is parsed with an SAX parser, one can place a tag inside the logic of another tag and overwrite data without authorization. As an example:

```
<AccountInformation>
<AccountNumber>XJ12M</AccountNumber>
<Privileges>15</Privileges>
<FirstName>John</FirstName>
The attacker changes the XML to read as follows:
<AccountNumber>XJ12M</AccountNumber>
<Privileges>15</Privileges>
<FirstName>John<AccountNumber>XJ13M></AccountNumber>
</FirstName>
```

John's account number is now XJ13M.

Just as in URL manipulation, the parameters of a SOAP packet can be tampered with if they are not signed. Metacharacters can be injected into the parameters and break the services logic. Where data in the XML are not signed, one can often cause a denial of service within a service provider by mistyping the data expected in a tag.

Just as with any web application, Structured Query Language (SQL) injection and Lightweight Directory Access Protocol (LDAP) injection may reveal information in services exposed to the architecture but not designed to provide the information you request through the injection attack. If the underlying database or directory service does not properly check authorization, price lists, account information, and even password hashes and x509v3 private keys may be provided.

When web services leverage file systems and the underlying operating system, the SOAP packets can manipulate the web service to provide file data or execute code in the context of the account under which the web service is running.

### 6.1.3  Attacking Authentication

Security Assertion Markup Language (SAML) is a credential unique to service-oriented applications, and as it can be used to access multiple companies' resources, successful attacks against the protocol can result in a security breach to all organizations to which the credential has been authenticated. Where SAML assertions are sent over Secure Sockets Layers (SSLs), they are vulnerable to man-in-the-middle attacks. When the protocol was developed, those were considered theoretical, and insufficient rigor was placed into the protocol's design and recommendations to prevent these attacks from having an impact. Unfortunately, hackers have made the theoretical practical, and in fact, rather trivial to implement on wireless networks. Unless client-side certificates are used, SSL/TLS (Transport Layer Security) is not sufficient to prevent a successful man-in-the-middle attack, and some of the techniques will not even generate a certificate error.

To execute a man-in-the-middle attack successfully without errors, the attacker must deliberately target the service, not attack as the opportunity presents itself. The attacker must request from a known and trusted certification authority a server certificate. Unless the company you are attacking uses extended validation certificates, which is not likely, the intended victim will never notice that the certificate they encounter was signed by a different certification authority than prior certificates.

Because, by default, the SAML protocol does not ask for credentials upon subsequent connections within a defined period of time, but relies upon a shared secret, usually an SAML artifact, to indicate that the system and user presenting the assertion are the same system and user as the initial connection, it can be vulnerable to a replay attack. The replay attack depends upon a man-in-the-middle interception of the assertion, where the malicious user then uses the assertion from his/her computer to gain access.

For this attack to succeed, the attacker not only needs to capture the SAML assertion but also be able to duplicate the SAML artifact used to prove prior authentication. As you will no doubt remember from the SAML chapter, after a successful authentication, the service provider provides the client with a uniform resource identifier (URI) to get the artifact that SAML will use to prove prior authentication upon subsequent requests. However, this is something for which SAML by default does not authenticate, and by default, the request can be replayed. The artifacts are only good once, but if there is an error, good artifacts may still be available to grab and use.

To execute a replay attack, the malicious user must intercept the redirect to the destination site and replay it. At this point, there is no method to differentiate between the attacker and the legitimate client, and there is no authentication at this stage. The service will respond to the attacker with the same response it would provide to the originator and authorize the attacker to use the resources of the compromised user.

Another mechanism is to impersonate the intersite transfer URL of the source site to the client. The attacker simply erects a proxy and forwards on to the client all valid traffic until an unused SAML artifact is sent. Then, it forwards to the client an intersite transfer URL which points to the proxy and injects itself into the communications with the server. From that moment on, the malicious user can either take over the session or continue to act as a "man in the middle" passing traffic back and forth, while making calls of his own.

Another means to attack SAML, which also depends upon the ability to execute a man-in-the-middle attack, is to interrupt the response the provider sends to the browser, with the hope of generating an error with a link or HTTP redirect embedded within the error. These should provide access to unused artifacts, which can be used to establish and maintain the connection with the service provider. Those links and redirects will presume that authentication has already successfully happened.

All of these man-in-the-middle attacks can be prevented by requiring authentication where the protocol does not specify it but that may break interoperability. Enforcing the one-time-use property of artifacts will help. If all of your clients are applications, they can be programed to evaluate the certificate of the SSL/TLS connection to ensure it is the one that your organization has authorized the use thereof, but if your application will be accessed by browser-based clients, that option will not be available to you. I also want to note that executing a man-in-the-middle attack against an application remains very hard to do without notice or impact where the client is another application as the mechanisms for the attack would be either Border Gateway Protocol (BGP) hijacking of the IP address space or Domain Name System (DNS) hijacking. However, there are a number of tools that facilitate these attacks, and if carefully planned, both can be executed without notice on the part of either compromised party. Use of DNS Security Extensions (DNSSEC) can help mitigate the risk of DNS hijacking. If your client is browser based, the only means to prevent a man-in-the-middle attack is to use client-side certificates, also referred to as strongly authenticated or unilaterally authenticated SSL/TLS. Strongly authenticated SSL/TLS also remediates this threat where the client is not browser based, and as this is easier to implement for interapplication communications, I repeat my strong recommendation that organizations planning to use SAML for authentication use client certificates to strongly authenticate the SSL/TLS tunnels between companies.

Man-in-the-middle attacks against SAML are not the only way to attack the protocol. SAML is not easy to implement, and mistakes in the implementation can leave one open to attack. The most common vulnerability in SAML implementations is that they misapply the XML signature, leaving the protocol open to XML Signature Wrapping (XSW) attacks. That these attacks can succeed without executing a man-in-the-middle attack first makes them especially devastating to an organization that depends upon SAML for authentication, but to succeed, the attacker needs access to a single-signed SAML assertion. The attack will work even if the assertion is expired.

If the service they are trying to compromise does not allow for self-registration, then the execution of a man-in-the-middle attack may be required. If the attacker is very motivated, and another client of the service provider is the target, they can simply set up a shadow company, register as a real client, and execute the attack against the service provider to gain access to the client's data. Here the adversary is organized crime or a malicious nation state. Defending against such an adversary is part of the planning involved in any sound security architecture. Depending upon the company, and the goods being sold, this threat may be very real.

While such adversaries are real, they are not an issue for all corporations. However, this attack does not depend upon such determination. If the target service provider uses self-registration, the attacker can simply register, gain an SAML assertion, and become the real target: another person. If the target service provider does not use self-registration, then simply set up shop in a cafe where the customer of the service provider hangs out.

The key elements that must be understood are:

XML Schema validation: Some SAML frameworks check compliance to the underlying XML schema. Wrapped content must therefore be placed into XML schema extension points, and if the extension elements are not provided in the message, they must be explicitly included.

Order and position: The order and position of signed and executed elements in the message tree can force different processing modules to have inconsistent data views. Please remember, XML digital signatures generally only sign parts of the XML, and different signatures can sign different parts.

Processing of the IDs: Several SAML frameworks explicitly check the reference of the ID in the XML signature to ensure it matches the ID in the handled assertion.

Placement of the signature element: When executing the attack, it does not matter if the signature element is left in the original or the new malicious assertion; the important thing is to be consistent.

Signature exclusion: While SAML assertions may be signed, the signature is often not validated, not by design, but because of bugs which cause this step never to be executed.

Untrusted signatures: Not only is the signature often not validated, but the key used to sign the XML is not always validated. If the application just validates that XML is signed with the corresponding certificate in the keyElement, and the key is not validated, then any key can be used to sign XML.

Attacking XML signatures depends upon the fact that XML signatures are processed twice, once for validation and once by the business logic. If the attackers can cause these two divergent processes to use different parts of the message, then they can inject their own information into the signature without invalidating it. The verification routine validates the original signature, while the business logic uses the modified signature.

To execute the attack, first obtain an assertion. Add additional claims about the subject and submit. There are a number of techniques for adding the additional claims. How you insert your attack depends upon how the XML was signed. The XML signature may be a child of the SAML and only sign the assertion element. The XML signature may sign the entire protocol-binding element, with the signature placed either within this or in the protocol-binding root element. You may also combine them, with a signature protecting internal XML and a second protecting the entire protocol message.

The first attack works against applications and frameworks that do not validate a signature unless it is included. Called a Signature Exclusion Attack, it works well against older versions of Apache 2 Axis2 web services framework, Java Open Single Sign On (JOSSO), and Eduserv. If the organization is using a vulnerable version of Axis2, it does not validate the signature for the entire XML even if the signature is present. It just validates the signature of the timestamp and the SOAP body; so a modification may be made to the SOAP header without issue. Simply placing the malicious assertion off of the root allows for exploitation and compromise.

A second attack leverages XML's architecture. Because multiple signatures may be used to sign the same elements, this attack simply places a new assertion with a different ID element in front of the first, with its own signature, so that the original becomes a child assertion of the new and malicious assertion. Where XML schema validation is being performed, the attacker could bypass this by injecting this into the Object element, which allows arbitrary content. This attack does violate SAML but that does not prevent it from working against older versions of Higgins, IBM's XS 40 security gateway, SalesForce.com, OneLogin toolkit, and the OpenAM framework.

If the application uses an older version of OpenSAML, none of the attacks above would work because OpenSAML checks the ID of the signature validation with the ID of the processed assertion. However, exploiting a bug in the handling of xsd:any content allows for duplication of IDs inside an XML message. This allows the insertion of a second assertion, which is processed.

This last example underscores a key problem in application development: Even if you have solid application architectures and implements with strict conformance to the standards and protocols, your defenses may be circumvented by using a library that has a flaw.

To defend successfully against XSW, one must:

1. Validate XML schema
2. Extract assertions
3. Verify what is signed
4. Validate the signature
5. Process the assertion

Additional countermeasures include a number of approaches to system implementation that should be considered by every application architect where the use of SAML is mandated by their business requirements. The first is to only process what is hashed, or more specifically, only process what is signed. The hashed parts of an XML document are those that are serialized as an input to the hash function where the value is stored in a Reference element. While this is simple in theory, it is actually complex to implement.

A second countermeasure against this attack is to mark the signed elements. One marking technique is to alter the response to an XML Signature Verification by returning the complete document with a description of where the validly signed assertions may be located. Another approach to marking is to generate a random value, use this to mark the valid signed elements with this value, and then validate that all signed objects contain that random value. This approach depends upon the attacker not recognizing that the attribute, which would be common to all signed objects, has value related to the signature processing. Because SAML cannot be extended, the XML node type could be used to carry this information. This technique has been proposed to the XML Security Working Group.

A third countermeasure is to simply structure the application so that only those elements that were validated by the signature verification module are forwarded to the business logic module. Architecturally, this is the simplest and soundest approach. However, it relies upon all unsigned elements being properly extracted and would not work if the XML signature uses Extensible Stylesheet Language Transformations (XSLT) or XPath transformations. As it is against the recommendations of the WS-Security standard to use XSLT or XPath transformations, an SAML implementation within a WS-Security framework has a better chance of being resilient to these attacks if properly implemented.

Because this attack can work against one's application in a way that could compromise the confidentiality and integrity of a customer's information, it pays to ensure that your application is not vulnerable to this attack. It is always wise to perform internal vulnerability analysis of an application. The presence of a vulnerability to this attack can be tested using WS-Attacker.

It is interesting to me that the implementations that have strictly adhered to SAML's standards have proven to be the most resilient to attack. Sound standards' adherence is a good strategy for an architect. It is also interesting to note that the free implementations of openSAML and SimpleSAML.php were also the most resilient to attack though openSAML could be defeated through a very sophisticated version of the XSW attack. The only professional version that was resilient to the attacks was the Windows Identity Foundation implementation of SAML. Considering all the bad press that Microsoft has endured for years in the information security community, this is a pleasant change.

For the most part, after Somorovsky, Mayer, Schwenk, Kampmann, and Jensen published their findings on the XSW attack, the vendors tested work to address the bugs and architectural flaws in their implementations. While the security architect should always test an implementation, especially if your SOA depends upon third-party-provided tools or libraries, modern SAML implementations should be resilient to the XSW attacks. However, the only way to build resiliency into any protocol so it can survive a man-in-the-middle attack is to ensure the protocol is strongly authenticated.

### 6.1.4 Attacking Authorization

Attacking authorization is the game of elevation of privilege. An existing authenticated user tries to gain access to features and information for which there is no authorization. Unlike with authentication, where there are standard means to authenticate using standards-based protocols which can be evaluated, each application controls authorization uniquely unless it is built upon a framework, in which, perhaps, vulnerabilities within the underlying framework can be exploited. This is the hardest thing to accomplish in attacking an application but the most rewarding.

If you can identify a framework underneath the application, this may help identify a vulnerability that allows for elevation of privilege. As an example, if you discover that the application you are attacking is a Microsoft Sharepoint application, you can readily find out that some versions of Sharepoint allow privilege elevation if you can get the application to load a web service you have written. However, getting the application to load and run an external application is not something available to all users; so you may have to find another way to elevate privileges to execute this attack.

The most common technique to elevate permissions is impersonation. Through an attack proxy, you replace the information mapped to the security token with similar information from another user, injecting the values. This only works if the XML is not signed and the signature not properly validated. If the XML is signed and the signature is validated with each transaction, then the attack will fail. If, on the other hand, the signature is only validated upon authentication, then the techniques discussed to attack authentication will allow impersonation, and if a more privileged user is impersonated, then the attack may succeed. Too many application architects only validate the signature used to sign XML upon authentication.

The second most common means is to manipulate the presentation layer. Especially with Web 2.0 applications where a majority of the presentation layer code is loaded into the browser for fast access, there may be objects that are not exposed in the user interface unless variables are set. Through reading both the header and body of the interface of the application, the attacker may be able to identify parameters which expose these interfaces to the client and leverage functionalities that they are not authorized for. These attacks will work as long as the application does not validate on the server side the access to application functionality with each service call. If this is established only at authentication, then these attacks will succeed.

While XSS and SQL injection attacks are very common in normal web applications, they are less common in service-oriented applications mostly because XML is most often used as the data language, and with SOAP there is little need for scripting. However, when the service-oriented application is based on Representational State Transfer (REST) instead of SOAP, then the service calls may make calls through scripts, SQL, and perhaps even WebSockets, allowing for XSS and SQL injection, which are data layer attacks, to succeed.

### 6.1.5 Denial-of-Service Attacks

If the web service is using DOM, the DOM parser will read the entire XML into memory before processing. One can overload a DOM processor using complex XML structures and large envelopes. Once the DOM processor is overloaded, it is often possible to run arbitrary code or take down the service entirely.

If the web service is using an SAX parser, it is harder to make the processor go into a state where the processer is overloaded, as the processor executes the instructions one line at a time. The only effective means to get an SAX parser to go into a race condition is to alter the logic of the XML so that loops do not close properly and the application becomes stuck in an endless loop. This is more possible with WS-BPEL (Business Process Execution Language), where a scope can be manipulated into an endless loop as the business logic is exposed in the XML. Another viable attack against WS-BPEL is to ensure that all scopes fail on their last action and roll back their transactions, causing lost clock cycles as the processing is taken up by a never-ending need to start over from scratch.

Both attacks are readily defeated by the use of digital signatures and validation of the signature by the service or simply deploying a data layer firewall, which parses all XML before it attempts to execute, thus preventing such logic attacks.

### 6.1.6 Data Integrity

While I have repeatedly stressed the need for digital signatures and signature validation throughout this book, a sufficient number of application developers will forgo this simple control because the application is protected by SSL/TLS, and they view this as sufficient.

The first place to attack the integrity of data is through metacharacter injection. Injecting a single quote, double quote, or a hyphen into a SOAP query may produce a fault code with a fault string that reveals interesting information regarding the back-end database. This can be followed up with injecting traditional SQL injection strings such as the infamous 1 or 1 = 1 string (you will need to match the syntax of the underlying database for this to work). Instead of a fault, this may return data for which you were not authorized.

The venerable wsAudit tool can be used to inject such characters into the SOAP. This tool, created by Shreeraj Shah allows the automation of SQL, XPath, and SQL injection attacks. Injection can also be used to attack both the integrity and authenticity of data by simply substituting invalid strings for valid strings. Unless the data is signed, this attack is undetectable and can be devastating to the organization. All of these attacks are made trivial if the unsigned XML is sent from the client's browser to the back-end service provider if the client is a victim to a man-in-the-middle attack.

While SSL/TLS should prevent a man-in-the-middle attack, it can only do so if the end user serves a client certificate for authentication. Otherwise, an attacker can simply spin up a false site, decrypt and modify the traffic, and then recrypt and pass it on to the unsuspecting service provider. A well-planned attack will not even have a certificate error as a certificate can be requested and provided by an alternative certificate provider. Extended validation certificates mitigate this somewhat but only if the end users notice that although when they usually connect there is a green bar in the URL, on this particular day that is absent. It is a sad state of affairs that organizations pay all that money for an extended validation certificate and all they get is the color green as if the certificate authority is acknowledging the extra cost.

A potentially more devastating attack that depends upon a man-in-the-middle attack also succeeding is to access the underlying file system through SOAP. If the fault string you generate from your injection attack indicates that the SOAP cannot find the file, then you know that the service provider is reading files from the hard disk from the parameter provided. Files can then be queried by the simple expedient of providing the path and an appropriate wild card. If you get a fault of "unsuccessful command", then you know that the parameter you have injected was tried by the service provider as a command in the operating system. The easiest way to exploit this is first to use either the ls or dir command to enumerate the files available and then execute a fully qualified command.

### 6.1.7 *Malicious Use of Service or Logic Attacks*

You can think of this as the unintended use category. As an example, creating an account in an online service which validates a credit card and then canceling that service a few days later is an excellent technique used by crooks to validate that they have a valid credit card. This is a category of fraud that is impossible to protect against. The more checks you place onto the validation of identity, the more valuable your service becomes to identity thieves as they are able to more strongly validate the information that they have stolen.

Another example of malicious use of business logic, which is the use of the ability to transfer money from one account to another is often used by money launderers to move money so that it cannot be tracked. An account is opened, later, money is transferred into it, and then almost immediately the money is transferred onto a third account and the recently opened account is closed. If this is done often enough, it becomes very difficult for law enforcement to trace the movement of funds.

These are both examples of using normal business processes for alternative use cases. This is the hardest crime to prevent as it means putting in place checks that prevent the business process from happening as effectively as the business should desire. Thus, many businesses do not put any controls in place and live with the risk that their application might be used by organized crime to perform criminal activities.

The worst thing is that an organization can be blissfully unaware that its application has been put to such use, even with careful logging. A good fraud investigation looks for event correlation. Both of the cases I outlined above would have patterns of accounts being created and closed within days of each other or in the case of the second example, closed within days of the money being transferred out.

Any good security audit should be looking for patterns of use like this, where normative functionality could be potentially misused for malicious gain. Any good penetration test should test business logic to see if it is possible to abuse such business logic. If money cannot be transferred out of an account within so many days of being transferred in, or if there are ceilings on the amount that can be transferred. If an account cannot be closed within so many days after being used for a money transfer, then perhaps the ability to transfer money in and out of a personal account will no longer be useful to criminals.

The penetration test should attempt such alternative uses of business logic. A business should know if its application can be used to conduct criminal activities. An audit should look for evidence that such activities are taking place if there is a distinct possibility that the application is being misused.

### 6.1.8 Poisoning XML Schemas

While SQL or script injection through cross-site scripting (XSS) is not common, XML injection is. XML injection or XML poisoning can be done either on the input or output phase of the message delivery, either injecting unauthentic valued into the data stream. With XML, the attacker could also poison the XML schema by replacing or modifying it. This would allow the attacker to prevent the use of the application in the way it was designed, often without needing to compromise the application itself.

Because XML schemas are publicly located and shared, one technique for accomplishing this is to attack the DNS namespace for the schema repositories, allowing misdirection to an alternative and malicious schema. This could impact the use of the schema for all organizations that use those XML elements. Attacks against the namespace tend to be noticed rather quickly, precisely because of the global nature of the impact. Most organizations use local and known good copies, not the references to the schema provided in the XML. While this means that modifications of public copies or redirecting from public copies would not impact the targeted organization, this technique does not necessarily mitigate the risk.

The XML still needs to reference the location of the schema it is using, and those locations need to be available to all components that process that XML. If the attacker can gain access to these locations, it may be able to poison the schema, or if the attacker cannot gain access to the files, it could misdirect the application through DNS hijacking.

No matter how this attack is carried out, it is a relative noisy attack if the application performs any input validation. Sudden errors in data input would allow for speedy detection of an XML poisoning attack. It really depends on how serious the development team is about input validation. Typically in applications that I have tested, input validation consisted of format checking and required fields enforcing.

# 7

# DEFENDING AND
# DETECTING ATTACKS

Fortunately, web services have many excellent and robust controls that can be applied to diligently and proactively protect the service, data, and business process.

There are three layers to defend: the service container, the service, and the messages between the services.

## 7.1 SSL/TLS

SSL or Secure Sockets Layer version 3 is roughly equivalent to TLS or Transport Layer Security version 1. It is a technology that creates in essence a virtual private network between two computers, which allows HTTP and other protocols to transverse the network. There are two kinds of SSL/TLS tunnels: server-authenticated tunnels and client/server-authenticated tunnels. Server-authenticated tunnels are much more common, with a certificate authenticating the server to the client resting on the server. When the client connects, the server presents the public key of the certificate to the client for its inspection. Should the client accept the certificate, the traffic is encrypted.

The process of establishing this connection is called a handshake. During the handshake, the client and server follow the rules of the protocol for both validating the certificate and establishing the encrypted tunnel. First, the client sends to the server the version, ciphers, session-specific information, and other requirements to set up the tunnel. Then, the server returns the version, ciphers, session-specific information, and other information as required. The client uses these data to authenticate the server. For a complete authentication, it should look at many fields within the public key of the certificate, especially the expiration date, where to check to see if the certificate has been revoked using either a certificate revocation list (CRL) or an Online Certificate Status Protocol (OCSP), and if the certificate was issued by a trusted certification authority.

CRLs and OCSP are far from equivalent, but the difference is likely only important to those organizations that depend heavily on client certificates, which we have yet to discuss in this chapter. CRLs are a list of revoked certificates. Usually updated only once a day, if that frequently, they are not a very reliable mechanism to validate the certificate you have encountered that has not been revoked. However, as revocation of server certificates is a rare event, it is likely sufficient. OCSP is a mechanism for both publishing and checking real time that a certificate is valid. This is much more important when client certificates are in use as client certificates are much more likely to be revoked than server certificates. No matter what the mechanism listed is, it is very important that it be checked, not only for the certificate at hand but also for the certificates that were used to sign the certificate you are validating. There have been compromises of keys used to sign other keys in the past, and no key signed by a compromised key should be trusted as the actual compromise may have happened significantly before the time when the compromise was discovered.

Let us look at each of these elements individually. First, the subject. The subject, among other things, traditionally maps the certificate name to the Domain Name System (DNS) name of the host. With the advent to so-called wildcard certificates, this is no longer a strong mapping as the certificate may be used on any valid host in the DNS domain. To some degree, this has weakened the security of the protocol. It only works for a single subdomain of the DNS domain; thus, foo.bar.certificate.com cannot host a certificate for *.certificate.com, only *.bar.certificate.com. Extended validation certificates cannot be wildcard certificates. Wildcard certificates, however, are invaluable for organizations that use protocol load balancers.

It is possible to maintain the mapping to DNS hosts by using the subjectaltname field. This field is a multivariate field, allowing multiple hosts to be added but requires the certificate to be reissued with each new host added to the wildcard certificate. In this author's opinion, those certificate authorities which use the subjectaltname to record the host names have a vastly more secure product offering than those certificate authorities which do not. There is at least one certificate authority that uses this to issue all servers covered by the wildcard its own signed private/public key pair, using the subjectaltname field to map to the actual host name. Because I am not going to advertise for any company, you will have to research your certificate authorities to find out which ones support wildcard certificates without sacrificing security.

There is a third level of certificate issued by modern certification authorities, called extended validation certificates. There is no real improvement of technology here, but of process. When a certificate is requested, a member of the certification authority contacts the authorized approver within the requesting organization to validate that the request was authorized. This prevents the issuing of certificates that are valid to individuals who do not represent the organization.

This is done to defeat one of the main attacks against SSL/TLS: impersonation. In theory, any organization can contact a certificate authority and claim to be any company. Many do not bother to check properly, especially the cheaper organizations. This is why extended validation certificates are so important; you know the certification authority actually checked to make certain that the certificate belongs to the company associated with it. It is important to note that wildcard certificates are not available as extended validation certificates.

One way to get around this limitation is to terminate SSL/TLS at a protocol load balancer. This allows multiple hosts to have the same host name as far as the systems on the Internet are concerned, but only a single certificate is used amongst those hosts. However, should the load balancer go down, the hosts behind it will not answer with that certificate, creating a potential single point of failure for the organization.

The subject field may have more than the host and DNS domain name in it. They may contain the country (c), domain component (dc), state/province (s), locality (l), organization (o), organization unit (ou), and common name (cn). The common name should be the host name, the domain component should be the DNS name broken up. Thus, foo.bar.com would be dc = foo, dc = bar, dc = com. Organization must be the legal entity name of the organization requesting the certificate. Organizations may have multiple organizational units within the subject. This can give you ou = IT, ou = engineering, o = organization like structures. The subject cannot contain the same number of characters as a DNS domain; the certification authority may use the subjectalt-name to contain the entire DNS domain name.

After the validation of the certificate, the client takes the public key of the server and uses it to encrypt the premaster encryption key for the session. This key is used by both client and server to create the session keys. The server now informs the client that the next packets will be encrypted, as does the client to the server, and from that moment forward the traffic sent is encrypted.

I have spent much real estate in this book lauding the benefits of strongly authenticated SSL/TLS. If the server mandates that the client present a certificate, then the client signs something known by the server and sends this back with its certificate. The server performs the same validation procedures on the client certificate as those performed by the server. The differences are that there are no hostnames to DNS mappings, no wildcard certificates, and no extended validation.

The subject's common name is often the email address of the individual, but may also be other values, such as an account name, full name, nickname, or other means to identify that individual uniquely within the organization. In fact, it is more important that a fully laid-out subject be present for a client certificate than for a server certificate because many people can have the same name, even within a company, but less likely within an organization unit.

## 7.2 Firewalls, IDS, and IPS

There are three kinds of firewalls, network, application, and data firewalls. While there are many kinds of network-layer firewalls, they are mostly irrelevant as protections for service-layer applications. As the connections to most service-layer applications will be over encrypted tunnels allowed through the firewall, they will be unable to perform the deep packet inspection that they perform on most network traffic they permit into a company's perimeter.

Application-layer firewalls are designed to inspect traffic at the application layer and are designed to either be the terminal of an SSL/TLS tunnel or behind a protocol load balancer that terminates the tunnel. Thus, an application-layer firewall has the opportunity to inspect the packets at a deep layer and inspect the application instructions for malicious traffic.

This works rather well for applications that render the presentation interface over HTTP but not for SOAP as SOAP packets may also be encrypted. While encryption provides protection for application data, it may also provide protection for application-layer attacks. Most application-layer firewalls lack the capacity to inspect SOAP, even less to decrypt it to examine it. However, while SOAP is a protocol, the Extensible Markup Language (XML) it carries can be looked at as a data set. Therefore, it is worth looking at data firewalls, or more specifically, XML firewalls.

Good XML firewalls can decrypt the XML, parse it without executing the instruction set, and then recrypt it before sending it on or do this with a copy of the message and send on the original encrypted XML after the copy has passed inspection. This last step is very important as it preserves data confidentiality until the SOAP messages are delivered to the intended destination. The ability to decrypt and understand the instructions in the XML is critical; otherwise, it would be trivial for an attacker to send an encrypted XML, which attacked the service, bypassing all controls and detection mechanisms.

As for IDS and IPS systems, which are traditionally part of a security architecture as potentially both detective (IDS) and preventative (IPS) controls, they are less useful in protecting a service-oriented application than could be desired. This is due to the inability to decrypt traffic. Even if the SSL/TLS has been terminated before the traffic transverses the IPS or IDS system, which is not often, no IDS/IPS that I am aware of has the ability to decrypt the XML and recognize an attack. This role again falls upon the XML firewall, which must not only function as a preventative but also as a detective control and alert the organization to an attempt at compromise, if the risk tolerance of the organization includes the need to be alerted about data-layer attacks.

I would recommend that the security architect strongly urge the alerting of data-layer attacks. These tend to be the most damaging kinds of attacks and can impact not only the confidentiality of existing data but also their integrity or availability. XML attacks may put the data parser into a run state where it never completes the parsing, effectively creating a denial-of-service condition. XML attacks may inject data, breaking data authenticity. They may gain access to unauthorized data, and so on.

A word or two about service-oriented architecture (SOA) governance products. Some of these products claim to be able to operate as XML firewalls among their other features. For the most part, the market segment is one that tries to enforce the interoperability of products designed to be components of an SOA. They provide monitoring and reporting of the monitor's meeting of key metrics. As with any technology which claims to support a security function, in this case the defending of a SOA implementation, the claims need to be validated in a laboratory setting. Choosing not to implement an XML firewall because one's SOA governance solution claims to be able to provide this feature may or may not be the wisest of choices. Organizations' SOAs will be attacked; so if implementing an SOA governance solution is desirous, this should not take budget money away from also implementing a feature-rich XML firewall. If the application is important enough to the organization to be worth spending the money to ensure interoperability, then the data within the application is important enough to the organization to be worth protecting properly.

# 8

# ARCHITECTURE

Once the business requirements have been gathered and turned into policy, as applications are designed, threat profiling should be a defined phase of the application design. It provides to the application architect what is referred to as a malicious-use story. Penetration-testing strategies should inform this malicious-use story, driving security considerations as part of the feature set of the application. The application should be explicitly designed to fit into the larger security architecture so that the policies of the organization are readily supported and enforced.

The application architects I have worked the closest with developed their architectures by starting at the service layer, delineating what were going to be independent services and then looking at how they would interface with each other through the communications layer. Others, however, may start with the workflow or the data flow, as these most closely map to business requirements. I have even known one application architect and design team to start at the presentation layer, use that to detail how functionality would be rendered, and then work back from there into the execution. So the approach I am going to take in this chapter does not reflect how things must be done but should reflect the nature of the decisions that need to be made at each layer of application design and in determining the mechanisms for interlayer communications.

## 8.1 Example 1

The application we are going to use for our first example will be a business-to-business application, which provides review and testing of integrated circuit board designs for efficiency using mathematical algorithms proprietary to this imaginary company, which looks at the resistance in the copper on the circuit board based upon the design and tests mathematically before a single board is cut. As this imaginary company will be interfacing with many customers' design teams, they must ensure that these customers, who are often competitors, cannot access each other's designs and that the designs are not tampered with. They provide to their customers an existing database of chips, capacitors, resistors, and so on, so that each design may be properly tested with the components that will be soldered to the board. This means that the application has some data that are common and shared between customers and other data that are proprietary and not shared. It is in all the customers' interests that they maintain control over who has access to their design documents and schematics, and thus, a federated identity management system is imperative to the success of the design.

Now that we have captured the imaginary business requirements, let us take them apart and look at how we would meet them with a sound application design. Let us start with the service layer. We have a need for an analysis service, a customer data exchange service, an internal data exchange service, a presentation service, an authentication service, and an authorization service. The reason we have identified a need for an internal data service is that we may look to expand the business so that customers can use our database of design components to design their boards in our application. That would be future functionality, but keeping these future expansion plans will help as we design the data service, the presentation layer, as well as the security services.

Because we need strict segregation between customers, we are not going to implement a back-end message bus to connect all the application layers directly. While this will sacrifice some operational and design efficiencies as we will need to establish interfaces between all the service layers to communicate with each other, this will also allow us to impose authorization checks on these interfaces. If we had a centralized message bus, communications and workflow could be exposed as internal services, but we would be vulnerable to one of our customers paying one of our employees to look on the message bus for information regarding their competition. Planning for prevention of industrial espionage between our customers is an essential part of building trust with them. While the more nefarious of our customers will be disappointed that they cannot exploit our staff to gain information on their competition, most of our customers will be comforted to know that we have kept their data from our employees even when it is on our platform, because they do not trust us not to share their data. All internal communication between the layers will be over Secure Sockets Layer (SSL) encrypted tunnels, but that will be sufficient protection as the application will validate the keys of the server before initiating the connection.

While it is hard to enforce externally, your security architect has presented you with internally generated and trusted x509v3 certificates. These are used to authenticate both internal servers and the applications making connections to them, as well as the service endpoints listening for the application-programing interface (API) calls. By enforcing strong authentication between devices, you are able to ensure that no rogue system can connect to your databases. However, the use of strongly encrypted tunnels and the enforced Transport Layer Security (TLS)/SSL at the perimeter has reduced the effectiveness of your network intrusion detection system (IDS). You mitigate this somewhat by ensuring that the logs from your firewall, your application firewall, and your Extensible Markup Language (XML) firewall all send their logs to the IDS/IPS (intrusion protection system) for evaluation. The IDS/IPS will only be able to prevent network layer attacks. It is imperative that both the application and XML firewalls can inspect incoming packets and block attacks dynamically. The application-layer firewall will be the termination point for your SSL/TLS tunnel, and while you send to the destination over a newly initiated encrypted tunnel, that will be the XML firewall, which will decrypt any encrypted elements and parse the XML before it is sent to the application for execution. This ensures that any malicious XML is not executed by the application.

Because of a need to communicate directly between the presentation layer, data layer, and service layer, an internal account federation would allow each layer to authenticate the other and allow authorization checks at the data layer for access to both our data and the customer's data and authorization at the service layer for application functionality. This authorization can readily be accomplished if we use Security Assertion Markup Language (SAML) with attributes in metadata. The SAML assertions will show that the principle was authenticated at the presentation layer and provide both the data layer and the service layer the ability to evaluate independent of authentication the request for access.

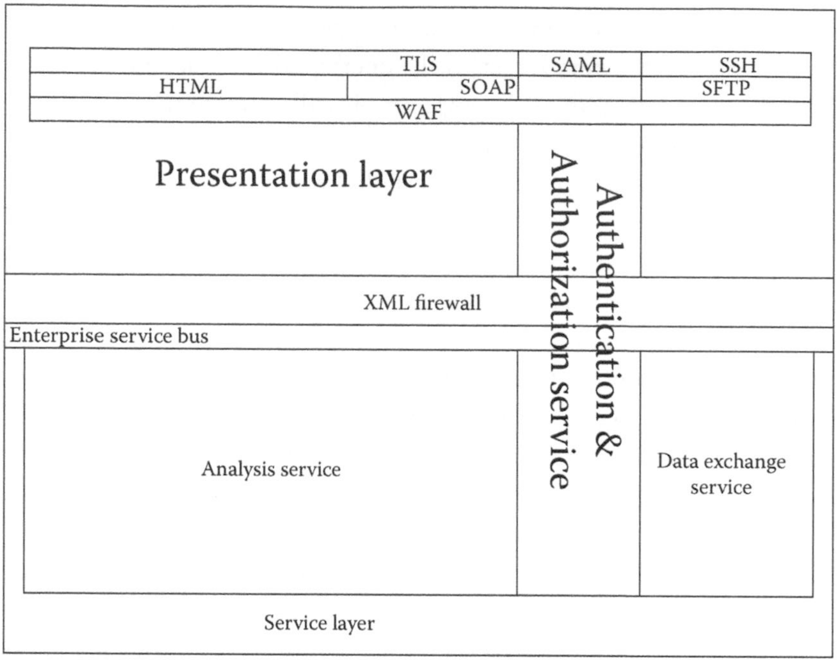

| | | TLS | SAML | SSH |
|---|---|---|---|---|
| HTML | | SOAP | | SFTP |
| | | WAF | | |

Presentation layer

Authentication & Authorization service

XML firewall

Enterprise service bus

Analysis service

Data exchange service

Service layer

**Exhibit 8.1**

## 8.2 Example 2

For this example, the corporation is looking to develop a business for a consumer travel and entertainment application that will be leveraging services provided by other providers. Maps will be provided by Google, weather information by the national weather service, and what to do by local conventions and visitors' bureaus, with the ability to make hotel reservations, train and airplane reservations, and book local rental car or taxi services or both. A key differentiator for this business is that it books mystery trips, where the person doing the booking has no idea where he/she will be going until the transaction is complete, but you as the service provider must be able to keep track and present enough information to allow an intelligent decision that meets the customer's budget and whims.

Anonymity will be important to preserve, not of the consumer, as you cannot make hotel or airline or train reservations without private and personal data regarding the consumer; however, as a mystery travel service, the names and locations of the hotels and the airline destinations will be kept anonymous until the booking is complete. While the application will not require any authentication to use, being a public application, private and personal data will be collected as part of the booking process, so security and compliance with both the Payment Card Industry Data Security Standard (PCI DSS) and international privacy regulations will be important. You will allow the customer to create an account with you to facilitate the ability to change or cancel any part or all of the mystery trip, because sometimes life changes and you cannot keep the plans you have made, for whatever reason, and you want your customers to know that they can change or cancel their reservations at any time. You will, however, allow various travel agencies to create accounts on your system so that they may make arrangements for their customers as you have no wish to lock out that important set of the travel and entertainment industry. The arrangements made by these agents must be able to be shared with the consumer. Lastly, you know that some of your customers will want to share their arrangements with family and friends via social networking sites, so you will provide the ability to authenticate to key social media sites.

The application workflow will be a critical factor in the success of your application as it must bring the consumer or travel agent throughout the reservation and booking process to produce a successful travel registration. The application architect will develop the entire application architecture around a workflow that will especially present to the consumer various ideas for a trip, such as an "Indiana Jones"-style treasure hunt with a jungle adventure, complete with ruins to explore and hidden treasure to find, or a "James Bond"-style adventure complete with casinos, fancy cars, and an evil villain to foil. Once they have selected from the many styles of mystery adventures, you will allow them to identify their budget and other constraints on the trip. Perhaps the entire trip must be in the country, as they do not want a passport or perhaps there are dietary or religious concerns such as days where they cannot travel or food that should not be presented.

Along with a workflow layer, this application will need two communication layers, an internal and an external. However, internally this can be handled with the same routines; simply specifying a destination should allow the application to either reach out to the internal message bus or to send messages to an externally facing message bus. Some architects would argue that a single message bus would suffice; however, the externally facing message bus will need to accept messages that originate at other organizations. As such, it will be vulnerable to a denial-of-service attack. By segregating that message bus from the internal message bus, you isolate internal application processing from this attack vector and reduce the exposure from denial-of-service attacks. The external message bus should have an XML firewall between it and public networks. In addition to traditional firewalls, this device will protect against both application and data layer attacks over XML. They parse the XML before sending it on to the message layer, looking for malformed XML.

The application will also need a service layer, a data layer, and a presentation layer. This presentation layer will be built dynamically by the workflow layer and will be composed of both the information from and interface into the service layers of many other companies' products. Thus, as the client indicates in the presentation layer that he/she does not want an adventure tour that will include any water adventures, then journeys to rediscover the lost city of Atlantis will no longer appear on the menu along with back-end connections to scuba tours.

As the application workflow captures the preferences of the prospective traveler, it will be writing the information into SAML metadata so that when he/she is ready to book, it can readily be shared with the service partners, both internally and externally. This way, the application cuts down on unnecessary writes into its own database, improving on both performance and data storage. If the booking is not finalized, the information is not kept, and the metadata is purged periodically and frequently.

The application itself, however, needs to authenticate to the external service providers to call the proper API. This is done over an external communications bus where SOAP messages are sent over Hypertext Transfer Protocol Secure (HTTPS). As the application will be communicating with the external service providers frequently, but only sharing sensitive data when a booking is ready to be made, the application authenticates with its own SAML assertion once daily with the first connection. However, when a booking is ready, the application reauthenticates using a different SAML assertion which has the signed and encrypted metadata of the client within it so that when it begins to forward the SOAP messages containing the booking details, the service provider not only authorizes the purchase but also sends the service initiator the requisite invoice for the services to be provided. These secure communications with the payment processors must be delivered, and the results must be returned. As such, the company has looked for payment processors, which support the WS-ReliableMessaging protocol, not so much because the transactions are going to have many steps to them, but rather so that there is reliable tracking and error handling, should a transaction not be delivered properly.

As other service providers may also need to call into our application, its presentation layer must also expose a services interface. This is where the application and security architects have decided to set up WS-Security, with WS-Trust and WS-Policy. Not only do they want to allow access to the provider's SAML assertions but they also wish to expose access to users of Facebook, LinkedIn, LiveJournal, Twitter, or Google accounts, so that authenticated users of those services can readily access your services. The company also wishes to allow these users of social media the ability to authenticate into their service transparently using their already existing authentication into the social media site they are using. To this end, the application must not only support SAML for their business partners, but also OpenID for their customers.

As your application will readily mine those social media sites for as much information about the prospective customers as possible with the intent of making adventure recommendations to them from posts or tweets, you develop a Platform for Privacy Preferences Project (P3P)-based privacy policy as well as specify very clear terms of service and privacy policy, which informs of your access to the account they have used to authenticate into your service so that you may provide them with the best travel adventure experience.

To ensure your customers' privacy, should they access your system using credentials from one of your supported social media partners, your WS-Policy requires that any connections initiated from these services are over SSL, and that the metadata provided by these social media connections are never sent over an unencrypted channel.

However, you also write this information into your own internal database right away, unlike with an unauthenticated client, as this way you can better market your services to them next time.

You use the same calls into your communications bus, but this time the calls are kept internal to your network. Because the internal communication's bus is behind a firewall, an application firewall, and an XML firewall, and inside a restricted network in a data center, your security architect has begrudgingly agreed that this bus does not need to transverse encrypted tunnels. After all, the only people who can sniff those networks is the same staff that needs to support the networks, and if an attacker is able to break through those defenses, encrypted tunnels will not protect your organization from the attackers' actions.

The presentation layer will build its interface from three contexts: is the principle a user, an authenticated user, or an application over the API. Where the principle is an application, the presentation layer will respond with well-formed XML over SOAP that is encrypted and signed to preserve the privacy of the request and its integrity. It will also communicate with the workflow layer using signed and encrypted XML to preserve the privacy of the communications and the integrity of the information. Where the client is an authenticated principle, the presentation layer renders the information over an HTTPS session to the principle, while calling the workflow layer using well-formed XML over SOAP that is encrypted and signed to preserve the client's privacy and the integrity of the requests. Where the principle is an anonymous user, the presentation layer will let the principle choose to use the service in the clear or over HTTPS. Where the user chooses to use the portal over HTTP, this state is marked as an SAML metatag, and communications with the workflow layer are not encrypted by the presentation layer. They are still signed so as to protect the integrity of the message more effectively than a checksum, as there is less chance of collision and you are reusing code used for your more security-conscious customers. In all cases, you capture information about the principle in SAML metadata so that it may be shared transparently with your business providers. You always sign this information so that your providers know that it comes from your application unaltered.

The application provides a slightly different workflow depending upon the source of the authentication information. Your application is an authentication partner with Facebook, LinkedIn, LiveJournal, Amazon, and so on. You also accept authentication from Ping Identity, Okta, and other identity providers. As your security architect is more comfortable with the rigor applied at the identity providers such as Ping and the others where maintaining an online identity is their business model, you offer these clients more flexible cancelation and refund policies than you do those who authenticate using a social media service. To those, you not only offer less flexible cancelation and refund policies but also require them to enter their payment information into your system and do a verification against both the profile sent over by the social media provider and a third-party fraud prevention service you subscribe to.

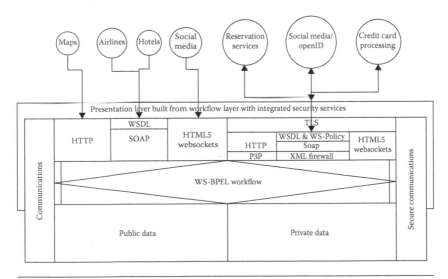

**Exhibit 8.2**

## 8.3 Example 3

The third sample service-oriented application architecture we are going to look at is one where the application provides updated commodities' prices for a commodities market upon request. This is a very simple service that can be accessed by individual traders or other service providers, which can wrap the information we provide into their platform. We do not accept orders nor can our users use our service to sell. We can, and do, however provide historical analysis for any time period since the founding of the exchange we are the front end for.

We will need to support two data feed models to support our diverse customer base: the push and the pull. Because we do not care who accesses our service to pull data from us, there is no need for an identity service provider or for an authentication front end. However, we must prove that the data we represent is ours to the organizations that require us to push the prices to them. It is for this reason that we are not supporting WebSockets at this time as there is no mechanism to demonstrate authenticity of the data. However, we are looking at the use of extended validated certificates to see if they meet our risk profile of our customers for sufficiently demonstrating authenticity and integrity of the data so that we can provide an HTML 5 WebSockets interface to our data.

Surprisingly, most of our customers require the push model as this is the most efficient means to provide updated prices. Unlike the pull model where they query the data periodically, and we then respond to the query with a SOAP message, with the push model we push out a SOAP message with each update to the price. Each of these messages will be signed with our private key, validated by our customers with our public key if they choose to ensure the integrity of the messages. Behind this service's presentation layer, we will need direct access to the business layer which intercepts updates to the data layer and spins off the SOAP messages to the communications layer for outbound data pushes. It is the communications layer that the presentation layer also goes to when it gets a request for an update. By intercepting the writes to the database, we are able to provide real-time price changes that create a high demand for our pricing service.

The main threats to the application are denial-of-service attacks and attacks against data integrity and data authenticity. The signing of the SOAP messages addresses the issues of data integrity and data authenticity. Protecting against a denial-of-service attack is always hard. We have hidden our presentation layer behind a service provider that provides distributed denial-of-service (DDoS) protection, and ensured that our Domain Name System (DNS) is registered with one of the better registers, signing the domain with DNS Security Extensions (DNSSEC). We have positioned both web application firewalls and XML firewalls in an array of highly available devices as well as put in place a network firewall, which only permits traffic inbound on ports 80 and 443. Our data center has multiple Internet service providers, brought into the facility over high-speed lines that are buried in concrete tubes. The data center manages its routers carefully, as do the ISPs, so attacks using Border Gateway Protocol (BGP) to reroute traffic to another facility will fail.

| Security layer |
|---|
| Presentation layer |

| Application layer |
|---|
| Communications layer |

| Data layer | Data warehouse |
|---|---|

Exhibit 8.3

## 8.4 Example 4

The next example we will explore is a distributed financial application for a large international bank. The bank has a legacy system on a mainframe that has been providing account management for its customers for decades. To compete effectively with other banks, as well as work with its business partners, it has decided to extend the power of this system through the Internet, providing access through a service-oriented application. The bank has deployed a message bus internally to govern and control all communications with the legacy system so that there would be a common interface from disparate systems and applications. This message bus is also used to control communications between the various client server, .net, and Java applications that have been deployed within the bank over the years. As all of this communication is to systems of different capabilities, maturities, and flexibilities, the data sent to the message bus is neither signed or encrypted nor does it transverse encrypted tunnels, as the speed and volume of the transactions exceed what even an SSL accelerator would permit.

The bank had two options regarding the conversion of the messages on the message bus to instructions that their legacy systems could both receive and respond to. The first was to install new software on the mainframe that translated the instructions, the second was to use a protocol gateway, or proxy, which translated the messages and then sent them on. As the mainframe was carefully tuned to run the software currently resident, and experts on big iron are no longer as common as they once were, the bank has elected to spin up a protocol gateway as a service provider on their message bus.

As the message bus has many systems communicating with it, it is imperative to the bank that ease of integration into their message bus is made available. As the entirety of the message bus is internal, they expose Universal Description, Discovery and Integration (UDDI) as well as Web Services Description Language (WSDL) on each service gateway and provider. The UDDI allows the easy integration of new applications and components onto the message bus. The developers do not need to know the system names or addresses of the systems that house the services they need to leverage. Instead, a service catalog can be accessed where the application can call the most appropriate service provider off the service bus to facilitate the distributed processing of information. More importantly, many of the systems on the service bus do not support the publication of a formal WSDL, and the presence of a UDDI allows the publication of the WSDL for that service without the need of service gateways. This allows the minimization of the service gateways to only those systems that do not natively support calls over the HTTP protocol.

Despite the lack of encrypted traffic and signed messages, the bank has strict requirements for security and audit. Thus, one of the services that all messages on the message bus must call is a centralized logging service. This provides the bank with a single repository for trans application logging and transaction auditing. All service providers on the service bus are required to verify that the message has been logged before processing it. By forcing logging to happen before the transaction means that in the event of a transaction rollback, that will also be logged. This captures a full audit history, but there may be a delay in processing because of this; however, this is viewed by the bank as a lower risk than the transaction happening without the transaction being logged.

Each application on the service bus interfaces with it through its own presentation layers. These are many and various and dependent upon the specifics of the application. We have already discussed the use of UDDI, WSDL, and application gateways. Each application is expected to expose either an HTTP or SOAP interface for service calls to be made. As most of the principles using the application are internal to the bank, these presentation layers expect that the HTTP or SOAP messages presented with have Kerberos tickets. The identities behind those Kerberos tickets are all stored within the corporate Lightweight Directory Access Protocol (LDAP) directory, and the authentication resident in the deployed Windows operating system is extended to authenticate the credentials into this distributed application. Authorization is checked by the individual services making LDAP calls to verify either attributes or group membership associated with the account depending upon the capabilities and requirements of each.

Because many of the bank's internal operations have dependencies on a variety of services on the message bus, they have implemented WS-Coordination with Ws-BusinessActivity. This allows the multistage transactions to move forward as more data is provided without data loss while waiting for related processes to provide the information needed to complete the process.

A subset of the application's functionality needs to be exposed to bank customers. This is done to individual customers through a web portal into the bank. Corporate customers can access a business-centric portal similar in design to the customer portal, or they may access the service through service calls of their own. Both require that the principle authenticate. As they are authenticating using credentials that are not stored in the centralized directory store, because the bank believes in segregating its accounts, the application needs to be designed to accept credentials from more than one identity store and authorize access based partly upon that context.

This is where the application and security architect have a very serious decision to make. SAML can be used to provide the capacity for multiple identity stores, but so can WS-Federation, but neither is truly necessary. The web portal could either generate Kerberos tickets using its own account and provide application-level access to application functionality while relying upon business logic to restrict access to data, or it could develop a secondary-access control system for the internal communication between the portal and the systems on that internal message bus.

Most banks will make the first choice as it allows reuse of existing capabilities, and the business logic should be sound enough to be used as a mechanism to restrict access. A history of application hackers manipulating business logic should, however, convince architects to reject that approach. Application code is too often easily tricked into supplying data for which the user is not authorized if there is no proper authorization check on the data requested against the privileges associated with the user. Simply put, basing your security strategy on business logic is a not a good decision.

To this end, these architects have worked together to develop an identity service specific to the portal and its customers which grants Kerberos tickets. These Kerberos tickets use a different source directory for storage of the accounts, but one in which similar attributes and groupings are available so that the systems and applications on the message bus can use the same logic for authorization checks but are directed against a different LDAP server for the information needed to provide the data required for an authorization decision. Now access can be granted or denied upon the principle of least privilege.

The bank is very committed to the idea of a business partnership as one wherein trusted transactions can enable business growth and as such exposes to its business partners a services interface so that a subset of the their business capability can be provided as a web service. Here they only expose a WSDL, not UDDI, and only to authenticated network sessions. They insist that their business partners use client certificates to authenticate the TLS session, and that both sides of the TLS handshake validate the certificates are still good using Online Certificate Status Protocol (OCSP). These client certificates, however, are not used for application authentication, just for establishing the network tunnel over which both application authentication and application data will flow. This allows multiple client sessions over the same encrypted tunnel.

Application authentication is through a one-time pad using time-synchronized tokens. These tokens are software, which generates a shared secret dynamically, which is constantly changed on a synchronous basis every so many seconds. These tokens do not authenticate the user, they authenticate the client, which is an institution. The bank uses SAML to have the client pass the authentication of their employees through to the bank. The bank's own identity store has a mapping for these SAML assertions and the LDAP directory entries, which creates some administrative overhead but allows the bank to continue to use Kerberos exclusively internally.

The bank requires that its institutional customers register their employees with the bank when they are authorized to use the bank's application service. This removes the administrative overhead for account creation, placing it where it belongs in any federated identity model. The customer is also required to notify the bank when that status changes, including when the access should be terminated. As the Bank is aware that some customers are not at all good about this, it builds into its contracts with their customers that the risk of unauthorized access of the customer's employees to bank resources or data is absorbed by the customer. In reality, this is something that all contracts with service providers and principles should have, and the bank's lawyers are good.

Individual customers have an even more restricted access to the bank's services. While the bank has made available cards with a time-synched one-time pad available to its individual customers, unlike with its business partners, this has not been made mandatory. In fact, being a bank, it forces its customers to pay for the privilege of better security than a password. The customer is forced to use a complex user account name and a complex password (even if they are using the one-time pad). A real risk to the bank is that it does not require its individual customers to use strongly authenticated network connections to its application. This leaves the individual accounts susceptible to compromise through interception, injection, and replay attacks, as well as to the various phishing schemes that execute those attacks.

To mitigate those risks somewhat, the bank has had its DNS signed through its registrar using DNSSEC, and uses an extended validation certificate with a high key strength. Its cookies expire quickly and are signed and encrypted with the bank's TLS private key. This provides some integrity protection.

The bank also sends periodic emails to its customers reminding them that the bank will never ask for an account number or a password in any official communication.

Because the bank has chosen to reuse code wherever possible to reduce the costs of software development, and leverage both off the shelf components and existing deployments, the presentation layer for the external portal is the same presentation layer as the internal portal. The difference in how it is displayed and what options are available are tied to the bank's authorization model for portal accounts.

I have already discussed how the bank uses metadata in its LDAP directory to authorize access to application functionality. This metadata is prepopulated so that it is not vulnerable to injection attacks during the application's session. The place where it is vulnerable is during account provisioning, especially for retail customers as the web portal is somewhat self-registering.

To provide proof of identity to the portal for the initial registration, the portal requires the presence and use of an account number already known by the bank and a shared secret that is pre-established upon account creation. Each account has a different kind of shared secret. In the case of a credit or debit card, there is a pre-existing PIN. In the case of a mortgage or other loan, the bank sends the client a PIN after the loan is established. This is sent by mail to the same address as the statements. The individual is then instructed to login to the portal and change the PIN to one he/she will remember.

Knowing fully well that PINs sent by mail may be intercepted, the PIN is not sufficient to self-register for access to the portal. The client is also asked to provide the value of the last month's bill and the branch where the loan was tendered. These values lower the risk that the person requesting access is not the person who should have access. The information requested is sent in a SOAP message into the message bus where it is directed to the various data sources containing the matching data. Some will be in the DB2 database in the mainframe, some will be in the LDAP directory, and others will be in smaller Structured Query Language (SQL) databases. The message bus updates the SOAP message at each datasource and when all pertinent datasources have been queried, the message bus returns the message to the authorization engine. If they match the records, then the registration is accepted.

The next thing the bank's registration application does is to ask the client to establish a shared secret. This allows the customer to choose three questions and the answers to the questions. It does not matter if the answers are the correct answers to the questions, and the bank's application's help system stresses to the client upon registration that what is truly important here is that the client remember how they answered those questions.

The system is designed, upon a successful registration to do three things: First, map the identity created with the accounts internal to the system to which it is authorized. Second, profile the computer used in the registration. This will allow the bank's application to recognize when that computer is used again to access the application. The third thing is to write an encrypted cookie. This cookie will also be used for authenticating the computer.

When the customer uses a different computer to access the bank's application, it recognizes from the different profile and the lack of the cookie that this is not the computer usually used for access. The bank's authentication engine then prompts the client with two of the three shared secret questions that were created upon registration. If the client cannot remember the answers, the use of the new computer is rejected, even if the credentials used match the credentials stored in the account store. In fact, the security architect has persuaded the application architect to mark those stored credentials as compromised and kick off a routine wherein the client is called by the bank in question.

While the details of profiling a computer are beyond the scope of this volume, they include noting the serial number, the media access control (MAC) address, the size of the hard disk and its manufacturer, the version of the operating system, and so many other small details. With each successful registration, these are all queried, and if any change, the new value is updated if the change is reasonable, such as an update to the operating system version. However, if too many of the variables change, and what is too many is a configurable parameter based upon the value of the account, then the system will prompt the client for the shared secrets established at registration.

The other thing, which is done with the profiling of the computer is that the computer is checked against a list of computers known to be involved in either botnet activity or criminal activity. As often the owner of the system is not aware of this, the application has two logic paths. If the system has been observed to have been involved with botnet activities, then the system owner is notified and the owner is granted the right to continue with the access, if he/she acknowledges that in doing so he/she may be compromising his/her own account. If they do continue, then the account will be locked after the termination of the session, and the options to transfer money or pay new creditors are not shown.

TLS/WAF/XML firewalls

| Security presentation layer | Presentation layer | | | Logging |
|---|---|---|---|---|
| One time pad/ SAML | Customer facing web 2.0 applications | Customer facing websockets | SFTP and FTP over HTTPS | Customer facing SOA applications |
| Kerberos | | | | |
| LDAP | | | | |
| External identity store | | | | |

Ws-coordinator & WS-business activity

Enterprise service bus

| UDDI/WSDL | UDDI/WSDL | UDDI/WSDL | UDDI/WSDL | UDDI/WSDL | UDDI/WSDL | UDDI/WSDL |
|---|---|---|---|---|---|---|
| Application gateway | Kerberos | Message que | Service oriented applications | Databases | Data warehouses | Logging |
| | LDAP | | | | | |
| Legacy applications | Identity store | | | | | |
| Client server applications | | | | | | |

Exhibit 8.4

What is related to the subject of this book is how that status relates to the calling and use of services. There are a number of approaches that could be taken to implement this complex authentication and authorization check, one of which is to make it into an authentication and authorization service that is called by the presentation layer. As, for the moment, the bank's portal is the only customer of this functionality, the question might be begged, what advantage is there in designing this single-purpose function into a service? Could it not just initiate a service call itself? While it could, there are several factors that make turning this into a service a distinct advantage.

First, the bank's design philosophy of develop for potential reuse has some merit. The complex service bus they have put into place to tie together diverse applications which are not service oriented is a hack. It is a well-designed and highly functional hack, but it is a hack that would be best avoided with future development. By making all new applications designed within the bank services, they can call each other readily. While they can still make use of the service bus, for them it becomes just a communications service.

Second, by designing the authorization and authentication system as a service, future application development can utilize it. Because it is rather complex, with checks on the account and on the computer, it is worth taking a moment to discuss the structure of this service on an abstract basis, or in other words, look at its architecture.

While it is called from the presentation layer of the bank's portal, it has its own presentation layer, which involves checking the computer being used and authenticating it using the profiling we have described above. The computer profiling can be something that the bank develops internally, or it can be an external service which the bank calls. If the profiling is leased as an external service, the results have to be aggregated with the results of the credentials' check. If they check positive, that the computer has been used before and the credentials match what is on record, the authentication is permitted and an authorization check is initiated. If, on the other hand, the computer cannot be identified, then an extended identity check through use of the shared services is initiated.

# Bibliography

Abadi, D., Madden, S., Hachem, N. Column-stores vs. row-stores: How different are they really? SIGMOD 08, Vancouver, Canada, 2008.

Al-Kofahi, M.M. *Service Oriented Architecture (SOA) Security Models*. Iowa State University Digital Repository, Ames, IA, 2011.

Alberts, C., Dorofee, A. *Managing Information Security Risks*. Boston, MA: Addison-Wesley, 2003.

Anonymous, 2004. WSDL—SOAP to CORBA internetworking version 1.0. http://www.omg.org/spec/WSDL2C/1.0/PDF/

Anonymous, 2006. The online community for the Universal Description, Discovery, and Integration OASIS standard. http://uddi.xml.org/uddi-101

Anonymous, 2007. Data Distribution Service for real-time systems. Version 1.2. http://www.omg.org/spec/DDS/1.2/PDF/

Anonymous, 2012. Workflow services overview. http://msdn.microsoft.com/en-us/library/dd456797.aspx

Anonymous, 2013. Hacking web services with Burp. https://www.netspi.com/blog/entryid/57/hacking-web-services-with-burp

Anonymous, 2013. MS-DCOM Distributed Component Object Model (DCOM) remote protocol. http://download.microsoft.com/download/9/5/E/95EF66AF-9026-4BB0-A41D-A4F81802D92C/[MS-DCOM].pdf

Anonymous, 2013. Removal of UDDI services from server operating system. http://msdn.microsoft.com/en-us/library/dd464641.aspx

Anonymous. Windows Live ID web authentication SDK. http://msdn.microsoft.com/en-us/library/bb676633.aspx. Accessed on September 1, 2013.

Anonymous. Passport authentication provider. http://msdn.microsoft.com/en-us/library/f8e50t0f(v=vs.85).aspx. Accessed on September 1, 2013.

Anonymous. Single sign-on for apps and websites. http://msdn.microsoft. com/en-us/library/live/hh826544.aspx. Accessed on September 1, 2013.

Bajaj, S., Box, D., Chappell, F., et al. 2006. Web services policy 1.2. http://www. w3.org/Submission/WS-Policy/

Bertino, E. *Security for Web Services and Service Oriented Architecture*. New York: Springer, 2010.

Boag, S., Chamberlin, D., Fernandez, M., et al. 2010. XQuery 1.0: An XML query language. http://www.w3.org/TR/xquery/

Bos, B. 1997. XML representation of a relational database. http://www.w3.org/ XML/RDB.html

Bournaee, B., *XML Security*. Berkeley, CA: McGraw-Hill, 2002.

Box, D., Christensen, E., Curbera, F. 2004. Web services addressing (WS-Addressing). http://www.w3.org/Submission/ws-addressing/

Bray, T., Paoli, J. Sperberg-McQueen, C.M., et al. 2006. *Extensible Markup Language (XML) 1.1* (Second Edition). http://www.w3.org/TR/2006/ REC-xml11-20060816

Brown, A., Fox, B., Hada, S., et al. 2001. SOAP security extensions: Digital signature. http://www.w3.org/TR/SOAP-dsig/

Calder, A., Watkins, S. *International IT Governance*. Philadelphia, PA: Kogan Page, 2006.

Cantor, S., Hirsch, F., Kemp, J., et al. 2005. Bindings for the OASIS Security Assertion Markup Language (SAML) V2.0. http://docs.oasis-open.org/ security/saml/v2.0/saml-bindings-2.0-os.pdf

Cantor, S., Hughes, J., Hodges, J., et al. 2005. Profiles for the OASIS Security Assertion Markup Language (SAML) V2.0. http://docs.oasis-open.org/ security/saml/v2.0/saml-profiles-2.0-os.pdf

Cantor, S., Kemp, J., Philpott, R., et al. Assertions and protocols for the OASIS Security Assertion Markup Language (SAML) V2.0. http://docs.oasis- open.org/security/saml/v2.0/saml-core-2.0-os.pdf

Cantor, S., Moreh, J., Philpott, R., et al. 2005. Metadata for the OASIS Security Assertion Markup Language (SAML) V2.0. http://docs.oasis-open.org/ security/saml/v2.0/saml-metadata-2.0-os.pdf

Chappell, D. *Enterprise Service Bus*. Sebastopol, CA: O'Reilly Media, 2004.

Christensen, E., Curbera, F., Meredith, G., Weerawarana, S. 2001. Web Services Description Language. http://www.w3.org/TR/wsdl

Chris. WS-Attacker. http://sourceforge.net/p/ws-attacker/wiki/Home/. Accessed on September 1, 2013.

Cranor, L., Dobbs, B., Egelman, S., et al. The platform for privacy preferences 1.1. http://www.w3.org/TR/P3P11/

Deutsch, A., Fernandez, M., Florescu, D., et al. 1998. XML-QL: A query language for XML. http://www.w3.org/TR/1998/ NOTE-xml-ql-19980819

Eastlake, D., Reagle, J., Solo, D., et al. 2008. *XML Signature Syntax and Processing* (Second Edition). http://www.w3.org/TR/2008/ REC-xmldsig-core-20080610/

Edlich, S. NoSQL: Your ultimate guide to the non-relational universe. http:// nosql-database.org/. Accessed on September 23, 2013.

Erl, T. *Service-Oriented Architecture: A Field Guide to Integrating XML and Web Services*. Upper Saddle River, NJ: Prentice Hall, 2004.

Ferraiolo, D., Kuhn, D., Chandramouli, R. *Role-Based Access Control*. Boston, MA: Artech House, 2003.

Fielding, R., Gettys, J., Mogul, J., et al. 1999. Hypertext Transfer Protocol HTTP/1.1. http://www.w3.org/Protocols/rfc2616/rfc2616.html

Fielding, T. 2000. Architectural styles and the design of network-based software architectures, Chapter 5. http://www.ics.uci.edu/~fielding/pubs/dissertation/rest_arch_style.htm

Fremantle, P., Patil, S. 2009. Web Services Reliable Messaging (WS-Reliable Messaging), version 1.2. http://docs.oasis-open.org/ws-rx/wsrm/200702/wsrm-1.2-spec-os.pdf

Garman, J. *Kerberos: The Definitive Guide*. Sebastopol, CA: O'Reilly & Associates, 2003.

Gross, T. 2003. Security analysis of the SAML single sign-on browser/artifact profile. http://www.acsac.org/2003/papers/73.pdf

Gudgin, M., Hadley, M., Mendelsohn, N. 2007. SOAP version 1.2 Part 1: Messaging framework. http://www.w3.org/TR/2007/REC-soap12-part1-20070427/

Gudgin, M., Hadley, M., Mendelsohn, N., et al. 2007. SOAP version 1.2 Part 2: Adjuncts. http://www.w3.org/TR/2007/REC-soap12-part2-20070427/

Gudgin, M., Hadley, M., Mendelsohn, N., et al. 2007. SOAP version 1.2 Part 2: Adjuncts data model. http://www.w3.org/TR/soap12-part2/#datamodel

Hallam-Baker, P., Shivaram, H. 2005. XML Key management specification. http://www.w3.org/TR/2005/REC-xkms2-20050628/

Herold, R. *Managing an Information Security and Privacy Awareness Training Program* (Second Edition). Boca Raton, FL: Auerbach Publications, 2012.

Hickson, I. 2013. The web socket API. http://dev.w3.org/html5/websockets/

Hirsh, F., Datta, P. 2012. XML signature best practices. http://www.w3.org/TR/2012/NOTE-xmldsig-bestpractices-20120710/#denial-of-service

Hirsh, F., Philpott, R., Maier, E. 2005. Security and privacy considerations for the OASIS Security Assertion Markup Language (SAML) V2.0. http://docs.oasis-open.org/security/saml/v2.0/saml-sec-consider-2.0-os.pdf

Holmes, T. *What is Application Architecture?* Conjecture Corporation, Sparks, NV, 2013. http://www.wisegeek.org/what-is-application-architecture.htm

Imamura, T., Dillaway, B., Simon, E. 2002. XML encryption syntax and processing. http://www.w3.org/TR/2002/REC-xmlenc-core-20021210/

INCITS/ISO/IEC 27001-2005. *Information Technology—Security Techniques—Information Security Management Systems—Requirements*. Information Technology Industry Council (ITI), Washington, DC, 2006.

Johnson, K. 2011. Attacking web services Pt 1—SOAP. http://resources.infosecinstitute.com/soap-attack-1/

Johnson, K. 2011. Attacking web services Pt 2—SOAP. http://resources.infosecinstitute.com/soap-attack-2/

Jordan, D., Evdemon, J. 2007. Web Services Business Process Execution Language Version 2.0. http://docs.oasis-open.org/wsbpel/2.0/OS/wsbpel-v2.0-OS.html

Juric, M. *Business Process Execution Language for Web Services.* Birmingham, UK: Packt Publishing, 2006.

Kaeo, M. *Designing Network Security.* Indianapolis, IN: Macmillan Technical Publishing, 1999.

Kakimus, N., Bradley, P., Jones, M., et al. 2013. OpenID connect basic client profile 1.0—Draft 28. http://openid.net/specs/openid-connect-basic-1_0-28.html

Kaler, C., McIntosh, M. 2009. Web Services Federation Language (WS-Federation) 1.2. http://docs.oasis-open.org/wsfed/federation/v1.2/os/ws-federation-1.2-spec-os.html

Kemp, J., Cantor, S., Mishra, P., et al. 2005. Authentication context for the OASIS Security Assertion Markup Language (SAML) V2.0. http://docs.oasis-open.org/security/saml/v2.0/saml-authn-context-2.0-os.pdf

King, C., Dalton, C., Osmanoglu, T. *Security Architecture.* Berkeley, CA: McGraw-Hill, 2001.

Krafzig, D., Banke, K., Slama, D. Enterprise SOA. In *Service-Oriented Architecture Best Practices.* Upper Saddle River, NJ: Prentice Hall, 2005.

Kurtzban, S. Implementation of access controls. In *Information Security Management Handbook,* 432–447. Boca Raton, FL: Auerbach Publications, 2009.

Landoll, D. *The Security Risk Assessment Handbook.* Boca Raton, FL: Auerbach Publications, 2006.

Lawrence, K., Kaler, C. 2004. Web services security. https://www.oasis-open.org/committees/download.php/16790/wss-v1.1-spec-os-SOAPMessag-eSecurity.pdf

Lawrence, K., Kaler, C. 2007. WS-SecureConversation 1.3. http://docs.oasis-open.org/ws-sx/ws-secureconversation/v1.3/ws-secureconversation.html

Mandia, K., Prosise, C., Pepe, M. *Incident Response.* New York: McGraw-Hill, 2003.

Meier, J.D., Hill, D., Homer, A., et al. 2009. *Microsoft Application Architecture Guide* (Second Edition). Microsoft Press. http://www.microsoft.com/downloads/details.aspx?FamilyID=ce40e4e1-9838-4c89-a197-a373b2a60df2&DisplayLang=en

Nash, A., Duane, W., Joseph, C., Brink, D. *PKI: Implementing and Managing E-Security.* New York: McGraw-Hill, 2001.

Newcomer, I., Robinson, I. 2009. Web Services Atomic Transaction (WS-AtomicTransaction) Version 1.2. http://docs.oasis-open.org/ws-tx/wstx-wsat-1.2-spec-os.pdf

Newcomer, I., Robinson, I. 2009. Web Services Coordination (WS-Coordination) Version 1.2. http://docs.oasis-open.org/ws-tx/wstx-wscoor-1.2-spec-os.pdf

O'Reilly, T. 2005. What is Web 2.0? http://oreilly.com/web2/archive/what-is-web-20.html

Parker, D. *Fighting Computer Crime.* New York: John Wiley & Sons, 1998.

Peltier, T. *Information Security Policies, Procedures, and Standards.* Boca Raton, FL: Auerbach Publications, 2002.

Preibush, S. 2006. Privacy negotiations with P3P. http://www.w3.org/2006/07/privacy-ws/papers/24-preibusch negotiation-p3p/

Reese, G. *Cloud Application Architectures.* Sebastopol, CA: O'Reilly Media, Inc., 2009.

Rosenberg, J., Remy, D. *Securing Web Services with WS-Security.* Indianapolis, IN: SAMS Publishing, 2004.

SAP News Desk. 2005. Microsoft, IBM, SAP to discontinue UDDI web services registry effort. http://soa.sys-con.com/node/164624

Shreeraj, S. *Hacking Web Services.* Boston, MA: Charles River Media, 2007.

Smorovsky, J., Mayer, A., Schwenk, J., et al. 2012. On breaking SAML: Be whoever you want to be. https://www.usenix.org/system/files/conference/usenixsecurity12/sec12-final91.pdf

Tudor, J., *Information Security Architecture.* Boca Raton, FL: CRC Press LLC, 2001.

Weerawarana, S., Curbera, F., Leymann, F., et al. *Web Services Platform Architecture.* Upper Saddle River, NJ: Pearson Education, Inc., 2005.

# Index